D1132659

*Garden Flowers from Seed*

SB405.L58 1994
Lloyd, Christopher, 1921-
Garden flowers from seed

P73690

South Puget Sound Community College

WITHDRAWN

LIBRARY-MEDIA CENTER
SOUTH PUGET SOUND COMM. COLLEGE
2011 MOTTMAN RD SW
OLYMPIA, WA 98512-6292

50397
DEMCO

*Books by Christopher Lloyd*

The Mixed Border
Shrubs and Trees for Small Gardens
Hardy Perennials
Gardening on Chalk and Lime
The Well-Tempered Garden
Foliage Plants
The Adventurous Gardener
The Year at Great Dixter
Clematis (revised edition with Tom Bennett)

*Books by Graham Rice*

The Gardener's Guide to Growing Hellebores
(with Elizabeth Strangman)
A Handbook of Annuals and Bedding Plants
Plants for Problem Places
Perfect Plants

# Garden Flowers from Seed

## CHRISTOPHER LLOYD
## AND GRAHAM RICE

TIMBER PRESS
*Portland, Oregon*

LIBRARY-MEDIA CENTER
SOUTH PUGET SOUND COMM. COLLEGE
2011 MOTTMAN RD SW
OLYMPIA, WA 98512-6292

WITHDRAWN

Paperback edition first published in North America in 1994
by Timber Press, Inc.
The Haseltine Building
133 S.W. Second Avenue, Suite 450
Portland, Oregon 97204–3527, USA.
phone 1–800–327–5680 (USA and Canada only)

Reprinted 1995

ISBN 0–88192–296–x

Copyright © Christopher Lloyd and Graham Rice, 1991

The moral right of the authors has been asserted

All rights reserved.
Without limiting the rights under copyright
reserved above, no part of this publication may be
reproduced, stored in or introduced into a retrieval system,
or transmitted, in any form or by any means (electronic, mechanical,
photocopying, recording or otherwise), without the prior
written permission of both the copyright owner and
the above publisher of this book

Set in 11/13¼ Lasercomp Garamond
Printed in Great Britain by Butler & Tanner Ltd, Frome and London

LIBRARY MEDIA CENTER
SOUTH PUGET SOUND COMM COLLEGE
2011 MOTTMAN RD SW
OLYMPIA, WA 98512-6292

P73690

# Contents

# List of Illustrations

All photographs are by the authors except where indicated.

# Table of Conversions

| | | |
|---|---|---|
| $\frac{3}{4}$ in | = | 2 cm |
| 1 in | = | 3 cm |
| $1\frac{1}{2}$ in | = | 4 cm |
| 2 in | = | 5 cm |
| $2\frac{1}{4}$ in | = | 6 cm |
| $2\frac{3}{4}$ in | = | 7 cm |
| 3 in | = | 8 cm |
| $3\frac{1}{2}$ in | = | 9 cm |
| 4 in | = | 10 cm |
| 8 in | = | 20 cm |
| 12 in | = | 30 cm |
| 1 ft | = | .3 m |
| $1\frac{1}{2}$ ft | = | .5 m |
| 2 ft | = | .6 m |
| 2 ft | = | .7 m |
| $2\frac{1}{2}$ ft | = | .8 m |
| 3 ft | = | .9 m |
| 3 ft | = | 1 m |
| 5 ft | = | 1.5 m |
| 6 ft | = | 2 m |
| 8 ft | = | 2.5 m |
| 10 ft | = | 3 m |
| 11 ft | = | 3.5 m |
| 13 ft | = | 4 m |
| 15 ft | = | 4.5 m |
| 16 ft | = | 5 m |
| 18 ft | = | 5.5 m |
| 20 ft | = | 6 m |
| 23 ft | = | 7 m |
| 26 ft | = | 8 m |
| 30 ft | = | 9 m |

# *Acknowledgements*

*GR:* I would like to thank all my friends in the seed trade for their continuing help and advice, and especially Sue and my Mum for their helpful comments on my text.

*CL/GR:* We would both like to thank Dr Alan Leslie, who has clarified some of the trickier points of nomenclature for us. Thanks also to Eleo Gordon, our editor, for being so patient.

# Introduction by Christopher Lloyd

Why should I be writing this book in collaboration with Graham Rice? Why should I (Graham will have his own explanations) be writing it at all? Well, I just love raising young plants, from seed or any other way. Anyone with an addiction, benign or malign, wants to share it with others. So that's how it is. Writing is another act of creativity that I enjoy (though it becomes a burden at times). So writing about some aspect of plant propagation is just a matter of putting two and two together.

I first heard of Graham through being sent a review copy of his book on *Annuals and Bedding Plants* by Helm, the publishers. Far too many gardening books are written, and most of them are so dismally boring that they send me straight to sleep. This is not a good thing, as I'm no insomniac and the days are precious when you reach my age. But this book made me sit up. Furthermore, it often made me laugh. Here was a genuine voice putting across one of my favourite themes with verve and with professional expertise. It made me want to meet the author.

Graham arrived for a weekend, backed up by a friend to soften and dilute the traumatic experience! During their stay I had a brainwave (let's call it that), and this book is the result.

Between us, on a subject dear to both our hearts, we can cover the ground more comprehensively than either of us could alone. In many respects our experience is complementary. Graham is, as befits a young man, more up-to-date than I, while I have had the years and the opportunity in which to grow a wide variety of plants. In many respects our experiences run parallel, so that we can comment the one upon the other's, conducting a kind of dialogue. Our editor took a good bit of persuading about the wisdom of this approach: rather awkward from her point of view in its presentation, and even at the time of writing this introduction which, as usual, is done after pretty well everything else, I'm not sure that she's any too happy. Let's hope it all turns out well in the event.

From Graham's and my point of view I think I can say, inclusively, that it's been a thoroughly harmonious exercise, neither of us getting cross with the other nor showing impatience (though Graham has had just cause, because I limit my book-writing to a short winter period). I think it should come across in the results that we each hold a great respect, not unmixed with affection, for the other.

How do you define and limit the boundaries of such a huge subject? We knew for a start that we wanted to write about annuals, biennials and perennials (in the popular sense), because these are the areas wherein our personal experience is most concentrated. We have tried to follow the obvious precept of writing about what we know from having done it ourselves, rather than merely regurgitating someone else's writing.

This may mean sometimes that we haven't dealt with those very plants about which you most wanted to read. Too bad; further reading will be necessary. I am so sorry for you. However, it must be admitted – and certainly the publishers will agree – that the book is quite long enough. And, without using too much padding (padding always shows up as just what it is, whatever the self-indulgent author imagines to the contrary), it is surely better to discuss a fairly limited number of plants in some detail, treating them as personal friends (or enemies) rather than as mere cogs in a wheel, than to cover a great deal of ground inadequately.

Obviously there are trees and shrubs that we enthusiastically grow from seed. What better than to have raised your own walnut tree, for instance, from a nut that you picked up (without permission) from under its owner's tree while holidaying in France? But we have left out trees, we have left out alpines, which barely come within our range of experience, and we have left out greenhouse flowers from seed, which are a book in themselves (that book is being written by Raymond Waite who, currently in charge of glass at the RHS garden, Wisley, has a vast fund of knowledge on this fascinating subject).

The flowers we have embraced are among the freshest and most endearing that you can grow in a garden. That is the way we see them, anyway, and we hope to communicate a similar feeling to others. We are both intensely interested in colour and form and in the possibilities for using plants effectively in the garden, so there are a good many suggestions along these lines. Plants should never be thought of in a vacuum – the context matters as much as the plant itself.

Many keen gardeners have never got around to sowing seeds themselves. This is simply through lack of confidence and it is a great shame, because they are missing out on one of life's big thrills. True, they can point at me and observe, correctly, that I've never parented a human child. But there are too many humans around already and seedlings are no bad alternative. So I hope that we'll have brought some more seed-sowers into the world. I could ask no better.

# Introduction by Graham Rice

Although the prospect of visiting Dixter was a little daunting, Christopher proved indulgent to one whose experience was rather more limited than his own. But alarm, and delight, took over when he suggested we write this book together.

There were two problems. The first was that I kept losing myself in his large labyrinthine house. On a later visit Christopher played a mischievous trick on me – or maybe it was less than deliberate. He retired to bed one night, leaving me reading by the fire, and switched off every single light in the house – it was as black as a 'Molly Sanderson' pansy – blacker! I had enough trouble finding the way to my room in the daytime – in the pitch black it was hopeless. I felt round the walls, trying not to bash my shins on oak chests, knock over clocks or fall down the stairs. At last I found a switch, and it was with some relief that I eventually reached my room (whose chief reading matter, I might say, seemed to consist of ancient year-books produced by the International Plant Propagators' Society – bedtime reading indeed). Tackling Christopher about this 'oversight' when I found my way to breakfast in the morning, 'Did I? Oh dear' was the innocent response!

The idea, however, of Christopher and me combining our definite, though not always synonymous, views in one text seemed an entertaining prospect for authors and readers alike. And so, for me certainly, it has turned out. We've stuck to our self-imposed brief fairly well, although a few shrubs that one or other of us especially likes have crept in. But what are rules for?

Our quite different circumstances make for a diversity of recommendations, from which readers in most situations can draw ideas. Christopher maintains a large garden which is open to the public, as well as a small nursery. He has someone to wash his pots for him. I'm making a new garden on land which, on my arrival, was little more than an unkempt field of 4-ft grass with a few crumbling fruit trees. I have no staff. More than one of my previous gardens would fit on to the terrace at Dixter.

Christopher is almost thirty years older than I, and it's clear from his contributions that many of the techniques he's been using since before I was born are still invaluable. (Followers of fashion should take note.) I may be more up to date with the latest research and the new varieties, so we complement each other well. We don't always agree on what plants to grow, how to raise them or what to do with them afterwards – why should we? But we've learned from each other's methods and tastes.

There are times when it seems ludicrous to suggest that the dust in the corner of a packet of begonia seed will eventually be transformed into big bushy plants. And sometimes, of course, this fear can turn out to be well founded: as I write, in March, I have 157 pots of seed waiting to germinate, and some have been sitting there for over two and a half years. Many more have germinated, been pricked out and grown on. But just as congestion threatens a clear-out, leaves will appear in some forlorn and almost forgotten seed-pot. When counting the pots just now, I spotted two new seedlings of a red-flowered *Tropaeolum polyphyllum,* collected in Chile, which had suddenly come through after two years.

Of course some of my seed-pots will never produce seedlings. The seed itself may be infertile (this is especially likely with seed collected in the wild or received from society seed lists). Or I may have inadvertently given it the wrong conditions – easily done with unfamiliar species. We cannot tell you how to make dud seed burst into life. But we have explained our methods in the hope that they will boost your success rate. And not only have we enthused about plants which we feel you should grow and warned you off less worthy varieties, but we've made suggestions for good 'uns to set alongside them once they're ready for planting.

Reading *Foliage Plants,* by my esteemed collaborator,* first made me realize that a book on plants could be funny as well as inspiring – not just a place to look things up. The way in which Christopher's ideas are expressed is almost as important as the ideas themselves. So writing with him is a privilege, if an unnerving one. A first draft littered with his almost indecipherable suggestions can be less than heartening. (But then I didn't always take any notice.)

The second problem? Well, at times I've again felt as if I was lost in

* Christopher Lloyd, *Foliage Plants,* Viking, London, 1985.

the dark, with little hope of finding light or rest. For progress came in fits and starts (I'd have a fit and he'd start), and sometimes I wondered if we'd ever finish the book. But we made it.

# Sowing in Protection

*GR:* Few seeds have an absolute requirement for supplementary heat and protection during their germination period. Many of those that we treat as half-hardy by sowing them in a heated propagator will germinate in a cold frame or outside in the open garden. So why use extra heat?

There are some seeds, F1 hybrid impatiens, for example, which will not germinate successfully unless kept at a fairly high temperature. Others are happy with less heat but need such a long growing season that by the time the ambient temperature outdoors reaches the necessary level for germination, it's too late for the plants to develop fully before the weather cools again.

*CL:* Not entirely true, at least in the South, Graham. If I sow impatiens in a double-glazed cold frame during May, I'll get decent germination and the plants will be ready to put out as a follow-on to sweet williams or other biennials, giving a fine display up to late October. There is extra heat, admittedly, but only the sun's, which is trapped by the glass.

*GR:* Then there are those seeds, such as F1 hybrid geraniums, which will germinate at temperatures lower than those usually maintained in a propagator but do so slowly and erratically. While germinating so slowly, they may rot or develop dormancy.

So a heated propagator or propagating bench will provide the high temperature that some plants need and will also encourage those satisfied with a lower temperature to germinate more quickly. In addition, hardy annuals and perennials which have no need of artificial heat can be given higher temperatures and will often germinate more quickly. This may well make all the difference between success or failure, as the sooner they germinate, the less time there is for rots to attack. But as they also germinate perfectly well in a cold frame or the open garden, the relatively limited propagator space which most of us are stuck with can be better utilized for those plants that need it.

## Timing

*GR:* My propagator usually gets a thorough clean-out around Christmas, after the very last of the late summer cuttings have rooted, and then starts filling up with seed in January. It's full of seed for some months with never a gap, then cuttings take over again. Another big scrub down and sterilization takes place in early September, followed by another burst of activity, this time for cuttings of half-hardy perennials. The expertise of a juggler is necessary all through the spring to ensure that the seeds that need the heat get it at the time they require it.

How you go about this depends on your facilities. I have a thermostatically controlled propagator, set so that the temperature at seed level in the pots is 70°F. I also have a large heated mat for weaning, and this too is thermostatically controlled so that the temperature at seed level is rather less than in the propagator. A partition divides the greenhouse into heated and unheated sections. The heated part houses the propagator and mat and is kept at a minimum of about 35°F. Research has shown that if you keep the *roots* of bedding plants warm after pricking out you can lower the air temperature significantly. This allows you to save greatly on heating bills without lowering the quality of the plants you grow.

I have an all too small cold frame outside, and a standing-out area. My advice is always to double the amount of frame and standing-out space you think you need. I make more just about every winter.

My point in mentioning all this is that having such a variety of situations provides a very helpful flexibility, in that growth can be slowed or quickened by moving the plants to cooler or warmer places. For example, I sow F1 hybrid geraniums in January. After germination and a few days' weaning on the heated mat they are potted up, and spend another couple of months on the mat before moving on to the nearby bench. By April at the latest they are ready to go into the unheated section, where they are safe in most seasons, and finally they go into the frame to harden off in early May. So I have sown them early and then grown them on slowly – which also helps keep them bushy.

Fibrous- and tuberous-rooted begonias are less hardy, and I sow these in late February or early March, pricking them out and growing them on in the warm part of the greenhouse until early May before moving them to cooler conditions. So these are sown later but grow more quickly in warmer conditions.

Generally speaking, the slow-growing or slow-germinating plants are sown first, and their position in the greenhouse is adjusted according to their progress and the demands of other plants. Quicker-germinating and speedier-growing plants like marigolds can be sown much later. If space gets too tight, marigolds and even dahlias can be sown in the unheated greenhouse and will germinate reasonably well.

But the converse of this rule is that easy, quick-growing plants should not be sown too early. Marigolds sown in February will need to be in 5-in* pots by May, and unless you have a particular reason for wanting to grow them in this way it pays to wait. So in general I would suggest not being too eager to get seeds in.

My one rule is always to keep the propagator full during the crucial spring period. For there's no doubt that apart from one or two plants like primulas and lettuce, in which dormancy is induced by high temperatures, a little heat improves germination and this means you can sow fewer seeds in smaller pots, thereby saving on space and compost. So as soon as a few pots are removed to the heated mat for weaning, more varieties are sown. Pots that show no sign of germination after a reasonable period are removed to an unheated propagator in the warm part of the greenhouse, otherwise, as in some seasons when I've grown unusual and unknown plants, the propagator can be in danger of filling up with pots which never produce any seedlings!

After the spring rush of half-hardy plants has left the propagator, it can be used for sowing seeds of bedding plants to fill late summer gaps, for sowing perennials or for summer cuttings.

## Containers

*GR:* Do not sow seeds in seed-trays. Heresy? Think about it. A seed-tray is large enough to contain thousands of seedlings, and very few of us need so many seedlings of one variety, even assuming that the seed-packets contained enough seeds. My propagator will hold three

---

* We use imperial measurements throughout the book, except in a very few cases where the metric measurement is necessary. A metric conversion table will be found on page x.

standard seed-trays with a little space left over; it will hold fifty seed-pots. There really isn't an argument.

There's one job which I absolutely hate (even supposing I had the time to do it) and that's pot-washing. So I buy the thinnest, cheapest plastic pots. I used to throw them away when I'd used them once, but now they go to the local hospital for the patients' gardening groups. Most annuals, bedding plants and other plants raised in the propagator are sown in square pots which are $2\frac{1}{2}$ in across and $2\frac{1}{4}$ in deep. They hold enough seeds for me and enough compost for the seeds. I sow those seeds which are going to over-winter in the cold frame in larger, deeper pots, so that they have extra moisture-holding capacity and I don't have to water them so often.

This way not only can I get fifty different varieties in my propagator instead of three, but when I take them out to wean them they can be fitted into small gaps wherever there happen to be some – I don't have to clear a large space. And they are *square* pots – round ones take up more room for the same amount of compost and surface area. Mathematicians among you can work it out.

For pricking out I use the same two sizes of pots. I used to use seed-trays if I needed a large quantity of one variety, but find that the flexibility of using individual pots in a crowded greenhouse is a great boon, as they can be arranged to fill every inch. I prick out the required number of seedlings individually and then add two or three pots with three seedlings in each in case friends want a few, there are plant sales coming up or simply 'in case'.

Plants that resent disturbance, such as many of the *Papaveraceae*, zinnias and so on, can be sown in Propapaks or one of the many other trays divided into small sections. Two or three seeds are sown in each cell and then thinned down to one after germination, and when they are well established the young plants are either set out directly into the garden with the minimum of root disturbance or potted on.

Some large seeds like ricinus are sown in pots individually, and go on the heated mat. Sweet peas are sown five seeds to a 5-in pot; although these pots too are available in disposable flimsy plastic, they are rather fragile when full of compost so I use standard rigid plastic pots instead – and wash them after use.

## Temperatures

*GR:* I keep my propagator so that it maintains a temperature at seed level of 70°F. This is easier said than done, particularly as some heated propagators have no thermostat. Those that do are usually calibrated in meaningless numbers, so you need a thermometer to help. Simply placing a max/min thermometer alongside the seed-pots will not always give a true reading. You have to bury it in a tray of compost to gauge the correct setting for the thermostat.

The heated mat for weaning is kept at a slightly lower temperature, and a similar ruse is needed to set this accurately. Again, the heat probe can be buried in a pot of compost to get the most accurate reading. The use of this heated mat, which primarily warms the roots of the plants, enables the ambient temperature to be kept lower than would otherwise be necessary – another technique which will lower overall running costs.

Temperatures in the propagator can reach very high levels on sunny days, and shading will be necessary. The greenhouse should be shaded with blinds or paint from early April onwards, and brown paper should be available for extra shading of the propagator itself on sunny days. The lid of the propagator can be painted with shading paint in early May if you wish. Automatic ventilators are also helpful.

## Composts

*GR:* This is a subject which causes great controversy.

Time was when all seed was sown in John Innes seed compost. Few people now make this themselves, and the standard of the compost available ready-mixed in garden centres is so variable that it does not pay to rely on it. I still buy ready-mixed John Innes seed compost, but I inspect it closely before using it and more often than not add grit or sharp sand to improve the drainage. Unlike the compost I used as recently as ten years ago, I also find that it pays to firm it only very gently, otherwise it compacts to such an extent that the water lies on the surface for some minutes before finally soaking in. I think this deterioration in quality is due mainly to the use of inferior loam – often it seems more like third-rate top-soil.

Ready-mixed peat-based sowing composts are now widely used, but these too can be disappointing. Not only do pieces of bark, twig and knots of fibres cause the occasional surprise, but they can also be unaccountably lumpy – hardly ideal when sowing fine seed. Some are made up of nothing but sedge or moss peat; some also contain vermiculite, grit, sharp sand or perlite. You will often need to add more drainage material.

The manufacturers of these products will say that their John Innes or their peat-based compost leaves their mixing plant in perfect condition and that adding extra materials upsets the carefully researched balance of ingredients. Well, you and I know that these composts are not always suitable for seed-sowing when we open the bag and that we must do something about it.

Christopher runs a nursery, so building a loam stack or buying bulk loads of good loam and making his own John Innes compost makes sense. But for most of us it is impossible to buy a bag or two of sterilized loam to use in our own mixes, so we are stuck with what comes in a bag from the garden centre.

Various other materials are sometimes recommended as compost ingredients, but only vermiculite has any virtue used alone. For drainage, perlite, various grits and sharp sand are recommended, and which you use depends largely on what is easily available in your area. But vermiculite can be useful on its own. It has a unique combination of characteristics. It allows penetration of air, it holds a lot of moisture, but it also allows surplus moisture to drain away promptly. On the debit side, it contains no nutrients whatsoever.

I prefer not to sow in pure vermiculite, but it can be added to peat-based composts to improve the drainage without reducing the water-holding capacity too much, and I have recently tried using it as a covering to seed sown on normal compost. This gives the great advantage of allowing you to water far more often than you would normally, so ensuring that the seed never dries out. But even with all this watering there is no risk of washing the seed away or over-saturating it – unless you let the vermiculite dry out, in which case even when using a fine rose it will all wash to one side of the pot – seed and all.

If you prefer, you can make up your own peat-based compost mixes using fine or medium grade moss peat and perlite for drainage plus a seed base – a fertilizer formulated specially for seed composts. I tend to make up a few big batches of this economical mixture for spring potting, but use ready-mixed composts, which often have the extra advantage of an added wetting agent, for sowing.

Vermiculite is also useful for seeds which take a very long time to germinate. Peonies, aroids and many shrub seeds can be mixed with a little moist vermiculite, closed in a small plastic lunch-box or even a 35mm film canister, and left in the cold frame or the fridge. Regular inspection is necessary, of course, but this technique completely eliminates problems of algal, moss and liverwort growth on pots standing outside for many months or even years. It also removes danger from natural hazards such as dogs and cats, which can overturn pots, and ensures that the seed stays constantly moist even in summer.

For pricking out there are again two choices of compost – soil-based and peat-based. Contrary to what all the books tell you, it is not necessary to prick out using the same type of compost into which the seed was sown. I always prefer to use a compost with at least some loam and also extra drainage. I manage this by keeping in my potting-shed (as well as a radio for the test matches) a bag of John Innes No. 2 compost, a bag of peat-based compost, a bag of grit and a bag of perlite.

When pricking out I gather my seed-pots into groups and make up batches of compost accordingly. Sometimes, I might need to make a small mix for just a few seedlings and the ingredients can then be measured in 3-in or 5-in plastic pots and mixed by hand. Most bedding plants go into my home-mixed peat-based compost, or possibly into branded peat compost plus peat-based compost plus extra grit. This is in spite of the fact that many new varieties of bedding plants are bred to be grown in standard bagged composts. With so many different plants, having different requirements and all growing together, the extra drainage is certainly a big help.

Bedding plants which are actually perennials and have a chance of surviving the winter, and which I'm putting in large pots, get a compost with loam and good drainage. The water held in the peat around the crown can cause rot in wet spells.

Most perennials go into a loam-based mixture, often with extra drainage, but woodland and shade-loving plants often have extra peat too.

This too is an approach which will infuriate the makers of branded composts, but it is based entirely on personal experience, especially the frustration of opening compost bags to be disappointed by the contents.

Finally, feeding. Most annuals and bedding plants, especially those pricked out into pots where the roots have plenty of compost to run through, will get by with no feeding at all until planting time. But it should be said that if you do add grit to bought composts you thin out the nutrients, so you may need to feed.

I usually give all these plants a couple of liquid feeds from a can during their last month before planting, just to ensure that they're quick off the starting blocks once planted out. Anything that remains in a pot for more than three months after pricking out is fed every fortnight from April to September with Maxicrop – if I remember.

PEAT

Now that we have become aware of the extent to which our wetlands are being destroyed to provide peat for gardeners, I have been trying alternatives. So far, although coir or coco fibre looks very promising, it's too early to make definite recommendations for all the plants we cover in this book. However, I would certainly suggest trying it for half-hardy annuals and bedding plants.

SEED COMPOST RECIPES

*John Innes seed compost*

> 2 parts sterilized loam
> 1 part moss peat
> 1 part sharp sand (up to $\frac{1}{8}$ in)

The loam and peat are put through a $\frac{3}{8}$-in sieve and to each bushel is added $1\frac{1}{2}$ oz of superphosphate. Unless acid-loving plants are to be sown, $\frac{3}{4}$ oz of ground limestone is also added.

*Peat-based compost*

> 3 parts moss peat
> 1 part grit or perlite

Fine-grade moss peat is used, or sedge peat which is usually milled fine. To each 2-gallon bucketful of mixture add one (130-gm) sachet of Chempak seed base.

PRICKING OUT AND POTTING COMPOST RECIPES

*John Innes potting compost*

> 7 parts sterilized loam
> 3 parts moss peat
> 2 parts sharp sand (up to $\frac{1}{8}$ in)

The loam and peat are put through a $\frac{3}{8}$-in sieve and to each bushel $\frac{3}{4}$ oz of ground limestone is also added, unless acid-loving plants are to be grown. The addition of 4 oz of John Innes base fertilizer gives potting compost No. 1. This is doubled for No. 2 and trebled for No. 3.

*Peat-based compost*

> 3 parts moss or sedge peat
> 1 part sharp sand, grit or perlite

To each 8 2-gallon bucketfuls of mixture add one 795-gm pack of Chempak potting base.

## Seed-sowing techniques

*GR:* Some gardeners are remarkably careless about how exactly they sow their seeds. It's not surprising, then, that seed companies are pestered with phone calls from gardeners who insist that the seed is useless when in fact it's the sowing technique which is at fault, not the seed.

Home-made compost should be thoroughly and evenly mixed to ensure a uniform distribution of ingredients; if necessary, bought compost should be sieved to remove lumps. When you come to sow, it should be moist but not sodden. Moisten it well in advance if necessary.

Filling the seed-pots is the first stage, and even this can be done badly. Seed-pots should be filled evenly without air pockets and then firmed carefully. Over-enthusiastic firming, which prevents good drainage, is a worse fault than too light firming; it is usually sufficient to fill the pots loosely, level with the rim, and then to firm down about $\frac{1}{4}$ in.

A specially cut board which will leave a smooth surface is more satisfactory than the base of an empty pot.

People disagree about the best way to get the seed from the packet to the compost. I have my favourite method, which I will describe; Christopher's may be different. Cut off the top of the packet containing the seeds with a pair of scissors. Make a sharp crease down one side and hold the packet between your thumb and first finger, with your new crease in the middle of the lower side. Tilt the packet slightly and tap it with your second finger to encourage the seed to slide along your crease. As it drops out, move the packet across the surface of the compost to give an even coverage. This technique works well even with fine seeds, as you can watch them drop, and by moving the packet as necessary the seed can be sown evenly. Personally I find mixing fine seed with silver sand, as is sometimes suggested, less than helpful. [So do I. – CL]

The technique that I find least likely to result in an even distribution of seed is to tip some of the seed into the palm of one hand, take a pinch of seed between two fingers of the other hand and rub the two fingers together slightly to release the seed. This is an extremely unpredictable method and fine seed will stick to your hand. [Not my experience! – CL]

Next there's the problem of how to cover the seed. It's quite difficult to find a sieve with a suitable mesh size – most kitchen sieves are too fine and garden sieves are too coarse. You can make one by knocking together a square wooden frame and tacking on a piece of stiff plastic shade netting. [A sheet of perforated zinc is also effective. – CL]

Using vermiculite solves the problem, as it's easy to handle, runs freely and it doesn't matter how deep, within reason, you put it on, as both light and air can penetrate. With very fine seed it's probably best to put the vermiculite on first and then sow the seed on top; watering it in (carefully!) will wash it into the vermiculite.

Seed which needs a cold period and which will be sitting in the cold frame all winter, and possibly for two winters, needs a covering of grit to discourage moss and liverwort growth and help keep the surface moist. Washed grit is greatly preferable to grit with sand particles, which impede the drainage. The depth is not crucial, as most seed will emerge through a covering up to $\frac{1}{4}$ in deep.

P73690

## Pricking out

*GR:* We are often told to prick out seedlings 'as soon as they are large enough to handle', and for many plants this is sensible advice. But I often think that the speed with which small seedlings establish themselves in ideal conditions is balanced by the ease with which they're damaged when so young, and the less than perfect compost that they sometimes have to tolerate. Larger seedlings are less fragile and so more likely to survive.

Of course, sowing in small pots as I suggest does mean that you cannot leave them in those pots for long periods, because they will simply crowd themselves too much and become too leggy and drawn. The roots will also become intertwined, making it more difficult to separate them. So there are many things to weigh up; I'm sure you see the problems and can decide for yourself at which stage to do the job.

If you have very few seeds and sow perhaps just three in a pot, these can be left to grow on for some weeks before moving each into a pot of its own. Conversely lobelia, which is a tiny seed that usually comes in generous quantities, germinates well, and the seedlings are so small that they are usually pricked out in patches.

At college they always tell you to orientate all the seed-leaves of the seedlings in the same direction when pricking out. This is not just to obtain an even-looking box (although some tutors seem to think this in itself is important). Rather, the fact that each seedling is orientated the same way implies a regular, ordered and systematic approach to the job and this of course saves time. On commercial nurseries experienced workers can prick out a full box of seedlings in a minute and a half!

There is always a certain amount of discussion about how much to firm seedlings. Usually, if the compost is good, gentle firming followed by watering in well will settle the compost around the roots thoroughly. Over-firming can damage the neck of the seedlings, and rots will then attack promptly.

Some plants are best if they're not pricked out. Fritillarias and some other bulbs fatten up more quickly if the whole seed-pot is simply potted on. Plants of this sort are probably best sown in larger pots to start with, to allow them greater root space. Regular liquid feeding is a great help, and the growing season can be extended by an early start into growth in the greenhouse before moving the pots outside. This all helps to bring bulb seedlings to flowering size quickly.

SOUTH PUGET SOUND LIBRARY

I find that small pots, the same as those I use for seed-sowing, are the most practical containers for most seedlings. They help you utilize your space effectively, roots are not disturbed when planting out, and you can easily give the odd plants away to friends. Only alpines and other plants that will stay in their pots for a long period should go into pots which are more elegant as well as more sturdy.

## Hardening off

*GR:* For gardeners with limited facilities, hardening off can be difficult to manage. But plants must be accustomed to the outside world before planting, otherwise they will surely suffer.

The ideal arrangement is to have a cold frame which can be used to acclimatize the young plants. You need to be around every night and morning, however, to put the lights in place and remove them as necessary, and this is not always possible. If you do not have a frame, you need to increase the ventilation steadily in the cold greenhouse before moving plants to a very sheltered place outside. If you concentrate on perennials and alpines which need no heat, the problem does not arise.

## Problems

### Chlorotic seedlings

*GR:* Seedlings can emerge from the compost with a yellow or whitish tinge, and this is usually the result of germinating acid-loving plants in a limy compost. The food store in the seed will usually provide enough reserves to power the seed-leaves through, but as soon as the roots discover the nature of the compost the leaves will reveal all. Some seeds may never emerge at all. Even prompt transfer to a suitable compost is usually too late.

On the other hand, there is always the possibility of a variegated or yellow-leaved variant among your seedlings. So if pale-leaved seedlings survive, look after them well.

*CL:* Another possible reason for yellow leaves is that temperatures for

SOUTH FRONT SOUND LIBRARY

germination and for the young seedling were too low. This is particularly evident in dahlias, tithonias, zinnias and ipomoeas.

### Damping off

GR: This is the biggest problem for many gardeners. Various soil-borne fungi attack the germinating seeds and young seedlings, causing rapid collapse. Infection can be prevented by using clean pots, fresh compost with no garden soil added, and clean tools, and on no account using water from a rain-barrel. Copper-based fungicides and those based on benomyl, used alternately, are of limited benefit; unfortunately the most effective fungicides for damping off are not available to the home gardener.

### Drying out

GR: Seedlings in a propagator or on a heated mat can dry out unnoticed. The heat from below dries out the compost in the bottom half of the pot and if insufficient water is given from above it may not penetrate to the bottom. Take care.

### Etiolated growth

GR: Lank and leggy growth is usually the result of leaving newly germinated seed in shady, dark or very warm conditions for too long.

### Lack of germination

GR: This can be caused by seed which is not viable, though that is highly unlikely in the case of the more widely grown bedding plants, perennials and annuals bought from larger seed companies. Rarer and more obscure seed may suffer from the problem. The other main cause is giving the wrong conditions. Seeds which require a cold period will not germinate if placed straight in the propagator.

### Moss

GR: Moss and liverworts can be troublesome on pots of fern spores in the propagator and also on seed-pots left outside for the winter. Pots of fern spores are placed in trays of water containing potassium permanganate, which prevents the germination of moss spores. A shallow layer of sharp grit is spread on the surface of pots left outside for some time, to provide a dry surface which is inhospitable to moss.

### Scorch and shrivelling of seedlings

*GR:* Bright sunlight on young seedlings which have just been moved out from the shade is liable to cause scorch. This can also happen in an unshaded propagator.

### Weeds

*GR:* Weeds sometimes appear in seed-pots left outside, and these are almost always from wind-blown seeds. Keep control of the weeds in your garden and weed your seed-pots regularly – weeds can easily be removed while still small.

### Worms

*GR:* Sometimes pots left outside suffer from worms; casts appear on the grit and these soon host weeds. A small piece of perforated zinc or plastic mesh in the base of the pots prevents larger worms getting in. A layer of polythene on the soil before the covering of grit on which the pots are stood is also a sensible precaution.

# Sowing Outside

*CL:* For anyone unused to handling seed, sowing it where you want it to bloom has the greatest appeal. Graham describes this method at its simplest (under *Papaver*) for Shirley poppies: 'The last time I grew these I simply flung the seed in a wide arc across a mixed border and left it all to its own devices.' This, after all, is what happens in nature, and if you have plenty of seed you can afford to be wasteful, like Dame Nature herself (the silly old profligate). Furthermore, the poppy family, and a few others like it, have such fleshy, fragile roots that they loathe being transplanted. The direct sowing method obviates this.

Usually, because seed supplies are limited and because we need to know more precisely where our plants are destined to grow, we adopt a more exact sowing method.

Suppose it is a patch of love-in-a-mist (see under *Nigella*) that we'd like, at the margin of a mixed border. It can be sown either in autumn or in spring, nigella being very hardy. Spring is the more normal time for most seeds if their hardiness is questionable, in which case fork the ground over, leaving it rough, in autumn, at the same time incorporating garden compost or spent mushroom compost. In early spring, knock this down with the back of a fork and get a fine tilth with a rake. If it doesn't break down easily, tread about on it and rake again. The ground must not be so wet that you pick it up on your feet – if it is, wait till it has dried out more. Given the right conditions, late March is a good time in the south, and two or three weeks later in the north, where the soil is slower to warm up.

My preferred method of sowing is to broadcast the seed as evenly as I can but not in rows.

*GR:* I must disagree. Especially for the newcomer to seed-raising, sowing the seed in rows has one major advantage. For when the seeds come up the weeds come up too, and if your annuals are sown in rows the very fact that they are in a straight line helps you distinguish them from the seedling weeds, which can then be removed without disturbing your newly emerged seedlings. There is no need for the mature plants to look as if they are sown in rows as long as you thin them out sufficiently to allow them to develop their natural habit. They will then simply merge into a cohesive group

*CL:* I never sow straight from the packet, either in the open or on to containers.

*GR:* Sorry, Christopher, I don't agree with that either! See my comments under sowing technique on page 16.

*CL:* You have more control by tipping the contents of the packet into one hand and removing it in pinches (like snuff) for sowing with the other. Hold the sowing hand sufficiently high (6 in or so) above the soil to get an even spread as it falls. Don't choose a windy day.

Now rake the soil gently, so that the seed is a little covered, and then tump it down with the back of the rake (I often use the soles of my feet, again, for this). Graham will describe the slight variation in the method he learned at Kew.

*GR:* Well, I can if you like, but I've given up using it myself. The area to be sown is first raked deeply, then the loose soil is drawn away from the area you wish to sow, using the back of the rake and leaving ridges on either side. The seed is then broadcast over this slightly sunken area and the soil flicked back with the rake and gently tamped down. Since I described this in detail a few years ago in my book on annuals and bedding plants,* I've reverted entirely to the row method. And Kew have too!

*CL:* When you write a label, always note on the back the date of sowing, the seed source and the year of purchase or harvest (one sometimes uses old seed). These are valuable reminders later on for deciding whose seed germinates best, how long you can keep it, and whether or not the date you chose for sowing gave good results.

If you sow in autumn – September, or even early October in the south, where sowings can be made later than in the north (as they can earlier in the spring) – a far stronger plant will be obtained, if it survives the winter. If it doesn't, you still have the chance for a second attempt.

* Graham Rice, *A Handbook of Annuals and Bedding Plants,* Christopher Helm, 1986.

Before your autumn sowing you'll need to dig in more completely rotted garden or mushroom compost (if the latter still smells ammoniacal, it has not decomposed sufficiently). The seedlings, in spring, can be given a top dressing of Growmore at 2 oz to the square yard at the same time as all the other plants in a mixed border, but don't let the pellets lodge on foliage or they'll burn it. If it doesn't rain soon after, spray from a watering can.

The alternative method to broadcasting your seed is to sow it in short, parallel drills [That's more like it, read on. – GR], which subsequently makes it easier (a) to distinguish weeds from your own seedlings and (b) to hand-hoe between the rows. If you're sowing a bed with a range of different annuals, the drills can be taken out at different angles, in respect of different seeds, so as to minimize a regimented appearance. You never entirely eliminate this, however, as can be seen in the annual borders at Wisley.

By this method you draw out your rows, $\frac{1}{4}$ in deep, with the tip of a cane, kept straight and in position by running it along the edge of a board or of another piece of cane laid flat on the soil and held firm with one hand while you draw out the channel with the other. Then sow, at the rate of about four seeds to the 1-in run, close the channels with the back of the rake and tump firm.

If you're sowing an informal bed with different kinds of annuals, first mark the outline of each group to be sown with the tip of a stick and (since your feet may prematurely obliterate this channel) dribble some sand or grit or fine peat (something of a different colour from the soil itself) along the groove so made.

When your seeds germinate, so will weed seeds with them, but yours should be distinguishable by being the most numerous of any one kind. If you haven't a clue what to look for, get an experienced friend to help in identification.

Remember that comparatively few large plants of any annual will make a much better and more prolonged show than a lot of runts that have been starved either through competition or because you have fallen for the fallacy exposed by Graham in his book on annuals and bedding plants: 'There is a great and popular rumour that annuals like nothing better than a parched and impoverished soil. This is rubbish.' Weeds must be eliminated and your own seedlings must be thinned in stages, first to a spacing of 3 or 4 in, and finally to 6, 9, 12 or 18 in, according to the strength of the annual in question. A spacing of

9–12 in will be right for love-in-a-mist seedlings sown in the autumn.

When removing seedlings that are close to one you want to retain, there is a danger of all being lifted in the upheaval. To prevent this, place the index and middle finger of one hand on the soil either side of the seedling to be retained and press downwards while you pull out unwanted seedlings with the other hand. (I'm not saying left or right, as I'm never sure whether I'm left- or right-handed myself.)

The sowing of annuals outside need not be limited to hardy or nearly hardy kinds dealt with in autumn or in early spring. Quite tender annuals like zinnias or tithonias can be sown outside in suitable May weather. Quick developers like *Cynoglossum amabile*, cornflowers, larkspurs, eschscholzias and candytuft can be sown for flowering the same season right up to July or even August.

## Drawbacks to direct sowings

*CL:* Once you have learned to handle seeds and seedlings in pots and seed-trays, generally with the help of glass protection, albeit frequently unheated, you will appreciate how much more control and precision those methods give you.

A far greater proportion of your seeds will germinate, and this is all-important where F1 hybrids are in question and there are only a few, expensive seeds in a packet.

If your soil, like mine, is heavy, the fine tilth necessary for preparing a seed-bed will pan, following rain or irrigation, into a horrible hard crust. This will crack as it dries out, and is altogether thoroughly unfriendly to the germination and development of seeds and seedlings.

Another snag: sparrows love to take dust baths in a fine seed-bed, thereby completely ruining your arrangements. You'll need to forestall this by laying branches of brushwood or a criss-cross of cotton, held on sticks, over the sown area.

Third snag: a seed-bed for your seeds is also a seed-bed for weeds. All will germinate together and, as most weeds are stronger and faster-growing than anything we introduce, competition is hot, right from the outset. But if you're planting out a strong, ready-made seedling into weed-free ground, it has a head start.

*GR:* Fourth snag: you can't give away your spares. I always prick out a few extra seedlings into 3-in pots if I have them, and these go to friends or plant sales later in the spring. True, I could dig up a few and pot them up but I suspect I'd simply never get round to it.

## Annuals for picking

*CL:* Seeds of column stocks, cornflowers, larkspurs, everlasting flowers of various kinds, and others that you grow for picking, can be sown in rows in a spare plot. Prepare the ground in the usual way and draw out the rows with a cane or the corner of a drag hoe. If the row is long, make a garden line the guide against which to draw the row out. Don't make your channel too deep – $\frac{1}{4}$ in is sufficient – otherwise the seeds will never come through (and if they don't, that is the likeliest reason, not drought, crows, the neighbours' cats or the Conservative Government). If the ground is desperately dry, take out a slightly deeper channel and water it from the long spout of a Haws watering can (much the best design).

## Half-hardy annuals outside

*GR:* If you've a mind to, there are a number of plants usually recommended for sowing in the greenhouse or the propagator which grow perfectly well if sown outside when the soil has warmed up. Zinnias flower prolifically and never seem to suffer from unpredictable collapse when sown where they are to flower, and cosmos, nicotiana or even dwarf dahlias can be treated in the same way.

You will find that the F1 hybrid varieties have the vigour to help them make up for lost time. And those in the daisy family with large seeds, like zinnias and dahlias, also have the reserves to cope with the less than perfect conditions compared with sowing in trays of seed compost. A year or two ago when I sowed two packets, just over 40 seeds, of *Zinnia* 'Ruffles' outside in late May, almost all of them came up. Next time I'll sow just one packet and space-sow them further apart.

## Biennials

*CL:* Wallflowers are always sown in rows outside, usually in the brassica seed-bed. Other biennials such as foxgloves, verbascums, myosotis and bellis (daisies) can be similarly treated, though with tiny seeds such as these I prefer the use of containers.

Late May is a good time to sow wallflowers in the south, but in cold or exposed areas a smaller plant will be tougher and a later sowing, in June–July, is advisable.

*GR:* Sowing later to produce smaller, stockier plants is also advisable in very windy gardens, where large plants will be more easily buffeted by the winter gales we are now blasted with so often.

*CL:* Siberian wallflowers and *Erysimum linifolium* flower prematurely if sown before mid-June. July is early enough for winter- and spring-flowering pansies. Use the same sowing technique as for annuals in rows.

Transplant your seedlings when they are large enough to handle comfortably, spacing them in rows according to their vigour. Foxgloves and mulleins will take 18 in between plants; for daisies, 6 in will be enough.

These operations tend to take place in hot weather. Try to do them in the evening and make sure, by judicious use of polythene, and also by lifting plants with plenty of soil attached, that the roots never get dry. Water in thoroughly. Subsequent irrigations are often a great help.

# Sowing in Cold Frames

*CL:* Unlike Graham, I have many cold frames and only enough heated glass to keep the frost out of a greenhouse where slightly tender plants and cuttings are over-wintering.

All my spring-sown seedlings are germinated under cold glass. This means that my principal sowings, when more than 100 different varieties are dealt with, take place in the first half of April. There are more at the turn of April–May and some as late as June.

From early April sowings, most seedlings will be ready to plant out in eight weeks' time, following nicely on spring bedding and finding the ground warmed up so that they zoom ahead. To gain my objectives, I'm using the sun's heat without supplementary electricity.

### The frames

*CL:* The first essential, when germinating seeds, is that the frames should be snug. No need to whack up their heat to dizzy heights by day, but most important to retain their heat at night. Glass-sided frames, which are the easiest to buy, do not hold heat once the sun is off them. They are OK for hardening seedlings off after pricking out, but not in the earlier stages. You may have to construct your own.

The simplest sort of frame can be made with grass turves, of whatever dimensions you please, laying your lights across the top. These need rebuilding every couple of years, but they are amazingly cosy. [But where do those of us without meadows find the turves – do we dig up the lawn? – *GR*] [Turves are not hard to buy – or filch – *CL*]

Better is the frame with concrete or breeze-block walls, tailored so as to be higher along the back than the front. Then your lights (I use Dutch lights which are fairly easy to handle and have a single pane of glass) will throw off the rain.

But for better warmth retention and quick germination (or rooting of cuttings), I have a double-walled frame and double glazing. The walls are built of thin concrete blocks bedded on to a common concrete foundation. There is a gap of some 2 in between the walls. The inner wall has a level top. The lights to cover it were made to measure by a local carpenter. The outer wall is higher at the back than at the front and made to fit Dutch lights. It faces towards the sun but there are ash trees overhanging it. They come into leaf late in May. Shading is necessary in bright weather, especially in late spring, but very little is needed once the leaves have expanded. The shade cast by ashes is always light, but I would console those who cannot lay on this convenience by observing that they frequently shed small branches.

The point of the inner lights being horizontal is that condensation drops collect evenly on their undersurface but no moisture is lost. We spray weekly with fungicide, varying the chemical so that resistant fungus strains do not have the chance to develop.

*GR:* Insulation blocks are now available which can be cut with a bow saw, enabling you to create a cosy frame with gently sloping sides using just one set of blocks. Dutch lights are now hard to come by, unfortunately, but if you can build your own you could double-glaze them with polythene sheeting. Better still, use twin-skin polycarbonate, which also has the benefit of being so tough that it probably wouldn't break if a whole branch dropped off one of Christopher's ash trees. It's expensive, though.

## Composts and drainage

*CL:* As Graham has remarked, I can build my own turf heap from a neighbouring meadow (which we then re-sow), and after a year this is in a fit state for providing loam for John Innes composts, so they are the ones I always use. The turf is roughly chopped off the heap, mechanically tilled and then riddled through a $\frac{3}{4}$-in sieve. Being full of grass roots, the texture is open. All makers of John Innes composts should use turf for their loam. Top soil simply does not provide the necessary drainage.

Three-quarter-inch soil lumps are on the large side, but none too large for my liking. I also use a very coarse grit from the local builders' merchants to comprise the sand ingredient. We sterilize the loam at least a day before use.

*GR:* For more remarks on John Innes composts, see page 14.

## Sowing

*CL:* For all sowings, as well as for pricking out, I use John Innes No. 1 potting compost, *not* the much weaker seed compost. If I made sowings in winter, when the light is feeble, the seed compost would be necessary, but by mid-March the light is strong, the days are long enough, natural sun warmth is there and all the seed varieties I require can cope with the stronger compost.

When filling pots and trays I have a large mound of compost on the bench in front of me, and using both hands back-sides down, I scoop a large volume into each container so that it overfills with a mound above the rim. Then I quickly rock the container a couple of times each way so that the largest lumps (which you don't want on the surface) roll off. Any that are left I float off with the side of my hand.

If the container is rigid, like a clay pot, or fairly rigid, like a wooden seed-tray (I don't use plastic trays; we soak the wooden ones when new in Cuprinol, and they last a long time), I first compress the compost with the tips of my fingers around the perimeter, roughly level the surface with the side of my hand, and finish off with a home-made pressing board, round, square or oblong, to suit the container type it's being used on. So as to finish with an even surface, a number of small pats are made all over to begin with, then comes a firm finishing pressure. Containers with rigid walls need greater firming pressure than those with plastic. Peat composts don't need this compressing, and it is mainly because my composts are very open and free-draining that they need a good bit. For seed-sowing, your compost needs to be a little on the dry side, so that your pressing board does not clog with bits of adhering soil, making the sowing of fine seeds impossible to do neatly.

If very fine seeds are to be sown, a fine sifting of compost through a home-made zinc sieve follows and another after sowing, unless the seeds are so small, like those of begonias and calceolarias, that they should not be covered at all. For efficient sieving it is again important that the compost should not be too wet.

Before sowing from any commercial packet (as against what I've collected and saved myself), I open it and tip the contents into a small, smooth-sided china, cat's drinking bowl. That shows me how much seed there is, whether I want to sow it all (there's no point in sowing a lot more than you need, and overcrowding at the seedling stage is harmful), and what size of pot to use. Unlike Graham, I have many sizes and I get someone to wash them for me! [Huh! – GR]

With any normal round seed, I sow the edge of the pot or box first, otherwise that area tends not to receive its fair share; then to and fro across the centre, as evenly as possible. I like to cup the seed in my right palm and take pinches (like snuff) with my left fingers and thumb. This generally retains reasonable control, but some seeds such as tagetes and cosmos are awkwardly shaped, and even distribution is less easy. Those that stick together, like anemones and clematis, have to be teased apart and pressed down before being covered and pressed again. Seeds that bounce out of position when being covered by compost I often press gently down with the board, first. Or else I mound the compost over the centre, and then spread it gently to the sides with my flattened fingers. (There is great sensuous satisfaction in these small refinements.)

## After-care

*CL:* To water my containers, I take them outside (in a round sieve) to a level bit of ground. Using a fine pot rose on a Haws watering can, which has a long spout and gives best control, I first rinse out the rose and the can, before filling it with water. If there's a wind, there's better control facing it than watering downwind. The first drops are always large and heavy. Hold the can to one side of the containers for a start, then water with an even, swishing motion to left and to right. Never allow water to float on the compost surface or your soil and seeds will shift. Always water from the top, however, never by soaking the containers from the bottom (who started that dreadful notion?).

Within the frame I cover with sheets of brown paper (old corn or poultry feed bags) to reduce water losses but *not* so as to exclude all light, as many seeds require this for even germination.

Some seeds germinate within three or four days. Close scrutiny of the containers is needed from an early stage, and as soon as action is noted, remove that container to another part of the frame, where it is light. Otherwise the seedlings will become leggy and drawn.

## Pricking out

*CL:* I prefer to prick out when the seedlings are still quite tiny, but they are first hardened off, initially in a single-walled close frame, then on the open greenhouse bench.

If the seedlings are sizeable, as with zinnias, stocks or tomatoes, I pot them individually straight away. Otherwise they go into seed-trays. If I want only a few seedlings, I divide the tray between two varieties of equal vigour (e.g. blue and white chimney bell-flowers – *Campanula pyramidalis*).

I believe in giving each seedling plenty of space, so that it can eventually be planted out with a large rootball and without undue destruction of roots. So in most cases I go in for a 7 × 4 spacing, but I use 8 × 5 for really small things like portulaca or leptosiphon, and also for seedlings that I intend to move soon into largish pots, rather than planting them out. The 7 × 4 seedlings are the ones that are going to be kept waiting longest.

With John Innes No. 1 composts, I do not find that feeding is necessary. The pricked-out seedlings go into a Rapley frame, which is a moveable metal structure made in sections, with one pane of square glass on the sides and four across the top. This needs a good bit of shading. At first kept closed, ventilation is soon admitted. Then the top panes are removed but the side panes remain for a good while as a protection against strong winds. However, the seedlings are fully hardened off before being planted out.

## Problems

*CL:* There are some seeds that I cannot handle satisfactorily without heat, notably bedding geraniums. Fibrous-rooted begonias and impatiens I can sow only in time for a late display (following biennials). Petunias I can do well because, from a late sowing, they grow so fast. Doubtless there are other snags, which I prefer not to think about, but I don't do badly.

*GR:* Christopher's heatless system is one which more people should consider. It depends on good frames and you may feel that by the time you have built them and made the lights you might as well have bought a cheap 8 × 6 ft greenhouse. But well insulated frames are warmer than most small greenhouses, not least because cheaper greenhouses tend to have very badly fitted glass and draughty doors. Frames also disrupt the scene in a small garden much less than an inelegant greenhouse.

# A to Z of Garden Flowers

## Acacia *(Leguminosae)*

*GR:* Some extraordinary techniques are recommended for germinating acacias. The problem is that the seed-coat is very hard and often stubbornly refuses to admit water; it also contains chemicals which inhibit germination. One of the more curious suggestions is to burn the seeds over a candle until they explode and then soak them in water before sowing. When I tried this they belched black smoke then finally cracked just as I was afraid they would burst into flames. Not one came up.

But be not disheartened, for here's a better way, and one that actually works. Put the seeds in a mug or bowl and fill it with boiling water. Put a saucer on top to keep in as much heat as possible, then put the bowl in a warm place – in the airing cupboard, near a boiler or in a propagator – for twenty-four hours. Next day you'll see that some of the seeds have swollen significantly, and these are ready for sowing. Pour the water and seeds through a tea-strainer to separate out the seeds, then wash them under warm water to remove the remains of any germination inhibitors. If you're not planning any spring picnics, use your thermos flask instead of the bowl and saucer as it keeps the heat in even longer.

The seeds can then be sown in John Innes seed compost at a temperature of about 70°F. Don't cover the seed, keep it in good light. They should be up in two to three weeks. Any that haven't swollen can have their tips cut off using a pair of nail clippers and then be soaked for another twenty-four hours. They should then plump up nicely – throw out any that don't.

The last acacia I tried this technique on was *A. baileyana*. Its fine, doubly divided leaves in a lacy silvery blue are about the best of all the genus, and then there are the flowers – puffy balls of yellow fluff gathered in brushes about 4 in long, which appear along the branches very early in the year. This is not the hardiest of species, but as a plant which used to grow in the botanic garden at Trinity College, Dublin, demonstrated, it will shoot strongly from below ground if hit by a savage winter. Or if ruthlessly pruned.

I tried both the smoky-purple-leaved version and the silvery species, but I'm afraid that about four out of five of what were supposed to be smoky ones came up silver. But they're still lovely.

## Acaena *(Rosaceae)*

*GR:* Be warned. The pea-green leaved *Acaena novae-zealandiae* germinates with all too little hesitation, and then shows as little caution as it promptly smothers more restrained treasures with its emerald foliage.

Generally acaenas need no special treatment. They self-sow easily and can be sown in spring in a cold greenhouse or cold frame; extra warmth will simply hasten their emergence.

They form pretty mats of miniature rose-like leaves, neatly toothed, from which rise stiff stalks carrying spherical heads of red, chestnut or sometimes silvery flowers, which Graham Thomas rather harshly calls 'insignificant'. Hooked burrs follow.

Acaenas are invaluable ground-huggers for gardeners who like their dwarf bulbs to grow through foliage, for they have no objection to the lengthening bulb foliage flopping on to them after flowering.

Even some of the hybrids come more or less true from seed, but only a few are available commercially. *A. caesiglauca* is silvery and neat, *A. microphylla* bronzed and neat, while the evil *A. novae-zealandiae* is only for the widest of open spaces.

*CL:* But this is the one with the most brilliant carmine red young burrs, in July; brighter by far than any acaena flower. Excellent for colonizing paving or a sunny bank where there are no treasures to be swamped.

## Acanthus *(Acanthaceae)*

*CL:* The only acanthus that has ever ripened seed in my garden is *A. balcanicus* (*A. longifolius*). This it does regularly, and it self-sows, which can be quite a nuisance because once the deep-rooting acanthus is established it is hard to eradicate. Every piece of root left behind makes a new plant. Indeed, the normal method of propagating this genus is from root cuttings, if not by division of crowns.

*A. mollis* is the species whose seed is offered commercially. In Britain, its disadvantage is that it often misses out on flowering. Handsome though the soap-smooth leaves are, even in winter, one would like those spikes of sinister, hooded flowers with their murky purple and off-white colouring. Presumably there is a climatic factor at work here, as acanthus of any sort will flower freely in the Mediterranean and throughout the United States. *A. balcanicus* is reliably free-flowering under all likely conditions, and so is *A. spinosus*. This last has prickly foliage but looks all the better for it. At anything up to 6 ft, the flowering stems can be awkward and need support. *A. balcanicus* and *A. mollis,* at 3 ft or so, are self-supporting.

*GR:* The even more prickly *A. spinosissimus* turns up in seed lists and catalogues occasionally, but some botanists consider it no different from *A. spinosus*; I suppose if it were simply a matter of degree of spininess then we might, just, accept their judgement. But *A. spinosissimus* really is exceptional, with spines on the midribs and leaf petioles too. And if you ever come across seed of *A. dioscoridis,* snap it up. It may not be spiny, but the dusky pink flowers are a real treat.

The clue to the flowering problem may be that in the Mediterranean acanthus often grow in hot and apparently dry places, although their roots surge deep into the soil so they are never short of water. But this combination of a baking and ample moisture is a little difficult to create in British gardens.

The seeds are big, only about five to the gram, and are flung out explosively for up to 20 ft. They are happy sown fairly cool, say in a cold frame or cold greenhouse, in spring.

## Aconitum *(Ranunculaceae)*

*CL:* As with delphiniums, the seed of aconitums, the poisonous monks-hoods, needs to be fresh if high percentage germination is to be obtained.

*GR:* Old seed or seed which has been stored for some time (i.e. most seed bought from seed companies) can be very slow to germinate. But four weeks in the bottom of the fridge or a winter in a cold frame will make quite a difference when the seed-pot is brought into the warm.

*CL:* The nugget-like, tuberous roots are so easily propagated by division that this is the normal method and ensures that the named varieties remain true.

*Aconitum volubile* is the exception. It is a herbaceous, climbing perennial, easily cultivated but not often seen. Perhaps the reason for this is that seedlings often give rise to disappointingly muddy flowered plants They *can* be a good deep monkshood blue, and your best hope of ensuring this is to beg seed off the owner of a plant which you have seen and liked.

This aconite flowers in late summer and autumn. Reaching a height of 6–8 ft, it associates particularly happily with the yellow lanterns of *Clematis orientalis, C. tangutica* or another of that group.

## Actaea *(Ranunculaceae)*

CL: This is a hardy genus of poisonous herbs. The flowers are insignificant but their berries, borne in dense, shortish spikes, ripen in August, are long held and can be extremely handsome. The plants grow to $2\frac{1}{2}$–3 ft tall and are excellent in moist shade.

Naming has been much chopped around. *Actaea pachypoda* (syn. *A. alba*) looks most unusual but pleasing, each white berry supported by an inflated, reddish stalk. In *A. spicata* 'Fructo-alba' the berries are pure white and larger. This looks well with the gleaming scarlet fruit of *A. erythrocarpa* (*A. spicata rubra*), but the latter is the more robust plant and might swamp its partner.

Sow fresh seed in autumn and allow frost to reach the container. There'll be free germination the following spring, with the first flowers and fruit the year after.

## Adonis *(Ranunculaceae)*

CL: So far as I know, all members of the *Ranunculaceae* are poisonous and this is no exception.

*Adonis aestivalis,* known as pheasant's eye, is a pretty cornfield weed with small red flowers, black-centred, and feathery foliage. Nice but not showy.

GR: Pheasant's eye is increasingly being cultivated as a cut flower. The usual hardy annual treatment suits it very well. But don't be tempted by varieties with names such as 'Scarlet Chalice', which seem to me no different from the wild species. A case of the seed companies trying to pull a fast one.

*CL:* The perennial members of the family are far more exciting, but I have no experience of growing them from seed. As they are from cold climates, their seed should be sown fresh and over-wintered where frost can reach the pots.

*GR:* The perennial *A. vernalis* is quite exquisite, and one of the most captivating of alpines for its big buttercups – so low on the ground and so early in the year. Germination can be slow, but unlike many members of the *Ranunculaceae,* no chilling is necessary if the seed is fresh.

## Agapanthus *(Amaryllidaceae)*

*CL:* Although easily raised from their shiny black seeds, the practice should not be encouraged unless rigid selection is enforced. There is an awful lot of seed-raised rubbish around, with dirty blue flowers. The 'Headbourne Hybrids' themselves, first bred and selected by the Hon. Lewis Palmer, have greatly degenerated as a strain. You may get almost anything under this title.

*GR:* The original 'Headbourne Hybrids' were a mixture of pure white, various lilacs and pale blues through to deep blue and violet, and had the added and welcome bonus of hardiness. Now in demand as a cut flower, high quality seed of this strain is again available, from Holland, and may well presage a return to better quality generally.

Sow in the propagator in spring. Germination will take four to six weeks. Prick out into 3-in pots, move into 5-in pots, then plant out. They'll probably take three years to flower.

## Ageratum *(Compositae)*

*CL:* These annual flowers derive mainly from the Central American *Ageratum houstonianum.* Something quite close to the wilding can be bought under a variety of names such as 'Blue Bouquet', 'Wonder' or simply 'Tall Blue'. It makes an informal 2-ft plant, and flowers without becoming weary from midsummer till the first frosts (and you'll get self-sown seedlings for years afterwards). It goes uncommonly well with tall African marigolds, its own colour (always described as blue) being lavender blue.

But the most popular ageratums are dumpy, squat little things, ideal for edging where you are frightened of the edging plant encroaching on your precious lawn. No danger of that with ageratums. If I admit to loathing these 6 to 8-in pygmies, that is just my prejudice in favour of a plant that grows more as nature intended. The public gets what it deserves and desires.

*GR:* 'Blue Ribbon' gets away from the blocky, flat-topped look to some extent, making a much more rounded, dome-shaped plant, and if planted about 10 in apart makes a rolling edge rather than the more familiar squarish, flat-topped strip.

*CL:* 'Blue Mink' grows up to a foot tall and makes a self-respecting plant. Mixtures are rather charming, with various shades of blue, purple, lilac, old rose and white combined. The plants will also vary considerably in height, so that a carpet of them undulates. This characteristic would rule out an award in any seed trial, but is the kind of informality that suits many gardens and gardeners.

*GR:* There has been one great advance in ageratums in recent years – bicolours are now available. These are delightful – the filaments in the flower retain their sharp, blue colour but are backed by a pure white cushion. And the result is stunning. Three varieties seem to be available. 'Bavaria', a tetraploid, has been around the longest but almost no one listed it. 'Southern Cross' was launched a few years ago with a great fanfare, and 'Capri' has also now appeared – though the true 'Capri' should be deep blue. Not yet having grown all three side by side, I hesitate to insist that they're all the same but it looks that way.

And Christopher would even approve of their habit – slightly uneven, with the flower-heads held on stems which stand up slightly above the foliage and which don't merge into a blanket of colour. All we need is a tall cut-flower version and life will be complete.

## Agrostemma *(Caryophyllaceae)*

*GR:* The corn cockle, *Agrostemma githago,* is one of Britain's rarest cornfield weeds. Now restricted to only two sites, the limited viability of the seeds, and changes in agricultural practice, have doubtless contributed to its decline.

A pretty cut flower, its tall spindly growth and long narrow foliage also make it a fine self-sowing annual for sunny borders; it disrupts none of its neighbours wherever it appears. The named varieties normally grown have 2-in, open, five-petalled, rather floppy flowers, prettily lined and spotted, each with a white eye. The pale plummy 'Milas' is named after the town in Turkey where it was found, just inland from the coast facing Kos and Rhodes. 'Milas Cerise' is darker. These may well be the same as 'Rose Queen' and 'Purple Queen'.

Treat it as a hardy annual. If you keep the seed it will lose its viability by the second spring after harvest.

*CL:* 'Milas' makes a splendid pot plant, treated like cornflowers. Sow in autumn, over-winter under cold glass, and move the seedlings on into 7-in pots. They'll grow to 4 ft and need a stake per plant.

## Alcea (syn. Althaea) *(Malvaceae)*

*GR:* If only they didn't succumb to rust. Spires of single hollyhocks used to be such a feature of English gardens, but rust and then poor selection by seed producers led to their ever-increasing rarity. As rust discouraged people from growing them, so seed companies put less effort into keeping both the single-flowered mixture and the older doubles like 'Chater's Doubles' up to standard. Poor roguing leads to deteriorating quality.

Now that they are being used a little more as cut flowers on the Continent, the quality is improving again. And as cut flowers they really are breathtaking. To commercial growers 'Chater's Doubles' are available in eight separate colours; we have only a mixture.

It is when they are treated as biennial that rust strikes, over-wintering on the foliage and leaf petioles and reinfecting the plant as growth starts in the spring. The answer is to cut off the foliage and drench the plant with a fungicide containing propiconazole, such as Murphy Tumbleblite. Alternatively, treat hollyhocks as half-hardy annuals and sow them in February for planting in May. 'Summer Carnival' is a double mixture specially bred for this purpose.

There are also some curious dwarf doubles reaching only about 3 ft in height. 'Powderpuffs' is one such, and this also lacks the usual leaves among the flowers – which are shown off rather better as a result. In dry summers like 1989, all these dwarf doubles seemed to produce shorter leaf petioles and this too can help reveal the flowers. But it's still difficult to take them really seriously – they just don't seem like hollyhocks at all without that tall swaying exuberance.

Far more worthy are two less familiar ones. *Althaea rosea* 'Nigra' may not be as black as the name suggests, but its rich purplish-maroon flowers, each with a yellow throat, are very fetching. *A. rugosa* (*A. ficifolia*) is the softest yellow. An elegant, noticeably branching plant with the flowers widely spaced on the stems, it seems less prone to rust than most and over-winters happily and healthily. As I write in December, its deeply-veined leaves are a rich, almost emerald green. It sets seed freely too.

*CL:* Yes, this is a winner.

## Alchemilla *(Rosaceae)*

*CL: Alchemilla mollis* is one of those hardy perennials that propagates itself compulsively from seed, whether you want it to or not. Sometimes the seedlings place themselves most attractively: between paving cracks under a garden seat, for example, or in paving where it would be difficult to establish deliberately, forming a frieze around a statue, sundial or birdbath. The scalloped, dewdrop-catching leaves and cool lime-green flower sprays are wonderfully fresh in early summer. Funny that we never heard of this plant until after the last war (there's no entry for *Alchemilla* in William Robinson's *The English Flower Garden*), and now it's everywhere. This makes one wonder what the favourites of the twenty-first century will be.

*GR: A. mollis* is in danger of going the way of aubrieta and becoming derided for being too common, partly because it does self-sow so enthusiastically. It's a wonderful plant – use it thoughtfully. Few of the other alchemilla species are available in seed lists. 'Robustica' is a taller, larger-flowered form, intended for cutting, which is occasionally available.

*CL:* When *A. mollis* sows itself into groups of other perennials, its tenacious roots quickly make it difficult to extract without damage to the involuntary host. To prevent seeding, and also because the plant flops all over the place and turns a horrid dirty colour, it is important to cut it right to the ground at the end of July. For a few weeks it will look bare, but it will then refurnish itself with a comely crop of new foliage.

Should you wish to sow seed yourself, autumn is the best time (as for all *Rosaceae*), leaving the container to be frosted. *A. alpina* is on offer and is a pretty, if unexciting, rock garden plant with a thin white rim to each leaf.

## Allium *(Liliaceae)*

*CL:* With only a few exceptions, alliums are hardy and their seed can be sown when ripe in autumn. It will often germinate with one wiggly thread-fine cotyledon, as early as the following February.

Alliums are onions and chives, all having the typical aroma to a more or less appetizing or disgusting degree. [*Almost* all are oniony, *A. cowanii* is actually rather sweetly scented. – GR] We call them alliums when we intend to admire them with our eyes rather than our stomachs.

The clump-forming kinds are easily increased by division, while some of the bulb-formers increase themselves with alarming enthusiasm, either by numerous offsets at or just below ground level or by making bulbils in the inflorescence.

But you have to start somewhere, and seed may be easier to come by than a vegetatively produced piece of plant. With the giant chives, *A. schoenoprasum sibiricum,* there is the definite advantage of slightly differing shades of colour in the pink to mauve range between one seedling and the next. The flower-heads are not unlike scabious and are extremely showy in their May season. After that, and before they can self-sow too abundantly, you slash the plants to the ground with a few vicious strokes of a large pruning knife (or the kitchen carver, if you can get away with it [and your shins get away with it too – GR]) and within a week your plants will be green again with tasty young foliage.

There'll be a second, weaker flowering, and even a third, by autumn's arrival.

Having a similar, non-bulbous rootstock, Chinese chives, *A. tuberosum,* is a good late summer species, with heads of white flowers at 15 in. *A. montanum* (*A. senescens*) is another August flowerer, with grey, spirally twisted foliage on a 6-in, clump-forming plant. The mauve flowers are especially popular with butterflies.

The flowers of *A. pulchellum* are typically rose-purple (though there is an albino form), and it carries whiskery bracts above the inflorescence on a slender, 18-in stem. In a border this can look and behave a bit weedy (ideal if you cultivate the fashionable cottage garden image), but I'm specially fond of it in paving cracks, where it can self-sow to its heart's content.

*A. neapolitanum* and *A. murrayanum* (now *A. acuminatum*) are dormant in summer, start growing in autumn and are green all winter, flowering in May; the former pearly white, the latter an excellent shade of pink. If you don't want them to self-sow (and it can be an embarrassment), yank their flowering stems out with a sharp tug, immediately after the performance. They are a foot tall and can be planted alongside things like *Sedum* 'Ruby Glow' or *Geranium wallichianum* 'Buxton's Blue', which will take over in the summer.

Tall (3 ft) and stately, *A. siculum* (now *Nectaroscordum siculum*) is popular with flower arrangers both for its pendent green and chestnut bells, in May, and for the upright, clustered seed-heads which follow. The bulbs smell revolting. A good self-seeder. And so is *A. christophii* (*A. albopilosum*), which I consider the best of the bunch. Its large mauve flower-heads on 18-in stems, in early June, are composed of tough, spiky mauve stars. These harden and bleach but remain on the plant all through the summer. They are a long-lasting asset and can also be culled for dried-flower arrangements. If left in the border, the heads will eventually detach themselves from the stems and blow around till they find an obstacle to lodge in for the winter. By early spring, a little clutch of seedlings will be found germinating beneath each seed-head.

*GR: A. christophii* is sensational growing through the smaller, blue-leaved hostas such as those raised and introduced by Eric Smith. The short stature and neat habit of 'Halcyon', 'Hadspen Heron' and the like allows the football heads to sit just over the hosta foliage – which conveniently masks the old allium leaves.

*CL:* Two species on offer that should be avoided as uncontrollable weeds, unless you actually enjoy losing control, are *A. triquetrum* and our native ramsons or wild garlic, *A. ursinum.*

*GR:* I would only add two species, *A. flavum* and what we grow as *A. narcissiflorum* – it's usually *A. insubricum.* The former has bell-shaped, bright yellow flowers with protruding stamens; the outer flowers tend to hang, the central ones are more erect. The foliage is rather dark. Seed is sometimes available of a dwarf form of *A. flavum* which only reaches about 5 in, half the height of the standard sort. Two-in forms occur in the wild, and some are said to be fragrant. A well-drained raised bed is ideal.

*A. narcissiflorum* is not yellow but pinkish-purple, and the pendulous flowers, which are up to $\frac{3}{4}$ in long, hang in attractive heads. Again, a raised bed is the best site.

## Alonsoa *(Scrophulariaceae)*

*CL:* Of the several species of alonsoa listed in dictionaries, *A. war-scewiczii* is the only one of this genus of tender Andean plants that is available. It is treated as a half-hardy annual and is one that I enjoy returning to every few years. Its habit is naturally spindly, so if you spot a compact form in the seed lists, you need have no fear that it will have been reduced to a nonentity like certain ageratums. It will still make 18 in of height and will flower for a long time, looking a bit like a nemesia, though the fact of the flower being twisted on its pedicel so as to be presented upside down (by normal standards) is intriguing.

The colour is a bright, clear, yet soft shade of scarlet. (From the description in the Chiltern Seeds catalogue, 'bearing a mass of brilliant scarlet flowers that provide a blaze of colour', you might expect something like *Salvia splendens.*) I like it with the rich blue of *Salvia patens,* at roughly its own height, or with the blue pimpernel, *Anagallis linifolia,* forming a mat at its feet.

Alonsoa seedlings benefit from being pinched in youth [which is more than I did! – *GR*] and the plants from having their height reduced by half, midway through the flowering season.

*GR:* Two new ones have recently appeared in catalogues, *A. linearis* and *A.* × *meridionalis* – though I'd be a little sceptical about the correct name for the latter. *A. linearis* is similar to the compact form of *A. warscewiczii*, except that the flowers are slightly more orange and have black spots in the throat. I found it exceptionally long-flowering and good for cutting too. *A.* × *meridionalis* 'Firestone Jewels' is the one listed, said to be a mixture of scarlet, orange, salmon, pink and white, though mine were mostly red. This range of colours is reflected in the colour of the stems – white-flowered plants have fresh green stems, those in the darkest colours are strongly red-tinted.

These alonsoas are actually perennials, so if you happen to like, say, the white-flowered form from the mixture you can take cuttings in September to keep it going for next year.

## Alstroemeria *(Liliaceae)*

*CL:* At one time the only alstroemeria in cultivation was the Peruvian lily, *A. aurantiaca,* which is yellowish-orange and a fiendish weed under border conditions. 'Dover Orange' is the improved version of this and it is a rich colour, not to be despised. For the past forty years it is the 'Ligtu Hybrids' that have been making the running. They flower in June–July but with the freshness of an azalea and they come in a range of delightful shades: not orange but pink, carmine, flame and biscuit. They are excellent cut flowers and will last in water for two weeks in the hottest weather.

Even more dramatic as cut flowers, and hitherto the reserve of florists but now released to the public, notably through Mr P. J. Smith, is a named range of much larger-flowered, longer-stemmed alstroemerias which he calls 'Princess Lilies'. They have no royal connections, however, and are not true lilies, so I find the name unfortunate. Mr Smith opines that alstroemeria is a difficult word for the public to cope with, but they seem to have done pretty well up to now and find it rather less daunting than antirrhinum. [Florists sometimes label them 'Ulster Mary'! – *GR*] Anyway, these giant alstroemerias are most exciting and they are clump-formers, with no tendency to invade their neighbours. We shall hear more of them.

They can be increased by division but most alstroemerias, including the 'Ligtu Hybrids', are intensely sensitive to any sort of disturbance. They make fleshy, deep-questing roots, covered with the finest hair, which it is all too easy to bruise. If you raise them from seed, disturbance is unnecessary. Sow 12–18 seeds in a 5-in pot of John Innes No. 1, in April, and place it in a cold frame covered with brown paper to prevent drying out in the course of a sunny day. Germination is promoted by the alternation of warm days and cold, even frosty nights, so don't imagine you're doing them a good turn by keeping them warm all the time. Germination will be in exactly a calendar month from sowing. You can then remove the paper, gradually harden them off, and by the early autumn there may even be a few flowers. In a severe winter the roots are frost-tender, so if you plant in the autumn, set them rather deep. Don't break up the ball of roots. Plant them tenderly, just as they turn out of the pot. A triangle of three potsful at 2-ft spacing should make a good patch in time, their eventual height being 3 ft.

The roots will find their way to a considerable depth. After flowering, in late July, you can yank the old stems out without damaging the roots at all and then plant something like annuals or bedding plants on top of them, to give you interest for the rest of the season. A sunny position is best.

*GR:* In recent years research has been under way to pinpoint precisely the conditions which lead to the best germination of alstroemeria in the quickest time. Julia Kerley at Unwin's Seeds has come up with the following regime which will ensure that every viable seed germinates.

She recommends sowing between January and April, putting three seeds $\frac{1}{4}$ in deep in each 3-in pot of peat-based compost. The pots are then wrapped in polythene bags and placed in a propagator or greenhouse at a temperature of 70°F. After three weeks move them to the bottom of the fridge, at about 40°F for three more weeks. Finally move them back to 70°F, and germination will start in ten to fourteen days. Be sure not to over-water the compost. She too recommends planting the whole potful of compost rather than splitting up the root ball.

## Alyssum *(Cruciferae)*

*GR:* The honey-like scent of sweet alyssum, correctly *Lobularia maritima,* is as much a reason for growing this pretty little plant as the flowers. Indeed, one seed company lists a variety called 'Sweet White', which is supposed to be the most fragrant – not that everyone notices the scent.

Varieties like 'Carpet of Snow' and 'Little Dorrit' have been around for years, and 'Little Dorrit' is a poor thing compared with modern strains. The flower-heads are open and the branching less dense. You may not think this matters, but it means that the brown and green stems and leaves show through from underneath, creating a rather dirty look.

New varieties like 'Snow Crystals' claim to have larger flowers and be longer lasting, and it's true that if you look closely they do seem better. But the truth is that seed stocks of the same variety of alyssum from different sources vary as much as the different varieties. At least 'Snow Crystals', being available only from the raiser, should always be the same.

A variety called 'Morning Mist', also sold as 'Pastel Carpet', recently appeared with a new colour – creamy yellow. A little less floriferous than the more familiar whites and pinks, it has now appeared as a separate colour, as 'Creamery'. In truth, though, this seems no more than the reintroduction of var. *lutescens,* a variety grown in the 1950s – when there was also a variegated variety with a white edge to the leaf, and double forms too.

New on the scene is an impressive mixture bred in Britain called 'Easter Bonnet' which, though without a cream, has a full range of colours from deep purple to sparkling white.

A useful tip with this and other alyssum mixtures is to prick them out in clumps of two or three seedlings, like lobelia. This will give you a really mixed mixture of colours – if that's what you like.

The pink alyssums generally leave me rather cold, but the deep purple 'Oriental Night' is good.

*CL:* The prim alternation of alyssum and lobelia as a bedding-out edging has become horribly predictable and unimaginative. But when sweet alyssum is allowed to self-sow in paving cracks from year to year it becomes a most endearing plant.

*GR:* In spite of mildew. There are two problems with all alyssum – mildew and burn-out. Downy mildew generally affects plants sown where they are to flower and not thinned out, or those left in seed-pots for too long. In wet seasons, mature plants suffer and over-wintering self-sown seedlings are often infected too. In hot seasons, plants can burn out during the summer leaving brown and charred remains which need instant removal and replacement in order to avoid causing offence to the gardener's delicate sensibilities. Fortunately they flower in only a few weeks from seed.

Of course there are some perennial alyssums too ...

*CL:* The dazzling mustard-yellow *Alyssum saxatile* is one of our most popular rock garden plants for spring flowering, and is often seen alternated with purple aubrieta. That's a bit excessive with repetition; once should be enough. Those with delicate nerve ends prefer 'Citrinum' (alias 'Silver Queen'), with soft, sulphur-yellow flowers on a much less robust plant. From a spring sowing, flowers will be borne a year later.

### Amaranthus *(Amaranthaceae)*

*CL:* The best-known amaranthus is the hardy annual love-lies-bleeding, *A. caudatus,* which makes drooping tail-like tassels, typically magenta but green in 'Viridis'. It forms quite a large plant, $2\frac{1}{2}$ ft tall by as much across, and gives a nice tropical effect combined with castor oil (ricinus), datura and cannas. A pity the large, coarse leaves are so self-declamatory. [Both make splendid specimens in 8 to 10-in terracotta pots. – GR]

In the British climate the kinds that make a virtue of their leaves are probably best raised in the greenhouse as pot plants (a 6-in pot is suitable), where root restriction ensures that the colours are fully developed. Combined in this way with lilies, begonias, salpiglossis and other foliage plants, 'Flaming Fountains' and 'Molten Fire' (colourful forms of *A. tricolor*) have made a good show for me in front of my porch in late summer and autumn. I particularly like the former, with its narrow leaves and jazzy mixture of orange and carmine.

*GR:* I find that it is pointless growing varieties in this group except in a conservatory or the sunniest, most sheltered spots outside. A sunny porch sounds ideal. They also need raising in the greenhouse, and can be a bit miffy even so.

I've also grown two varieties of *A. hypochondriacus* – 'Green Thumb' and the dwarf 'Pygmy Torch'. Both make dwarf plants, but unless started in warmth and planted out, rather than sown outside, tend to produce just one stem with one short upright plume. 'Green Thumb' makes about 2 ft, with much-divided green plumes, and is a splendid cut and dried flower and a good harmonious filler for unexpected border gaps, especially in front of variegated and yellow-leaved shrubs. 'Pygmy Torch' is only half the size, with dusky maroon foliage and denser heads in a similar shade. It looks startling with *Plectranthus hirtus* 'Variegatus' at the front of a subtropical scheme.

The *caudatus* types are easy to raise as hardy annuals, self-sow prolifically, and unless you're a demon hoer a few seedlings are usually around to pot up or move to the required spot. The *hypochondriacus* varieties are less fecund, and are best raised in pots anyway.

## Ammi *(Umbelliferae)*

*CL: Ammi majus* has only come on the scene in recent years. It is 2–3 ft tall, a hardy annual requiring no special treatment, obviously related to cow parsley, with umbels of singularly pure white (hence the sometimes added selling title 'Snowflake'). Lovely for cutting. One would like to sow a row of it to flower *in situ,* but there is little seed in a packet. The answer is to save your own!

This is a flower that was popular in the European markets long before we became aware of it.

## Ammobium *(Compositae)*

*GR: Ammobium alatum* is a pretty everlasting, usually grown only for drying but sometimes used in annual or mixed borders. The green winged stems are distinctive and the flowers intriguing, as the orange disc develops from its initial flat profile to a rounded cushion at the same time as the papery white petals become increasingly reflexed.

Raise them in the greenhouse with the usual half-hardy annual treatment, or sow outside in May. Plants make a broad flat rosette and then throw up a surge of flanged shoots, making a bright green stand for the clusters of white and orange flowers.

Dry them by the simple expedient of cutting them just as the flowers are starting to open and hanging them upside down in that much sought-after dry airy spot.

## Anagallis *(Primulaceae)*

*CL:* We never lose our childhood love of the scarlet pimpernel, even though it is a weed. Its flowers have the endearing habit of opening on sunny summer mornings. But they are small.

*GR:* This is *Anagallis arvensis,* and in Greece I've seen both scarlet and shining blue growing together in roughly cultivated fields along with a pale pink form. As usual, nature shows us how it's done and produces them in great sprawling mats.

*CL:* As a garden plant, the blue-flowered pimpernel is far more telling but not well known. It will always arouse inquiries from visitors to my garden, who think it is a gentian. Tell them it is an annual and their interest evaporates forthwith. In fact it is perennial but seldom survives our winters.

The plant in commerce was long known as *A. linifolia* 'Phillipsii', but the same thing is now listed by Thompson & Morgan [Now as 'Gentian Blue' – GR] as simply *A. linifolia*. The flowers, on a prostrate, mat-forming plant, are $\frac{3}{4}$ in across, deep blue, with a dusky reddish ring around the centre. They open only when the weather is right, but have a very long season and make nice edging plants or a carpet for something like the red flax, *Linum grandiflorum* 'Rubrum', or the clear yellow tulip poppy, *Hunnemannia fumariifolia*.

The red strain, 'Parksii', seems no longer to be around, but is found in a mixture with the blue. The two go well together. Treat as half-hardy annuals.

## Anchusa *(Boraginaceae)*

*GR:* Anchusa blue is an especially intense and vibrant shade. I've no experience of growing the perennials from seed, but I've grown the South African annual *A. capensis* and, apart from anything else, it seems to be exceptionally popular with bees.

Dryish conditions and full sun are required, and anchusas make good companions for argemones. The pure white *Argemone grandiflora* behind the intense *Anchusa* 'Blue Angel' is quite something. 'Blue Bird' has a purplish tinge and can be twice the height of 'Blue Angel' at 18 in.

Recently the red edge to the flowers and the white throat of the wild species has been developed to give us pink- and white-flowered forms, which together with various blues and lavenders make up the 'Dawn' mixture. The simple blue is more effective.

*CL:* The perennial *A. azurea* (*A. italica*) is excellent treated as a biennial from a late spring sowing and lined out for the summer. Plant into its flowering position in autumn and it will make great sprays of rich blue flowers next May–June on a 5-ft plant. You will need a single cane and tie for each plant. It can be dazzlingly combined with the blinding white daisy bush, *Olearia* × *scilloniensis* (Graham and I seem to have a blue and white syndrome). These anchusas are perennial, but are so much at their best at the first flowering that I scrap them and follow with a late-sown annual at the end of June.

## Anemone *(Ranunculaceae)*

*GR:* As with so many members of the buttercup family, sowing fresh seed makes a real difference for many anemone species – but acquiring fresh seed can be a problem unless you harvest your own. And even collecting your own can be trickier than you would suppose, as the dwarf tuberous and rhizomatous types like *Anemone apennina, A. blanda, A. nemorosa* and *A. ranunculoides* all shed their seed when it still appears green and unripe. So it's easy to be fooled into waiting until it's too late.

A well-drained, soil-based compost such as John Innes seed compost suits most of them quite well. Sown fresh, some species will germinate in a couple of months; others take up to six months. If you buy seed from a seed company or order it through a society seed list, give the seed-pots a winter outdoors. Should seed not arrive until spring, give the seed-pots two months in the bottom of the fridge to avoid missing a year.

Fresh seed seems to be essential for the delicate little white *A. baldensis* and the shining pink *A.* × *lesseri* (a hybrid between *A. multifida* and *A. sylvestris*). Some don't need the chilling that most demand, so *A.* × *lesseri* and the pretty yellow *A. ranunculoides* (such a useful woodland carpeter) may well germinate without cold treatment.

The simplest approach with all these dwarf types is to sow in John

Innes seed compost as soon as you have the seed. Cover the seed with grit and place the pots outside or in an open frame. As soon as germination starts, bring them into a cold greenhouse.

Cut-flower types have not usually been raised from seed until recent years, when two strains appeared at about the same time, the American 'Mona Lisa' and the British 'Royal Event' from the John Innes Institute. The latter seems to have vanished without trace, while 'Mona Lisa' is becoming increasingly widely grown by the cut-flower trade, though less so by gardeners.

*CL:* My mother used to grow a prize strain of St Brigid anemones from seed every year in the 1920s and 30s.

*GR:* There are seven groups of shades, rather than pure colours, with long 18-in stems, and they are not only relatively disease-free but have the unique characteristic of flowering from late August to early May from a spring sowing if the temperature is kept at a minimum of 45°F all winter. Unfortunately for the home gardener, they thrive best and produce the most flowers when grown in the greenhouse border rather than in pots, something which is difficult for most of us to manage. But just a few plants in 8- or 10-in pots can provide fresh flowers all winter.

Germination should be at no more than 65°F, and the seed and seedlings kept well shaded until pricked out. Most anemones have a white cottony covering to the seed, which can make it difficult to sow evenly. Seed companies will remove this before packing the seed, but if you save your own it can be removed by rubbing it in dry sand.

## Anthemis *(Compositae)*

*CL:* Within this genus of daisy flowers there are a number of good garden perennials, although they tend to be fairly short-lived. *Anthemis nobilis* is chamomile; this is nice-smelling, but as a lawn it usually lets you down (except in the south and west of Ireland, where it actually takes over from grass). When it compulsively runs up to make its white flowers, in early summer, mowing tends to kill it out. The non-flowering strain is preferred nowadays, but that cannot be raised from seed. Either way a chamomile lawn is hell to keep free of clover and grass. Forget it.

*GR:* Having spent many days teasing annual meadow grass out of somebody else's chamomile lawn, I couldn't agree more.

*CL: A. cupaniana* is a white marguerite-style daisy borne at 15 in on a loose, grey-leaved mat. May is its season, and it is spectacular as a carpet for tulips, especially late-flowering orange or yellow tulips like 'Dillenburg' or 'Texas Gold'.

*GR:* It often flowers right through to the autumn and is a plant I could not do without. Lovely in front of white argemones.

*CL:* On light soils *A. cupaniana* seeds itself, but it tends to sudden death on soggy clay. It is usually propagated from cuttings.

*A. tinctoria* is a well-known border perennial, mainly July-flowering but continuing into autumn if dead-headed. Whether from seed or from cuttings, plants are best in their first flowering year (the year after sowing), being then 3 ft tall and less liable to powdery mildew than old stock, which also grows to an inconvenient and floppy 6 ft. The colour is pale or rich butter-yellow. 'Kelwayi' is fairly pale, which looks good with delphiniums of any shade of blue.

*A. sancti-johannis,* as sold, is a handsomer plant with longer rays than the true wild species. It is a light, bright and altogether dazzling shade of orange that many gardeners are frightened to handle. If you really want to startle the well-bred community (there's a good cause), grow it with the magenta cranesbill, *Geranium psilostemon* (*G. armenum*). I do much the same as this by allowing the weaving *Geranium* 'Ann Folkard' to thread its way through this anthemis. In its June season it is smashing, but it is so short-lived a plant as to be best treated as a biennial and replaced with bedding plants in July. Sow in a pot in the spring of the previous year and grow the plants on in a row.

## Antirrhinum *(Scrophulariaceae)*

*GR:* Where do I start? Well, I suppose I could begin by saying that generally speaking I feel very friendly towards antirrhinums.

*CL:* Me too; just to catch a whiff of their characteristic smell on the air turns me on.

*GR:* They have character, and in spite of the breeders' attempts to 'marigoldize' them (a word Christopher will hate) they refuse to be turned into blocky little plants with garish flowers. That's not to say that there are no dwarf varieties or that the colours are not bright, but they all seem to retain a little style.

*CL:* There's not much style left in the ultra-dwarf 'Carpet' strains, which have eliminated the spike and replaced it with tiny clusters of two or three blooms. [But they're not as bad as those dumpy little marigolds. – GR]

*GR:* So I'm predisposed to tolerate their susceptibility to rust and the fact that their flowering can be intermittent – to say the least.

Rust, yes. The first thing to say is that if a variety or a series of varieties is described in a catalogue as rust-resistant, don't believe a word of it. Some years ago a large trial was undertaken at Wisley and it was discovered that there were indeed some resistant varieties. But, although some colours in, say, the 'Coronette' series proved resistant, others were wiped out. Since then the supposedly resistant colours have all succumbed at one time or another, as the rust fungus has mutated to produce strains which overcome the resistance in the plant. So I've found that it's safest to assume your antirrhinums will get rust, although it's true that in some years it won't appear at all; in others every plant will be wiped out. Be warned. Or be prepared, as thorough and regular spraying with a fungicide containing propiconazole (Murphy Tumbleblite) will keep rust at bay.

The other problem is that most varieties seem unable to flower continuously, and as constant flowering is a characteristic which we have been conditioned to demand of our bedding plants, we are often disappointed. But surely it's a matter of planning for this eventuality rather than giving up antirrhinums altogether or tolerating an unsatisfactory display. In short, grow them in the mixed border and not in a bedding scheme. And dead-head them if you possibly can.

*CL:* Graham is right, of course, about lack of continuity in their flowering, but even so I do enjoy a big bed of nothing but antirrhinums, choosing separate colours and juxtaposing them in groups to suit my own tastes. The jumble of colours in complete mixtures tend to cancel each other out.

*GR:* Choosing varieties can be a nightmare. But if, as I would suggest, you turn your back scornfully on the azalea-flowered and double-flowered varieties, which abandon the most endearing characteristic of the plant (what use is a snapdragon that doesn't snap?), you will find things much simpler.

*CL:* I have to confess that when I'm calling them antirrhinums and forget about the snap, I like the double rosettes of the 'Butterfly' series, as in 'Mme Butterfly Mixed'. Neither ungainly nor lumpy, they make nice, old-fashioned-looking, sturdy plants, $2\frac{1}{2}$–3 ft tall.

*GR:* In this case there is something to be said for the restricted range available in catalogues for home gardeners. One commercial catalogue lists 131 different varieties just for cut flowers, although most are for greenhouse growing. And they are well worth growing for cutting, though the superb tall 'Rocket' and 'Forerunner' are probably the only ones you'll find in catalogues for home gardeners. Their long spikes are so impressive that you really should try them.

For antirrhinums to grow in a mixed border, the single colours are essential. 'White Wonder' is pure white with clear green foliage and at about 18 in fits well into the middle ground. Try it planted among the blue-leaved *Elymus hispidus* (until recently *Agropyron pubiflorum*), a well-behaved and decidedly attractive relative of the couch grass and a most adaptable plant. [But so susceptible to rust. – *CL*] [Mine has never been attacked! – *GR*] Alternatively set it behind the fashionable *Heuchera* 'Palace Purple' or the narrow-leaved red beetroot 'MacGregor's Favourite'; in front of the creamy-variegated philadelphus it should be just right.

'Black Prince' is deep, deep red and the foliage is a rich purplish-bronze. A lovely colour, although the foliage can be a little variable. A mixed planting with 'White Wonder' can look very striking, and it also looks well behind one of the dwarf variegated euonymus.

If you like colours which are more flamboyant, then two varieties from the American 'Princess' series might appeal. 'Princess White with Purple Eye' and 'Princess Yellow with Red Eye' may have singularly cumbersome names, but at least we can thank the seed companies for not simply changing them to 'Yellow Sparkler' or something equally imprecise. Both are at their best when placed among plants which will set them off. So shrubs and perennials which are not in flower but which provide a good background green are ideal neighbours. This is often the best policy with plants that feature startling colour combinations, and is the safest approach with many mixtures. I suppose you can express this thought by using that tired old phrase 'brightens a dull corner'. The recently re-introduced Victorian striped varieties, now listed as 'Brighton Rock', will certainly do that.

One other that I especially like is 'Delice', in an unusual and most appealing soft apricot colour. It's a very short variety which spreads well, and if you set three plants in a 10-in earthenware pot they will fall gently over the edge, the reddish pot setting off the flowers beautifully.

But for character and sheer delight all these are comprehensively beaten by the wild species from south-west Europe. *Antirrhinum hispanicum* is a rather sticky, slightly shrubby plant with spreading stems from which arise upright shoots about 9 in high, each with a spike of delicate pink and white flowers with darker pink streaks on the lower lip. *A. glutinosum* is similar but a little smaller, and has yellow and white flowers, while the flowers of *A. braun-blanquettii* are cream with purplish streaks on the upper lip. There are more, but seed is rarely available.

All need Mediterranean conditions – well-drained soil, a hot, sunny site and shelter in winter. They set seed generously, and are easily raised by sowing in spring in the usual way in a soil-based seed compost. They are not entirely hardy, so saving seed is a wise precaution. If anything, they are less prone to damping off than bedding antirrhinums.

*CL:* When growing and self-sowing in a wall, antirrhinums, like wallflowers, become much hardier, with individual plants living for several years.

## Aquilegia *(Ranunculaceae)*

⟨ *l* · These are very hardy, poisonous perennials, the sepals as colourful as the petals, or more so. Each petal has a backwardly directed, nectar-secreting spur, and this feature has been much developed in the long-spurred hybrids.

Among the principal parents of the long-spurred aquilegias are three American species: *A. caerulea, A. formosa* (coral-red and yellow, similar to *A. canadensis* and charming along roadsides in the Pacific North-west states) and *A. chrysantha* (yellow in both sepals and petals – well worth growing).

In the long-spurred hybrids, the incurved petal limbs are nearly always white or yellow, while the spurs and sepals are often (not always) of some other colour: blue, mauve, pink, cherry or red. Thus you already have an intrinsic bicolour effect, even in single colour strains like 'Azure Fairy' (blue and white) or 'Coral' (coral-red and yellow). In my view this is mixture enough, and is more striking in the garden scene than deliberate mixtures in which all possible aquilegia colours are found. They tend, at a distance, to cancel each other out.

However, when grown as pot plants, which they most effectively can be, a mixture like F1 'Music' comes into its own, because you can grade and arrange your colours to taste when the plants start flowering. And anyway they'll be seen close to eye level, so that your vision can easily concentrate on detail.

Long-spurred aquilegia plants *can* be long-lived but have a general tendency to be at their strongest and largest-flowered when young, dying out after a few years. I therefore like to use them for bedding. They can be interplanted with tulips; these will flower a little earlier, but the aquilegia foliage makes a decorative setting. By the time the aquilegias themselves are flowering, the tulips, dead-headed, will not show.

Or you can interplant with Dutch iris bulbs, which will flower simultaneously. The only snag here is that even if top-sized bulbs are purchased, quite a high percentage are always blind and that makes for a patchy result.

To get large long-spurred aquilegia plants in one season you need to be on the ball. Sow in March under cold glass, but be prepared for uneven germination. Prick off into seed trays and then line out into well-nourished soil for the summer. Bed out in the autumn.

*GR:* If you're saving your own seed, sow it the minute it's ripe in late July or August. Prick the seedlings out into boxes as Christopher suggests, space them well, leave them in their boxes in a cold frame for the winter, and plant out in March.

*CL:* Our native columbine, *A. vulgaris,* is a cottage garden plant of long standing. It grows wild, usually on lime-rich soils, in light woodland and in rather wet places, so it is a good plant to naturalize in similar garden habitats, where it will self-sow freely. The flowers are nodding with short spurs, typically deep blue but including white, pinky-mauve and old rose shades. 'Nora Barlow', 3 ft tall and spurless, is double pink, deepest at the centre, pale at the tips. It self-sows more or less true to type and makes a change, but in the long run I find its company tiring.

*GR:* The number and variety of columbines is staggering. Unfortunately their promiscuity is notorious, so if you, or your neighbours, grow more than one variety you will end up with a mixture if you allow them to self-sow. They can be divided but only with care; buying in fresh seed is the safest way.

One of the plants of the moment is *A. viridiflora,* a dainty little species reaching only about 12 in, with bell-shaped darkest olive flowers and short spurs. This unusual colour is quite something, and I have it growing with the tiny annual *Saxifraga cymbalaria.*

*A. viridiflora* is slightly scented, and other scented columbines are also occasionally to be found. I have not yet grown *A. fragrans,* from the Himalayas, but I'm told it smells of apples, and I have a blue and white form of *A. vulgaris* with a remarkable ripe mango scent. Look out for them.

## Arabis *(Cruciferae)*

*CL:* Closely related to aubrieta, arabis can be treated similarly – as bedding plants, rock plants or for colonizing steps and dry-stone walls. Aubrietas have no known albinos (which is surprising), so arabis fulfils this need. Coloured arabis, on the other hand, always look dirty. [Couldn't agree more. – *GR*]

Double and variegated arabis do not come within our terms of reference. The strain to shout about is *A. alpina* 'Snow Peak' or 'Snowcap' (don't ask me the difference). These are sometimes referred to as *A. caucasica* (syn. *A. albida*). From a spring sowing under cold glass, lining the seedlings out for the summer, you will have large, compact, dome-shaped plants by the autumn, ideal for bedding out.

The display will start in February and is at its peak in March and early April, thereafter falling off quickly. Interplant with an early tulip like the scented, single yellow 'Bellona'. This arrangement would be ideal for a follow-on of antirrhinums sown the previous August and ready to plant out in April.

I have had trouble from wood pigeons eating the arabis flowers and buds just as they were building up to their climax. Pigeons don't fly down to their food but walk into it. By stretching a single horizontal line of 2-ply fillis on pieces of cane at about 6 in high around the bed, the birds were foiled. [You can use the same trick with brassicas. – GR]

*GR: A. blepharophylla* is another case altogether. A true rock garden plant and altogether daintier, the leaves are dark green, the flowers deep rose. Sow seed in July in a cold frame or greenhouse and pot the seedlings up when still very small, as they hate being shuffled about after the roots have developed.

## Arctotis *(Compositae)*

*CL:* Arctotis are half-hardy daisy annuals from South Africa. They are considerably hybridized and are often sold as hybrids, 12–18 in tall, in a range of cream, apricot, orange and brownish-red shades. Some plants you wish you had more of; others you could do without (like the people in our lives). The whitish and skimmed-milk blue *A. grandis,* 2 ft tall, is a dull thing. My favourite is the dwarf *A. acaulis,* which has a good colour range and makes compact plants some 9 in high.

*GR:* One taller strain not only has the extraordinary name of 'Circus-Circus', but its foliage is silvery green, as is that of some of the wild species occasionally listed.

## Argemone *(Papaveraceae)*

*GR:* The prickly poppies fall among the unsung heroes of the huge poppy family. Hardly anyone grows them, but their long succession of flowers makes them one of the most desirable of plants for well-drained, sunny but not inhospitable borders.

Argemones are naturally perennials but are too tender to survive British winters, so we grow them as half-hardy annuals, and they're very easy. I sow them into compartmentalized trays in April, two seeds to each section, thin out to one, and they are ready to plant out in May. It's fairly straightforward. If you prefer, they can be sown outside where they are to flower, but they dislike root disturbance.

There are a number of white-flowered species with attractive, slightly glaucous foliage. I grow *A. squarrosa,* but *A. grandiflora* and *A. platyceras* are similar. They have flat poppy-like flowers, which can be up to 4 in across; these first appear on quite small plants soon after planting out, then continue for many months as each new stem overtops the fading flowers. It encourages them to flower more prolifically if you dead-head them regularly. Mine were still flowering in November.

*CL:* *A. mexicana* has pretty foliage with white markings, but the yellow flowers, which last only the inside of a day, are small and wispy and will scarcely muster the necessary flower power to satisfy most of us.

*GR:* A new silky-yellow form of the tangerine *A. mexicana* called 'Yellow Lustre' has just appeared on the market and sounds stunning.

The argemones' most characteristic feature is, of course, the spines, which are especially dense on the seed-pods. Fortunately it is not until the pods dry off and the seeds ripen that they become really vicious. If you want to collect and clean your own seed you'll need stout gloves and a pair of tweezers!

## Arum *(Araceae)*

*GR:* Growing arums from seed can be a tricky business. First of all the seed has to be stored in optimum conditions, otherwise it loses its viability. Unlike most seed, it is best stored cool and damp; soaking the seed and then storing it at about 45 °F is reckoned to be ideal.

Sow the seed in the autumn and leave the pots exposed to frost, though in the spring you will see no signs of growth. What happens is that in early spring the fine root emerges from the seed, then a tiny tuber is formed together with a growing tip; then growth stops. In late summer new roots start to grow and pull the young tuber down into the soil. In loose soil these contractile roots have been known to pull a tuber 2 in lower into the soil in as little as a week.

Further development rather depends on the species. In *A. italicum* and other species which start to grow towards the end of the year, autumn sees the appearance of the first leaves above ground – about a year after sowing. But in *A. maculatum* and other species which normally start to grow in the spring, emergence will be delayed until then. It can take seven years of steadily more substantial growth before the plants flower.

In practice the routine should be to sow fresh seed, well spaced out, in a pan of leafy compost as soon as it is harvested, and to leave it in a cold frame for the frost to do its work. If immediate sowing is not possible, store the seed as described above. Bought seed is best soaked in warm water for twenty-four hours and then sown.

Knock the seedlings out of their pot in June, when the tubers are normally dormant, and repot individually.

Seed of few species is available. The white-veined foliage of *A. italicum* var. *pictum* makes it one of the most sought-after winter plants both for the garden and the vase.

*CL:* Don't be put off by the fact that in their early years the seedlings show little or no contrasting veining. This will develop later.

*GR: A. palaestium* is an altogether more curious plant, with creamy flowers, purple within, and a rudely protruding deep purple spadix. In the wild this plant comes in two versions. One smells of rotting fruit and attracts fruit flies for pollination; the other is pollinated by dung and carrion beetles and smells accordingly. A hybrid between the two would be intriguing.

## Aruncus *(Rosaceae)*

*GR:* Like vast spiraeas, the creamy plumes of *Aruncus sylvester* are at their most impressive in moist soil with perhaps a little shade, although they are tough enough to tolerate a wide range of conditions. Sow in early spring in a well-drained, peat-based compost which is kept moist but not sodden at a temperature of about 60°F. Prick out into boxes in a cold frame, and then move into pots before planting out in the autumn.

## Asarina *(Scrophulariaceae)*

*GR:* Sometimes included with the antirrhinums, *Asarina procumbens* is hardier and self-sows helpfully in dryish walls. It creeps along mortar joints in walls or in crevices between rocks and stones, but almost always on vertical faces, rarely on the flat. And not usually in full sun – wherever you start it off, by creeping and self-sowing it will tend to migrate to an open but sunless aspect, though not usually one shaded from overhead.

The leaves are rounded and hairy and its long-tubed yellow and white flowers last for many weeks.

Sow in spring at about 65°F, and germination will take about three weeks.

## Asclepias *(Asclepiadaceae)*

*CL:* Of the hardy members of this genus of perennials, the one to grow is *Asclepias tuberosa,* called butterfly weed in the central and eastern states of America, from where it hails. *A. syriaca* also comes from there. Linnaeus was mistaken in thinking it was from Syria; hence its misleading name. But it is a coarse plant, its leaves too large for the size and effectiveness of its flowers.

From fresh seed, *A. tuberosa* germinates freely and easily, as I discovered when brought some, freshly harvested, by an American friend. From a trade packet, two or three seedlings is as many as I have so far obtained, and similarly with the more variably coloured 'Gay Butterflies', which belong to this species.

*GR:* My experience with 'Gay Butterflies' is the same. A couple of months outside in the cold before bringing the seed-pots into the propagator in spring is reckoned to help.

*CL: A. tuberosa* is a long-lived perennial that does not need disturbing. It grows 18 in tall and flowers in August, with broad umbels of flowers in a most attractive orange shade, bright but not brash. It contrasts in every way, except height and season, with the loose spikes of deep blue *Salvia patens*. 'Gay Butterflies' includes red and bronze shades, all pleasing.

Asclepias flowers are fascinating. The petals compose a star but the filaments of the stamens are joined to form a central column from which the anthers radiate in a coronet. Altogether an undeservedly little-grown plant.

*GR:* I once came across a clump of *A. tuberosa* 10 ft across, in the south-facing border of a run-down walled kitchen garden. It had obviously been there many years, belying its reputation for not surviving bad winters. It was much appreciated by butterflies by day and moths by night.

## Asperula *(Rubiaceae)*

*CL: Asperula orientalis* (syn. *A. azurea*) is a cornfield weed in Syria and the Lebanon. It is a hardy annual that can be treated like annual candytuft and, like candytuft, it quickly runs to seed. The tubular, light blue flowers are borne in terminal umbels above whorls of linear leaves which clearly proclaim its close relationship to the bedstraws (*Galium*). Some seed strains are of a rather washed-out blue. They need reselecting [like many annuals – GR], because a definite sky-blue is within this charming annual's potential. The plant is upright to 1 ft, well-branched and open-textured.

*GR:* Contrary to what you may deduce from the conditions it must cope with in its natural home, annual woodruff is one of the few annuals which in the garden seems to prefer a slightly shaded spot, with a retentive soil. I've even seen it on the banks of a stream where, although growing rather lank, it made a pretty, foamy blue cloud.

## Asphodeline *(Liliaceae)*

*CL:* Long-lived perennials with grassy foliage and spikes of yellow star flowers, asphodelines are easily raised from spring-sown seed under cold glass and will take about three years to make flowering-sized plants.

The best known is *A. lutea,* long in cultivation and of cottage garden status. Its dense and sturdy 4-ft racemes open in May from a tough-rooted clump that needs little or no attention. Asphodels like sun, and I have planted a row to stand like sentinels along the top of a retaining wall.

*A. liburnica* is July-flowering, its 3-ft stems slender and the better for a little support near the base. The yellow stars open around four in the afternoon (unless it is wet) and close again at nightfall. It is a charming species, bringing an air of freshness to the summer's evening scene, and looks pretty with the spiky bracts and metallic blue colouring of *Eryngium* × *oliverianum.*

## Aster *(Compositae)*

*GR:* Michaelmas daisies and their various relatives are not worth growing from seed, as there are so many far better vegetatively propagated varieties. However, this may change, as breeders in Holland are improving their seed-raised strains.

So we pass straight on to the little alpine aster, *A. alpinus.* Easy to raise from an early summer sowing in John Innes seed compost in a cold frame, this is one of the tougher 'alpines' which will also thrive at the front of sunny well-drained borders. Tufted, slowly spreading growth produces bright orange-centred daisies in May and June. All reach about 12 in and at their best make rather flat domes of flowers.

The wild species is lilac-blue; 'Snowhite' and 'White Beauty' are lovely pure whites; 'Dark Beauty' has rather larger, deep blue flowers; 'Happy End' is bright pink. 'Trimix' is a mixture of rose, white and lavender.

## Astilbe *(Saxifragaceae)*

GR. Various mixtures derived from named astilbe varieties are listed in catalogues, but these can be unpredictable. And as the named clones themselves are so easy to split, there seems little point. But I would suggest raising the diminutive *Astilbe chinensis* var. *pumila*.

The plants you raise may end up a little variable in height (though 9 in will probably be the average), and in colour too, though they will always be a shade of pink.

Sow in December in a peaty mixture and leave outside until spring, when the pots can be brought into a frost-free greenhouse; germination should be both prompt and generous. There's no need to prick out at seed-leaf stage, but don't leave them beyond four true leaves. Again a peaty mixture should be used, and the seedlings should never be allowed to dry out. Plant out before they get pot-bound, in soil which does not dry out.

## Astrantia *(Umbelliferae)*

GR: Astrantias are demure but enchanting plants with good shining foliage, making domed clumps. The upright stems carry open heads of unusual flowers. Each soft cushion of tiny florets echoes the shape of the mound of foliage before the flowers come through, and is surrounded by a many-fingered star of papery bracts.

Most plants available seem to be seedlings of uncertain parentage, and the degree of variation could be seen at East Lambrook Manor, the garden in Somerset created by Margery Fish, where they had self-sown prolifically until kept a little more firmly in order by the new owner. The flowers come in dusky reds, pinks, whites and greens, and various combinations, with the starry collar also varying. The deeper the red, the weaker seems to be the growth.

Unfortunately, not only are there many seedlings in circulation but there is also some confusion over the nomenclature. Suffice it to say that most plants in gardens are varieties of *A. major* rather than *A. carniolica,* whose name they often carry.

White, deep rose, large-flowered and shaggy-collared varieties are listed, but all are rather variable and it pays to line them out and choose the best before planting in borders. There is also a creamy variegated version, which comes reasonably true from seed if the parent plant is grown in isolation. In Holland a variety called 'Remontant' is listed, said to flower continuously from May to October rather than the June to August of other varieties. But I've never seen it. 'Primadonna' is the deepest red yet available from seed. They all make splendid long-lasting cut flowers. [But they have an appalling smell. – *CL*]

Sow the seed in John Innes seed compost. The best germination is achieved by a short period of warmth before a rather longer cold period. Your seed will probably arrive from the seed company in winter. After sowing, keep in the house or in a propagator for a fortnight then move outside, and when germination starts a couple of months later, bring the pots into the protection of a cold greenhouse. Prick the seedlings out in late spring, and plant out later in the summer.

*CL:* Being specially at home in moist, semi-woodland conditions, astrantias combine handsomely with *Lilium martagon* in June.

### Atriplex *(Chenopodiaceae)*

*CL:* Orach (*Atriplex hortensis*) is a close relation of spinach, and its young leaves make a lively addition to early summer salads.

This is a hardy annual which self-sows abundantly. It is generally grown in its red- and purple-leaved forms, though the bright 'Green Spire' has lately come on the market. The others will be found listed under 'Rubra', 'Purpurea' and 'Cupriata', but there is some confusing overlap. If 'Rubra' is the carmine red that it should be, then it is the most effective garden plant, lovely with the sun shining through its foliage. The deeper, purple strain is the commonest, and it is also good, especially when rising from a substrate of grey foliage.

*GR:* Or peeping through pink shrub roses. Once there was 'Atrosanguinea' (dark crimson), 'Cupriata' (with deep red leaves and violet petioles), and 'Rosea' (with light red foliage and darker stems), as well as 'Purpurea', of course. But I agree, you can't really tell what you're buying until it grows. The answer is to do your own selection by heaving out all but those of your preferred shade before they seed.

On the Continent three varieties in buttery yellow, green and burgundy are sold for drying; the idea is that you remove the leaves and dry the flower spikes.

*CL: A. hortensis* grows 6 ft tall, and once you have it in a mixed border, where it is a handsome ingredient, your sole task will be to thin out its self-sown seedlings and remove them from where they will be too competitive. The unripe seed-pods look good in July and August but eventually make the plant top-heavy, at which point you had best pull the majority out before they seed. The few you leave can be staked at 3 ft.

## Aubrieta *(Cruciferae)*

*GR:* Raising aubrieta from seed may seem unnecessary when there are good varieties which are easy to raise from cuttings. The recent development of new varieties has been inspired by the needs of bedding-plant producers, who cannot fit production from cuttings into their system, which is based on seed-raising.

So we have 'Lilac Cascade' and 'Purple Cascade', which are very floriferous and widely-spreading, and 'Bengal Mixed', with semi-double flowers in various wine and purple shades. The newest on the scene is 'Novalis Blue', an F1 hybrid if you please, with very large, soft, sky-blue flowers, each with a tiny orange eye. In its early years it was most often listed in catalogues alongside the words 'crop failure', but supplies are now more reliable. 'Novalis Blue' is very expensive but it is good. Whether it was worth devoting such time and money to producing an F1 is open to question.

Sow in early summer at 65°F and germination will take about three weeks. Prick out into 3-in pots, move outside when established, and growth will be vigorous enough for good-sized plants to be set out in the autumn.

'Novalis Blue' looks good with a dwarf, pale lemon daffodil like 'Hawera'. For a bolder contrast try 'Purple Cascade' with the dwarfer and more buttery 'Small Fry'.

Incidentally, aubrieta makes an excellent spring bedding plant for hanging baskets, and if crocus, dwarf daffodils or grape hyacinths in appropriate shades are also put in the basket you can create very unusual and attractive spring displays.

*CL:* I like to use aubrieta seedlings, sown in April and grown on in a row, as a carpet in the following year for tulips. The lily-flowered tulip 'China Pink' looks good above a carpet of 'Purple Cascade', for example. You can subsequently cut your plants back and hold them in a reserve plot for another year.

## Baptisia *(Leguminosae)*

*CL: Baptisia australis,* a hardy perennial from the Eastern states of America, has the superficial appearance of a deep indigo-blue lupin. The flowers are more widely spaced on their spike and the whole plant, 3 ft tall, has a greater air of distinction. It never succumbs to mildew; after flowering May–June, the plant remains fresh-looking till autumn.

Easily germinated, seedlings flower from their third year.

*GR:* Not *that* easily. I find soaking the seeds for twelve hours before sowing helps soften the seed-coat, though this may only be necessary with bought seed. Freshly sown, home-collected seed is probably softer.

## Begonia *(Begoniaceae)*

*GR:* Can you tell one fibrous-rooted begonia mixture from another? Well, it is possible to recognize some, but a certain amount of confusion exists over the names, so it's not always easy to know exactly what you're getting. And who wants mixtures anyway? The serious gardener wants to plan a scheme, not to hope the unpredictable mixture turns out OK. The first catalogue I pick up lists fourteen different varieties, single colours and mixtures – not as many as there are impatiens, but considering the limited flower colours available, fourteen is quite enough.

But as readers who have reached this far will be aware, Christopher and I are not great fans of mixtures, so let's simplify matters and head unerringly for the single colours. The 'Coco' varieties might be so named for their red noses or their funny faces – in fact it's their dark bronze leaf colour. A well-established series of colours, at about 8 in they are a little taller than many modern, rather squat varieties.

'Coco Scarlet' is a wonderful edging for variegated chlorophytums interplanted with *Hibiscus* 'Coppertone' in bedding schemes; 'Coco Pink' can surround the pewtery fans of *Pyrethrum* (now *Tanacetum*) *ptarmiciflorum,* while pink-and-white-flowered 'Coco Ducolor' looks fine on its own.

'Danica Scarlet' is larger than 'Coco Scarlet' in every way and reaches about 12 in; this is the one to *interplant* with chlorophytums.

The more trailing habit of 'Pink Avalanche' makes it a better choice for baskets and tubs, and it's sterile so flowers even more prolifically than other varieties.

Finally in this brief selection I must include 'Thousand Wonders White', a pale-green-leaved, white-flowered variety for adding light to shadier spots.

These fibrous-rooted begonias are second only to impatiens as bedding plants for shade, but the problem is usually finding good companions. Few are sufficiently elegant in habit or substantial in stature to mix with perennial plants, but I've seen 'Thousand Wonders White' edging *Hosta lancifolia,* with its glossy green leaves overlapping like fish scales very prettily. And 'Coco Ducolor' is a surprisingly effective companion for the trailing grey-blue foliage of *Acaena adscendens*.

Fibrous-rooted begonias prefer a soil that doesn't dry out and is reasonably fertile, and if the shade draws up some of the midget varieties a little, well that is no bad thing; and they still won't flop.

The 'Non Stop' tuberous begonias, with neat double flowers in ten colours and an ability to flower while still in 3-in pots and *still* be flowering when cut down by the first frosts, are quite an achievement. They are excellent tub plants for sunny or shady sites – no companions are necessary. There are three other superficially similar varieties, all with fully double flowers, which are in fact quite distinct and with their own special uses.

'Musical' is the first to flower, on quite small plants. It has flowers about 2 in across and is the most branching of all, so is best in window-boxes and at the edge of tubs. 'Clips' flowers ten days later, is less branched, has slightly larger flowers and probably produces more than any of the varieties. It makes a sparkling spreading carpet.

'Non Stop' flowers next, with the widest range of colours, flowers about 4 in across and a more upright habit. It's a very adaptable variety, good for bedding and tubs. 'Memory' is the last to flower, with a very upright habit of growth and the largest flowers of all, at least 5 in.

'Illumination', a cascading type for tubs, has double, rather flat, pale pink flowers and seems to thrive best facing east, out of the hottest sun. Finally, from Holland, come the 'Midnight Beauties', in seven colours but with the lustrous addition of lovely bronze leaves which give them an intriguing tropical air. 'Non Stop Ornament' is a recent improvement.

A recent development from the breeders of the 'Non Stops' is 'Charisma', a B. *elatior* hybrid and the first of its type to be raised from seed. It was developed primarily as a pot plant, with a succession of 2-in double flowers in orange or coral. It grows to about 12 in in pots but rather smaller outside, where a warm sunny position suits it best.

But with tuberous-rooted types we're up against a familiar problem – almost invariably it's mixtures only. Fortunately, as they will be pricked out into 3-in pots and will be in flower when they're planted out, you should be able to tell which colours you have and plant those of one colour together if you prefer.

Many people have trouble raising begonias, both fibrous and tuberous, from seed. I like a peat-based compost with extra drainage material – the compost needs to be constantly moist but not sodden, and clingfilm stretched over the pot helps stop the surface of the compost drying out, for the seed must be left uncovered. Prick out into trays and then move tuberous types into 3-in pots.

Sowing time is worth thinking about carefully. Begonias grow slowly from their tiny seeds and it's sometimes tempting to sow soon after Christmas in order to get a good-sized plant by late spring. But can you keep the temperatures high enough after pricking out? Can you prevent botrytis? Take my advice – wait till February at the earliest.

With tuberous types there is another problem. In days shorter than twelve hours the plants tend to form tubers rather than produce shoots, so if, for example, you sow in December as is sometimes suggested, the tiny seedlings spend many weeks trying to form a tuber soon after germination even though they are not really ready for it. So delay sowing until at least February for both fibrous and tuberous types, and this will be less of a problem.

*CL:* Tuberous begonias have a big colour range and are altogether more exciting than the fibrous-rooted types derived from *Begonia semperflorens*.

The cascade types are tuberous, and although generally assigned to hanging baskets, they are pretty and graceful when bedded out.

If raising tuberous begonias without heat, sow them in June – there'll be no trouble over germination. Prick off the seedlings into a tray and leave them in this to over-winter, storing them under a bench in a frost-free greenhouse. Next spring, pack them into moist peat in any suitable container and place them in a close frame. When sprouting they'll also be rooting, and you can pot them individually, harden them off and finally plant them out for your summer display. [What a good idea, I wish I'd thought of that. – GR]

CL: Come the first frost, lift them and store them in a cool, frost-free spot again. When you've started them off the following spring, you can increase your stock by cutting the tubers into halves or quarters, but don't do this until the tubers are active. Should you forget to lift a tuber you'll not infrequently find that it survives the winter as dahlias do, but the onset of flowering will be very late.

## Bellis *(Compositae)*

CL: *Bellis perennis* is the common daisy of lawns, and no one should underrate the charm of a daisy lawn in full bloom. [Absolutely. – GR] But if you have a conscience about such matters then it is advisable not to plant the double cultivated strains of bellis next to a lawn into which they will freely seed long before their floral display is past.

The largest-flowered 'Monstrosas' are good carpeters for spring bedding, notably tulips. At close range they can be faulted as coarse and over-fed. For my money, the 'Pomponettes' every time. These make neat buttons with quilled petals – charming in window-boxes or for lining a path, interplanted with 'Blue Spike' grape hyacinths, and also for combining with 'China Pink' lily-flowered tulips (but the daisies will flower on into June). All come in separate colour strains, red, pink and white, or (more frequently in the retail trade) in a mixture.

GR: The cherryish-pink 'Kito' has perhaps the tightest heads of petals, unless you count the old-fashioned cottage strains that must be divided rather than raised from seed.

*CL:* The seed being small, sow it in a pot in early July, prick off the seedlings, then line them out until required for bedding. Don't worry if autumn blooms show a yellow centre and insufficient doubling; they'll be much fuller after the winter.

## Bergenia *(Saxifragaceae)*

*GR:* Growing bergenias from seed is something of a new proposition. Seed of 'Winter Flowering Mixed', or varieties with equally uninspiring names, is apt to produce similarly uninspiring plants – mainly because seed is simply collected from existing named varieties and put in a packet.

Recently 'Redstart' has appeared from Holland, developed specifically as a seed-raised variety. The flowers are deep red, though slightly variable, and are carried on stems tall enough for cutting. The foliage takes a purplish-red tint in winter.

Sow the seed at about 70°F in spring, plant out in early summer, and the first flowers will appear the following April. I'm sure Christopher has some thoughts on plants to grow alongside them ...

*CL:* I find something rather gloomy about the leathery foliage and relentless evergreenery of most bergenias, but they do contrast well with the pinnate leaves of ferns.

## Beta *(Chenopodiaceae)*

*GR:* The beetroot is not everyone's favourite bedding plant, and some will think me mad to suggest that a humble vegetable be allowed to flaunt its charms in such a way. But there are two excellent varieties available which are specially selected for their leaves; their deep, glossy, dare I say it, beetroot-red foliage is one of my summer bedding regulars.

Even as late as the 1950s there were varieties with red or green leaves and yellow veins, and also those with unmarked foliage in red, yellow, green and purple. Now all we have are 'Bull's Blood' and 'MacGregor's Favourite'.

'MacGregor's' is my favourite too. Narrow leaves not more than

1 in across lie in a graceful arc, making a fountain about 9 in high of the richest, glossiest beetroot red you can imagine. Surrounded by *Diascia* 'Ruby Field' it looks stunning; with the multicoloured 'Mrs Henry Cox' zonal geranium it looks extraordinary; with the dwarf blue 'Halcyon' hosta, each flatters the other.

'Bull's Blood' is about half as tall again, and the foliage is about the same shade but rather mottled and of a more familiar beetroot shape – it's decidedly wavy along the margins. With the relatively new dwarf peachy-yellow *Hemerocallis* 'Stella d'Oro' it makes a fine little group. But it tends to run to seed more quickly than 'MacGregor' and is a little coarser; or perhaps it's more charitable to say a little less refined. The roots are said to be 'of good culinary quality' – I must try them next year.

But stocks vary, I'm afraid, a symptom of the fact that so many flower-breeding companies are concentrating on F1 hybrids and abandoning their commitment to open-pollinated varieties.

Both varieties are easy enough to raise from seed. Treat them as other bedding plants by sowing in March and growing on fairly cool. The 'seeds' are actually clusters of seeds and so usually produce more than one seedling; try to prick out the seedlings singly so that you get more shapely plants.

And if you ever come across any of those old varieties, send me a few seeds. Thank you.

## Borago *(Boraginaceae)*

*CL:* The best reason for growing borage, *B. officinalis,* is that it is a pretty plant. Additional reasons are not hard to find. Bees like it, and its blue star flowers can be used to decorate a salad (with nasturtiums) after it has been dressed, or in a Pimms, cider or claret cup. A hardy annual, it self-sows freely, growing 2 ft high in good soil. If you aspire to a mini-Sissinghurst white garden or, even higher on the social ladder, to a white herb garden, a white-flowered borage is available.

*GR:* And if you spot a dazzling field of blue from the car or the train, it's more likely to be borage, now widely grown as an oil-seed crop, than linseed.

## Brachycome *(Compositae)*

*CL:* If you need a low-growing annual no more than 9 in tall, the Swan River daisy, *Brachycome iberidifolia*, is the sort to choose because this is its natural height and it shows none of the dumpy artificiality of dwarfed ageratums or marigolds, for instance. The season over which its dainty cineraria-like daisies are borne is months long.

Sixty years ago, as many as five distinct colour strains were being offered. Nowadays, 'Purple Splendour' is the only one. But the shades in a mixture all blend well – blue, rosy lilac, mauve, lavender and white (with a telling black disc). The foliage is filigree. A charming half-hardy annual. Sow under glass in March–April.

*GR:* 'Purple Splendour' is the perfect hanging basket and window-box plant, as it does not resent a little dryness, fills out well and tumbles over the edge without straggling, it flowers for months, has a sweet scent and is happy host for a plant or two of *Thunbergia alata*.

## Brassica *(Cruciferae)*

*GR:* Opinions are divided on the ornamental cabbages and kales. Some love them, some hate them. I think they're positively outrageous – pink and white cabbages! But every now and then I grow a few because they give me a good laugh at a time of year when it's especially welcome, and the youngest leaves are also valuable in winter salads – in small doses.

There's one important thing to remember about these curious plants. They don't colour up well until the autumn, when temperatures start to drop – night temperatures must consistently fall below 50°F before they colour well. So the best plan is to sow in early summer and transplant them to their display positions as you would other summer-sown brassicas. It's no good treating them as summer bedding plants. Taking care to plant them upright will ensure an even display.

Although for a good-sized head they should be planted about 15 in apart, they can also be grown much closer if you like the coloured leaves for cutting; about thirty-five plants per square yard is recommended. I've not yet tried this but it sounds worth a go.

There are now F1 hybrid varieties available, and 'Osaka Red' and

'Osaka White' are perhaps the best. Each makes flat heads with a ring of wavy green leaves surrounding a broad disc of red or white. They are quicker to make substantial plants so can be sown and planted later than the older types.

Ornamental brassicas are usually ruined by severe frost so are definitely autumn plants, though if you like the leaves in winter salads a few plants in the cold greenhouse will keep you supplied.

## Briza *(Graminae)*

*GR:* The quaking grasses are neatly divided into three species – *Briza maxima*, *B. media* and *B. minima*. The names tell you a fair amount about them but not everything, for the large and small are both annuals while the medium is a perennial.

The largest, in stature and flower size, is a fine self-sower for dryish mixed borders, its rough rustling heads bobbing in the breeze wherever the seed happens to grow. For drying, sow them outside and thin to about 8 in apart.

*CL:* The strongest plants are obtained from an autumn sowing. After flowering in May–June, plants quickly ripen their seed and disintegrate. They can be replaced by other bedding plants.

*GR:* The medium quaking grass, supposedly known as doddering dillies, is the perennial and is less often seen, both in borders and in dried arrangements. Perhaps this is because its flowers are a great deal smaller. It won't usually flower in its first year but is a good perennial thereafter.

*CL:* This is a charming ingredient for a meadow garden. Raise your seedlings in a separate plot and then plant them in, when established.

*GR:* The flowers of the small quaking grass are very small indeed, though at 9 in the plant is about half the height of the largest species. A delightfully neat and dainty plant, it looks after its own affairs, popping up among choicer plants. If it appears in flat cushions it may need removing.

All three species tend to grow naturally in dryish limy soils, but are not particular.

## Buphthalmum *(Compositae)*

*CL:* There are two perennial species of buphthalmum, both with yellow daisy flowers and both good border plants in sun or shade. *B. salicifolium*, which I first met wild in Austrian woodland, makes a low, clumpy, evergreen hummock, flowering from May onwards more or less continuously. The branching stems, only 18 in tall, are wiry, the daisies neat but improved by occasional dead-heading.

   *B. speciosum* (*Telekia speciosa*) grows to 5 ft and has large heart-shaped leaves. It is showy in its July season, but the flowers turn disagreeably black thereafter. It self-sows readily if not dead-headed. An excellent wild garden plant, but I also enjoy it in my main border at the foot of a purple *Clematis* × *jackmanii*.

## Calandrinia *(Portulacaceae)*

*GR:* In the UK you have to be something of an optimist to grow calandrinias outside. In the southern states of America, there's no need to worry.

   *C. umbellata* reaches just 6 in in height, with big magenta cups above succulent tufted foliage. In warm climates it is best treated as a winter annual and sown outside in later summer or early autumn. Otherwise grow it as a half-hardy annual, plant in the hottest, driest, most sheltered spot you have, and pot up one or two extras for the greenhouse.

*CL:* It is worth giving your plants the chance to survive a mild winter and do a second term. By then they'll be really strong and will start flowering much earlier.

*GR:* There are many other species of calandrinia, mainly from South America, but only *C. menziesii* seems to turn up in catalogues. This can reach about 2 ft and is covered in bright red or purplish flowers with a lovely satiny sheen. The same conditions are necessary as for *C. umbellata*.

   Germination of both is relatively speedy at about two weeks, and they are happy to be started off in temperatures as low as 55 °F.

## Calceolaria *(Scrophulariaceae)*

*GR:* I must say that I'm not too keen on the big blousy greenhouse varieties of calceolaria that look like the beloved bedroom slippers of a 1950s seaside landlady. But among the others there are a number of far more appealing varieties.

First, two hardy annual species which are likely to self-sow if given the chance. *C. tripartita* came to me as a surprise rogue in a packet of *Nicotiana langsdorffii*, just one seedling which was nurtured and planted out to see what would result. It proved a bushy plant, with very dark, almost lustrous, slightly bluish leaves and small, bright yellow slippers for most of the summer. To be honest, there was a little too much foliage and not enough flowers, but growing in front of the plant under whose name it originally masqueraded it made a pretty group. And it set and shed its seed copiously.

Rather smaller is *C. mexicana*, whose seed came from Christopher, and this too seems set to be a permanent fixture. It only made about 9 in in height, the yellow flowers were tiny, the foliage rough and it flowered all summer and thoughtfully popped up later among the *Heuchera* 'Palace Purple'.

Of the bedding types, I've more than once grown 'Midas', with its brilliant pure yellow pouches. On its own in a hanging basket it works a treat. The habit is just right – the stems trail down and then the flowering shoots stand up from them. 'Sunshine' is similar. In a sunny bed, bronze foliage makes a good foil.

Once germinated (at 65°F), and pricked out, 'Midas' is tough enough to be grown on in a cold frame until ready for planting. But you will need to sow fairly early, as growth will be slow in such cool conditions. Sometimes you will find that the foliage turns rather an anaemic yellowish shade, and this indicates a need for an iron supplement.

Finally, one to look out for in the future, 'Goldcut'. This variety is bred as a cut flower and reaches almost 18 in in height. It has also had the tendency to sticky stems bred out of it, a clever trick. Sow it in June for autumn cutting or in October for the spring.


## Calendula *(Compositae)*

*GR:* The pot marigold has undergone some changes in the last few years. *Calendula officinalis* used to be a 2-ft plant with 2-in orange flowers on long stems. One of the very earliest variations was the 'Hen and Chickens' form, with its ring of much smaller flowers like satellites orbiting the main flower. Technically this is var. *prolifera*.

The most recent developments, in the form of the 'Fiesta Gitana' mixture and 'Apricot Bon-Bon', are quite out of character. They are short, dumpy little plants reaching no more than 9 in sometimes, with the flowers carried in a plane across the top of the plants. Generally, these dwarf varieties flower in a great burst and then burn out well before the end of the summer. Unless rigorously rogued by the seed-grower, they also grow in an unattractively uneven way, and in hot summers they can be wiped out by powdery mildew before they finish flowering. Their densely branching habit, which prevents air circulation among the foliage, only encourages the disease.

So leaving these dwarfs to the fate they deserve, which varieties can we suggest for borders and for cutting? 'Indian Prince' is one of my special favourites – each deep orange petal shimmers with mahogany on the reverse. This gives the effect of a dark-eyed flower, as the central petals curl inwards to show off the dark tan on their backs. It looks good in front of a dark-leaved, orange-flowered dahlia such as 'David Howard'.

Of the others, 'Radio' is a brilliant orange cactus-flowered type while the 'Pacific' series has a number of unusual colours including apricot, pale lemon and cream with dark centres. 'Apricot Sherbet' has a dark orange centre, pale salmon edges and is peachy-yellow in between. Most are best as cut flowers, and if you grow them for this purpose you should try the recently introduced mixture 'A Touch of Class'. The oranges and yellows are complemented by peachy and almost pink shades, but grown together in a border the colours clash. Lined out for cutting, it doesn't really matter.

All are quick growers, happy with the usual hardy annual treatment; if you prefer a little more control, sow in March in pots in a cold frame and prick out into boxes, also in the frame.

*CL:* Very strong plants are obtained from autumn sowings of this hardy annual. Do use its colourful and tasty petals to scatter over a green salad *after* you have turned in the dressing. Some blue chicory flowers will further enliven the proceedings, but they must be used at lunch-time, having faded by the evening.

## Callistephus *(Compositae)*

GL: The China aster. If Everyman speaks of an aster, it is *C. chinensis* which he has in mind, not the michaelmas daisy, which is botanically *Aster*.

Annual asters are wonderful plants for late summer and autumn, their palette ranging from white and cream through lavender, purple (never true blue) and pink to crimson and magenta. But their popularity has waned over the years. In 1927 Suttons were offering 129 selected or mixed strains; in 1989 there were only eighteen, all in mixtures. Single colours are still available, mostly to the trade from wholesale outlets. They enable you to plan your colour effects, but mixtures are what the public mostly wants and the colours available all harmonize pretty well.

The sale of bedding plants through garden centres has worked against the aster, which can only be green at selling stage, never in flower. But it is good to grow such a showy annual whose peak is reached just when so many others are tired or finished.

Wilt disease of asters, caused by its own specific fungus and not attacking other genera, is a nuisance because it is soil-borne and long-lasting in the soil where it has once occurred. You should raise your plants in a sterilized compost (for all subjects, not just on this occasion). And if the trouble occurs, with plants suddenly dying in mid-season, grow them elsewhere for a good many years thereafter.

Or grow them in pots – the branching kinds make splendid specimens in 7-in or 8-in pots to flower on your patio or terrace or at your porch entrance. Each plant will require a cane and a single tie to steady it. Even in the border, some support of the taller kinds is advisable, yet those which make the biggest plants also give best value. The dwarfs are out and over in a very short while.

Some asters grow fairly tall, 2 ft or so, but have a narrow upswept habit which looks uncomfortable. Such are the 'Duchess' and pompon strains, while the powderpuffs are unstable and easily knocked askew. Although only a foot tall, 'Milady' asters are too bunched up.

'Princess' asters are among my favourites, with a wide colour range and tubular, anemone-centred florets in the middle of the flower. The well named 'Ostrich Plume' in a conscientiously selected mixture is excellent, and includes plenty of rich crimson plants. It is wide-branching and nearly 3 ft tall, so a few plants, well grown, go a long way. These long-stemmed asters are excellent for cutting, as also are the semi-single 'Madeleine', strong and bushy to $2\frac{1}{2}$ ft. A bed of these alone would make a great impression.

Sow under glass in March–April and watch for green aphids on the seedlings. Unless sprayed against, their damage can be crippling.

*GR:* Asters are occasionally listed as being wilt-resistant – have none of it. Once the soil is infected, as Christopher says, you're stuck with it. If you're desperate for asters in that bed, well, I dare say you're the sort of person who creates merry hell if your breakfast egg is not done (by somebody else) for exactly three and a half minutes. I can't imagine why you're reading this book.

Anyway, just for you, prick out your asters into 3-in pots and then on into 4-in or 5-in pots, depending on the variety, before planting out rather later than you would normally, after sweet williams perhaps. And be ready with the sprinkler.

A mention for two varieties raised in Holland as cut flowers, 'Riviera' and 'Teisa Stars'. 'Riviera' has fully double flowers with slightly incurved petals and reaches about 2 ft. Its great strengths are its range of colours, eight in all, and the fact that it branches extensively from the base to give the longest stems on the shortest plants. 'Teisa Stars' is unusual in having the finest quilled petals on plants about 12 in high so, at a pinch, it can be used for cutting or bedding. It comes in a mixture of nine colours.

## Campanula *(Campanulaceae)*

*CL:* The bell-flowers are among the most elegant and charming garden plants. Most are coloured white or blue, and their flowering season is centred on June and July, though *C. pyramidalis* and *C. isophylla* are notably later.

Seed is small and requires little or no cover. Neither should it be placed in total darkness. Most of the perennial campanulas can be raised from seed, when available. Indeed the 6-ft *C. lactiflora* and the only slightly less tall *C. latifolia* seed themselves freely in the garden. So does the peach-leaved bell-flower, *C. persicifolia*. Seed of this sown in the spring will produce magnificent flowering plants the year after. But with many selected cultivars, propagation has to be from cuttings or, where feasible, division.

The most important seed-raised campanulas are those grown as biennials. Rampion, *C. rapunculus*, whose fleshy roots, used either cooked or raw in salads, are its main purpose (though the galaxy of flowers in its second summer is delightful), is no longer easily obtained, though it is often available from wild flower specialists. It must not be confused with *C. rapunculoides*, a beautiful but terrifying weed, spreading both by underground runners and self-sowing. Seed tie is on offer. Don't be tempted.

*C. patula* is a delightful meadow ingredient in Eastern Europe. I should love to get it established in my own meadow and am still trying.

*GR:* New strains of *C. isophylla* have recently been appearing, and 'Krystal' and 'Stella', each in blue and white, are floriferous, neat in habit and wonderful basket plants. Seed is expensive and extremely tiny, so the seed companies also sell young plants.

*CL: C. pyramidalis*, the giant of the genus, is the chimney bell-flower, traditionally used for standing in front of the fireplace in August, when it is in flower but no fires are needed. It will also flourish in the garden, being perfectly hardy, and becomes, like antirrhinums, quite perennial where it seeds itself into the cracks of a wall.

It must be said, however, of this and of other campanulas that once their flowers have been fertilized by bees, they quickly fade. This happens in a matter of four days from the time of opening. But if unpollinated, each flower will last for weeks – three to four weeks in the case of *C. pyramidalis*, longer still with Canterbury bells. So there is a strong case for growing them, perfectly hard, as pot plants but bringing them indoors as soon as flowering commences. Keep them away from open windows. The plants will not demand light at this stage as they will be discarded after flowering anyway.

*C. pyramidalis* is blue or white and its seeds are dark or pale accordingly, so you can sort them out in a mixture, though it is still possible to buy the colours separately from at least one firm. Sow in April, prick off the seedlings, then pot them individually, moving them into their final 10-in or 12-in pots by August. Over-winter in a cold frame. Forcing is unnecessary (and undesirable) at any stage. Stand the pots outside somewhere sheltered from wind in the run up to flowering, and provide one cane for each plant. A single loose tie to this for each flowering shoot is all that's required. Flowering time, late July to mid-September, varies a little from plant to plant.

Canterbury Bells, *C. medium*, are treated in exactly the same way, though an 8-in pot is large enough for their 3-ft height, and they flower in June–July. In the garden, if you can be bothered, dead-heading by tweaking each faded bloom off ensures a second crop (with *C. persicifolia* also).

Most Canterbury bells are dependably biennial and will not flower at half-cock in the same year if sown in April. 'Bells of Holland' does behave as an annual but its flowers are on the small side. Of mainstream Canterbury bells there are three strains: single, cup-and-saucer (also know as 'Calycanthema') and double. The singles have a coloured bell (pink, mauve, purple or white) and a green calyx. In the cup-and-saucers, the calyx stands out horizontally like a ruff and is coloured like the bell. In the doubles, there are additionally petaloid stamens. These last give you most colour for your money. The cup-and-saucers are jolly in their way, but the singles have the greatest elegance and provide quite as much colour as any normal person needs.

Other biennial campanula species can be grown like Canterbury bells if and when you can obtain their seed. *C. incurva* makes a large, inflated, pale blue bell. A well-grown plant is marvellously symmetrical, with a vertical central flowering stem, all the rest forming a horizontal ring like spokes around it and spreading well beyond the rim of a 7-in pot. *C. formanekiana* is similar but has greater refinement.

*GR:* This is a large genus, with over 300 species, many of which are alpines. Some are available in seed catalogues, but rather more are to be found in the seed lists of the specialist societies. Some are difficult, some are monocarpic, but the simplest approach is to treat them as if they need some chilling before they will germinate. Sow in autumn or winter in equal parts of grit and John Innes seed compost, cover with only a thin layer of grit (many need light), and stand the pots in a north-facing frame.

As a quick guide, *C. lasiocarpa*, *C. raineri* (much seed will actually be crossed with *C. carpatica*, which seems to cross with everything), *C. waldsteiniana* and *C. zoysii* all need chilling, while *C. alpina*, *C. barbata*, and *C. formanekiana* do not. If in doubt, try the cold frame.

Many species will set plenty of seed, and for monocarpic species seed is the only way to keep them going. They will probably self-sow generously if allowed to do so, but it pays to cut the ripening heads with a length of stem and leave them in a paper bag to finish ripening. That way you can be sure of your seed.

## Cannabis *(Cannabinaceae)*

*CL:* Hemp is an ornamental annual foliage plant with fingered palmate leaves, and until comparatively recent times it was offered, without a blush, in our seed lists. Suttons (1915) quote an appreciation from Lt Col. R. A. Cartwright: 'I may also mention that the Hemp seed you sent me has produced plants which attained the height of 10ft 6in to 11 ft, with grand foliage. I have never before, during my twenty-four years here, had Hemp grow to this height.'

In Hungary I noticed it as a ubiquitous cornfield weed. It would be impossible to ban its cultivation there, as here it is of the opium poppy, *Papaver somniferum*, which is so widespread as a garden weed (and ornament) that you could not start to proscribe it. How ridiculous that we should no longer be allowed to grow hemp for ornamental purposes. The seed is not hard to come by, being an ingredient of bird-seed mixtures.

*GR:* It's not long since the seed was sold as fishing bait, to be boiled until it bursts but no longer. I've caught fat roach on it myself.

*CL:* I have grown it in pots to stand outside my porch in summer. A local junkie (he admitted it later) pinched out the inflorescence on one plant, thus spoiling its symmetry. I cannot imagine that he got kicks from that.

*GR:* Cannabis was still grown until recently in the Chelsea Physic Garden, and a fine plant it is too. It has not been grown at Kew for some years, but there is a plant called *Urtica cannabina* which is in the same family. Unkind members of staff, when nervous youths inquired where the cannabis was grown, directed them to this plant. They could then be seen glancing round shiftily before reaching out to pluck a shoot. You will guess the result. *Urtica cannabina* is a nettle and stings fiercely.

The rich blue spikes of *Salvia farinacea* 'Victoria' surround a large, overwintered plant of *Helichrysum petiolare*, raised from cuttings.

2. The butterfly weed, *Asclepias tuberosa*, hardy, perennial, August-flowering, with *Eryngium giganteum* behind.

3. The wild *Chrysanthemum coronarium* var. *disco[...]* from Greece is the forebear of a number of good annual chrysanthemums.

4. Mixed seedlings: *Osteospermum hyoseroides* (orange daisy), *Briza maxima* (quaking grass) and two species of campanula.

5. *Eucomis bicolor*, antirrhinum, *Nicotiana* 'Lime Green' and *Euphorbia characias*.

The single marigold 'Cinnabar' in a north-west-facing border, blending with *Helichrysum petiolare* 'Limelight', which likes it cool.

7. All daisy shapes: blue *Felicia amelloides* 'Santa Anita' (from cuttings), *Argyranthemum maderense* (from seed or cuttings) and *Mesembryanthemum* 'Lunette' (a short-lived annual).

8. The best germination of the Pasque flower, *Pulsatilla vulgaris*, is from fresh seed.

9. Aquilegias fill in among shrub roses in a Scottish garden.

Two forms of white foxglove. Graham Rice prefers the spotted, Christopher Lloyd likes them both.

11. *Lilium martagon* mixes well with astrantias in semi-shade, and both self-sow.

2. A dramatic stand of white dittany, *Dictamnus albus*, in the Van Duesen gardens, Vancouver, British Columbia.

13. Spikes of purple, cream and white foxgloves self-sown behind the rounded heads of *Allium christophii*.

14. The red (in this case pink) valerian, *Centranth. ruber,* probably self-sown, softens the severity of these terrace steps and balustrading.

15. The five-spot, *Nemophila maculata,* is hardy and flowers early from an autumn sowing among gi chives, *Allium schoenoprasum sibiricum.*

16. Dwarf blue hostas make just the right background for *Allium christophii*.

17. Thistly onopordum behind an oriental poppy, 'Cedric's Pink'.

18. A direct sowing of iberis, the annual candytuft, on the road side of a garden fence.

19. Spring bedding in the Parc de Bagatelle, Bois de Boulogne, Paris.

20. The dwarf lupin strain 'Minaret', treated a biennial and followed by late bedding, at Dixte

21. Double borders of annuals and dahlias in a Scottish garden, peaking in September.

## Cardiocrinum *(Liliaceae)*

*GR:* Sadly, the rather grand and imposing spikes of this tall lily are not within the reach of every gardener. First, cardiocrinums are a little fussy as to their soil, preferring a rich, leafy soil in dappled shade and shelter from spring frosts, which can damage the young growth. And second, they can take as many as seven years to flower from seed – after which the bulbs, rather unhelpfully, die. We don't all have the patience. It is true that on its departure it leaves behind a number of small bulblets, but although they flower rather more quickly than seed-raised plants, the flower spikes are generally less impressive.

If you want to raise some from seed, fresh seed sown straight away will usually germinate the following spring, but older seed which has dried off may take an extra year. You can then set the seedlings out in the back of a border, to grow on before planting them in their final homes. Insufferably well-organized gardeners sow seed every autumn and so after a number of years always have flowering-sized bulbs to plant out.

## Carex *(Cyperaceae)*

*GR:* A large number of previously unfamiliar *Carex* species, many from New Zealand, are appearing in nursery catalogues at the moment, but seed of them is still rather scarce.

The clumsily named pendulous sedge, *C. pendula*, is an old favourite which is easy to raise and very useful for shaded sites, especially on heavy soils. It's a tall plant, sometimes reaching 6 ft, with characteristic arching, dark green foliage and straight stems carrying long drooping flower spikes which hang vertically in early summer. This is a solid, self-reliant plant which will not be bullied by hostas or other broad-leaved plants, with which it looks so well. It self-sows too, and indeed in some gardens the enthusiasm with which it spreads can be irritating.

The only other sedge that seems to turn up in seed catalogues, though more are available in society seed lists, is *C. comans*. This extraordinary plant grows in dense tufts with fine, wiry, rather twisted leaves of an unusual shade sometimes described as 'milk chocolate'. Reaching only about a foot in height, it looks expecially good growing through gravel and is at its best in groups with, perhaps, variegated euonymus or the rather restrained *Lamium maculatum* 'Aureum'.

Both species are easy to raise from seed sown in gentle heat in spring, and in my experience there are no dormancy problems.

## Carlina *(Compositae)*

*CL: Carlina acaulis* is a 9 in perennial thistle carrying, in August, a large silvery-metallic inflorescence (bees love to forage on its disc) with a handsome surround of prickly involucral bracts. Each plant will carry six or eight of these. They close on themselves in damp weather and at night. They make excellent material for drying, and it is altogether a bold, eye-catching plant for a hot spot. It looks well in gravel.

*C. acaulis* is easily raised from seed, and so is the biennial *C. vulgaris*, which is a native of chalk, limestone and sand-dunes. 12 in tall, it carries three or four flower-heads to a single-stemmed plant, smaller than *C. acaulis* but still noticeable. It flowers in August and dries well.

## Celosia *(Amaranthaceae)*

*GR:* Sometimes it is quite fun being rude about a plant you really dislike, but there are always people (like Christopher, maybe) to whom the subject of your invective is real joy. So when I say that cockscombs, *Celosia cristata*, do not appeal, you will understand that I am moderating my language.

Quite different is *C. plumosa*, with its feathery flames of flowers. Mind you, although it is now being promoted as a bedding plant in the UK, our climate is not warm enough for it. In California, Florida and similarly balmy climes, celosias are a different proposition. They make resilient bedding plants, especially in humid areas, and impressive cut flowers too.

'Century Mixed', in scarlet and yellow and reaching 2 ft in height, and the deep orange 'Apricot Brandy' at a more modest 18 in, are All America Selections bronze medal winners. Don't bank on those heights in the UK. 'New Look', with dark, purplish foliage and deep red flowers, sounds interesting for bedding out in a sheltered spot.

Various cut-flower types are available in trade catalogues in both *cristata* and *plumosa* forms, plus a curious hybrid between the two, but they are rarely available to home gardeners. Most are intended to be grown as a single stem, so planting at 5 in apart is necessary. I especially fancy the pale salmon 'Halle', which is small-flowered but bushy.

The one crucial thing with all celosias is to prevent root disturbance, as this encourages them to flower when still tiny. The simplest method is either to prick out very early or to sow a number of seeds in a small peat pot, thin out the seedlings, then pot on when the roots appear through the side walls.

*CL:* I am no fonder of this flower as we see it in cultivation than Graham, but if we could reintroduce the wild *C. argentea*, from which all the modern cockscombs derive, I believe we should admire it. There would be grace in the plant and the astonishing sheen on the inflorescence would still be there. Also the leaves would be less coarse.

## Centaurea *(Compositae)*

*GR:* The wild cornflower, *Centaurea cyanus*, is one of the rarest and most beautiful of British wild flowers. However, like corn cockle and corn marigold, it still persists in a few areas, notably Scotland.

It has been 'improved' over the years – though I would not describe all developments as truly beneficial. Dark blue, violet and white versions were introduced direct from the wild, while in gardens and under the eye of plant-breeders various pinks, blues and deep purples have been added. The same colours are repeated in different varieties of various heights: 'Tall Mixed' (4 ft), 'King Size' (3 ft), 'Polka Dot' (15 in). 'King Size' has the largest flowers, and it is suggested by the raiser that the most spectacular cut flowers can be grown by disbudding.

'Frosty Mixed' is a little different in that the petals of all colours are tipped with white, while if you prefer to stick to the wild blue shade, 'Blue Diadem' at about 2 ft is the one to choose. The smallest available now and the one with the least charm is the blue 'Jubilee Gem'. Although the fully double 'Blue Bay', bred as a pot plant for commercial growers would you believe, could always be launched by some over-optimistic seed company. The new 'Ultra Dwarf Blue' sounds the same.

These hardy annuals are easy to raise if sown in spring where they are to flower and thinned out according to their eventual height. It is better to sow them in September, however, as this gives them more time to build up powerful rosettes and substantial food stores to fuel the surge of flower spikes the following year. I know Christopher grows the tall types as fine pot plants from an autumn sowing . . .

*CL:* Yes, from May to late June I like to make a show with them outside my porch. While they are in flower, dead-heading of the bleached, faded blooms every few days is essential in this prominent position.

To hit the right sowing date is the main problem, and much depends on the mildness of the autumn. Too early, and the seedlings will run up to flower before winter's arrival; too late and they won't make those 'powerful rosettes'. About the last week in September is a fair bet for me in Sussex – earlier in the north.

*GR:* Few separate colours in addition to the unique blue are available to the home gardener, which restricts their use in mixed borders. More are available to commercial growers, who always get the best colour choice in plants such as these.

Sadly, they tend to suffer from powdery mildew in hot summers.

The fluffy flowers of sweet sultan, *C. moschata*, start with the advantage of a sweet scent. The flowers, in pinks, lavenders, purples and white, have an appealing sheen to the petals. A naturally bushy plant, I've only grown it for cutting and found it very easy from a spring sowing outside. 'The Bride' is pure white with a creamy centre; the mixed is usually called simply that, or sometimes 'Imperialis Mixed'; and there is a yellow which is more correctly called *C. suaveolens*. Oh, and by the way – they are all more correctly known as *Amberboa*, but let's not worry about that.

*CL:* Seed is on offer of *C. gymnocarpa*, a perennial sub-shrub and potentially the most beautiful of all grey foliage bedding plants. In a good strain, the colour is very pale and silvery. The leaves are doubly pinnate and 9–12 in long, in loose rosettes on a 15-in tall, bushy plant.

The great idea, with this species, is to grow a strain that does *not* produce (or at least not freely) its wretched little thistle-like mauve flowers. Seed strains, alas, produce readily flowering plants and the leaves are not as pale as they should be. Better to acquire a vegetatively propagated clone of good appearance and to propagate it yourself, thereafter, from cuttings, never relying on its hardiness to bring an old plant through the winter. However well behaved, there'll be flowers in early summer, but if these are removed, leafy shoots will take over thereafter.

## Centranthus *(Valerianaceae)*

*GR:* Dry walls, dry hedge bottoms – anywhere dry and sunny suits *Centranthus ruber*, this opportunistic plant which sheds its wind-blown seeds in such vast numbers. Although red valerian is its common name, the dark pink seems to be the commonest: in a colony on a wall near me it makes up 90 per cent of the plants, with white and deep red filling the other 10 per cent. They flower all summer and are good bee and butterfly plants.

Although in some situations (with catmint for example) this is a very attractive plant, it can be a nuisance, and this irritation is multiplied when you discover how difficult the seedlings are to remove; they have an infuriating habit of breaking off just above the root and then regrowing.

*CL:* The best treatment, I find, is to cut the plants hard back to the base immediately after their first flowering and before they have had the chance to seed. This is approximately at the turn of June–July. Then you can be assured of a pristine second crop in September.

There is an attractive pale pink form which you rarely see in England, but which is common along the Galloway coast of south-west Scotland. Red valerian is as attractive to cats as catmint.

## Cephalaria *(Dipsacaceae)*

*CL: Cephalaria gigantea* (syn. *C. tatarica*) is the tree scabious, a hardy perennial 6 ft high with a branching inflorescence of greeny-yellow, scabious-like flower-heads. It associates well with the spikes of blue or purple delphiniums, which flower at the same time, and is long-lived and undemanding.

## Cheiranthus *(Cruciferae)*

*CL:* Several species and hybrids, including the Siberian wallflower, belong properly to *Erysimum*, although frequently listed as *Cheiranthus*. That leaves the wallflower, *Cheiranthus cheiri*, which is one of our most popular spring bedding plants, although by no means entirely hardy. Even in the Netherlands it is seldom used.

Wallflower seed is still widely available in separate colours, and although mixtures are exceedingly popular, far greater impact is obtained by using adjacent groups of two or three distinct colour strains. The individual plant is nothing much to look at and is easily knocked sideways by winter gales if isolated. The most effective policy is to mass the plants so that they are touching, and to use tulips in blocks among or behind them rather than scattered through them.

No grower could afford to market decent-sized wallflower plants at the meagre price which customers expect to pay. They get what they deserve. The only satisfactory way is to grow your own. I see no point in the dwarf strains. 'Nice bushy little plants', you might say of them, but a nice bushy big plant is preferable any day and can be accommodated in small gardens, only fewer of them will be needed.

*GR:* I find that dwarf varieties *are* useful, for they are good planted in front of the taller types which are without flowers for half their height. These smaller 'Bedder' types effectively hide the stems. A combination of 'Vulcan' or 'Blood Red' with yellow tulips ('West Point') behind and 'Primrose Bedder' in front is stunning.

I just think it's a shame that only one of the colours that have been developed in the Siberian wallflower is available to us. Wouldn't the apricot, pink, red, lilac and white be useful?

Double wallflowers are also available from seed, believe it or not, but they're not a patch on the delightful 'Harpur Crewe'. There are two varieties reaching 12 in and 2 ft, but even the smaller ones seem to flop. And the flowers are big, blousy and, frankly, a mess. It's a nice idea but ...

*CL:* The time to sow wallflowers is when you're hoiking out last year's plants at the end of May (not that I'm suggesting they should be grown *every* year; a change is a rest). A row of them can join the brassica seed-bed. When lining them out individually in July, be sure to allow a foot between plants in the row. Given the space, they'll fill it and you'll be proud of the results.

It is important when transplanting to their flowering positions to keep a ball of soil round their roots. Lift carefully with a broad trowel or, better, a spade, and press the soil around the roots so that it doesn't drop off (which can easily happen, as the roots are not fibrous). If you take care like this, wallflowers can be moved successfully even as late as January, but late October is the usual time. Do the job when their foliage is dry, otherwise you and they and everything around you will get in a fearful slimy mess.

*GR:* This advice on raising wallflowers is spot on. My only suggestion would be sowing a little later and transplanting slightly smaller plants if your situation is especially wind-blown.

*CL:* There are many colours to choose from. You'll need fewer of the light, bright, assertive ones than of the purples, browns and blood reds. A bed of 'Purple Queen' with regular dots of the brilliant 'Cloth of Gold' looks sumptuous. All varieties smell equally good to me. Avoid the double-flowered strains, which are very poorly selected these days.

Wallflowers are perennials, and it is nice to leave a few old plants somewhere so that they can seed themselves and carry on from year to year (though their tell-tale stripy blooms will proclaim the inroads of virus disease). They'll put up with a dry, starvation diet if need be, and are fun when growing in the cracks of a wall. These will be the earliest plants in bloom, and you can pick them to enjoy their warm scent in the house.

## Chrysanthemum *(Compositae)*

*GR:* Under the most recent botanical revision of the chrysanthemums, only a few Mediterranean annual species retain the name *Chrysanthemum*. The florist's types are now called (I hesitate to say 'are known as') *Dendranthema*; the shrubby species from the Canaries such as *C. frutescens* are now *Argyranthemum*; ox-eye daisies and shasta daisies are *Leucanthemum*; and feverfew is *Tanacetum*. And there are many more changes involving less familiar plants.

To avoid confusion we will keep them all together, although one day, when awareness of these changes is more widespread, they will have to be treated separately.

The three true chrysanthemum species are among the most colourful, reliable and exciting of hardy annuals – C. *carinatum*, C. *coronarium* and C. *segetum*, plus some hybrids.

C. *carinatum* comes from Morocco, and the flame colouring of the wild species is brought to such mixtures as the stunning 'Court Jesters', with their scarlet, orange, slightly rusty, yellow or white flowers with a contrasting red or yellow ring around the disc. Reaching about 2 ft, they are wonderful for cutting in armfuls, after which savage treatment they will simply throw up more flowers. But they need a fertile soil and not too many dry spells to withstand such culling.

From the Mediterranean region and Greece comes C. *coronarium* – the first sight of it growing wild in vast sheets is unforgettable. Like many annuals of this region this is a winter annual which germinates in autumn, grows slowly for most of the relatively mild winter, and can be in flower in March. In the coldest gardens spring sowing is more reliable, but as with cornflowers, autumn sowing gives the best plants.

Looking at fields full of these buttery flowers, you will notice the occasional flower which is different. This is usually the variety *discolor*, in which the outer half of the ray florets is cream or white. This is the sort of variation in the wild that can lead to new garden varieties. Two fine semi-double varieties are usually found in catalogues, 'Primrose Gem' and 'Golden Gem'.

The British native corn marigold, C. *segetum*, also behaves naturally as a winter annual. Being used to the tougher conditions in the UK (it thrives in the wild in Scotland), it is more reliable treated in this way. 'Prado' has flowers up to 3 in across with a dark, reddish disc, and its long-flowering qualities make it an ideal mixed border plant and a good companion for the earlier, rustier shades of helenium, perhaps in front of a purple smoke bush. There's also 'Eastern Star' in primrose with a dark centre, and 'Eldorado' in canary-yellow.

'Cecilia' is an especially productive hybrid between C. *coronarium* and C. *segetum*, with white flowers, the eye of each ringed with gold. Cut it in armfuls.

CL: One of my favourite annual chrysanthemums, only 6 in tall and therefore suitable for edging (with blue anagallis, for instance), is C. *multicaule* 'Gold Plate'. It flowers untiringly for many months, and the single yellow daisies have a ring of green dots around the disc. It is very prone to soil-borne fungus disease, which kills off the plants in mid-season, so you have to move it around the garden from year to year or give it a rest.

*GR:* New dwarf F1 hybrid shasta daisies have recently arrived. 'Snow Lady' is one, and these can be raised like bedding plants and will flower in their first summer. But the plants are so short, about 12 in, and the flowers so large, about 3 in, that the scale seems quite wrong.

In recent years the Japanese have worked hard at developing seed strains of various florist's chrysanthemums. The only ones I have tried are 'Super Jet', misleadingly said to be the equivalent of F1 pelargoniums. I found them to be very tall, lanky plants with a pyramid of fully double flowers perched on the top. When there are so many named varieties raised from cuttings which are so much better, I am inclined to ignore 'Super Jet'.

*CL:* The traditional florist's chrysanthemum that I regularly grow from seed (not sown till early April, though an earlier sowing might be preferable) is an F1 strain called 'Fanfare'. I find it wonderful to cut for the house in the autumn. Some flowers are fully double, others not. The mixture is pleasing, as are the colours, which include pink as well as traditional yellow and bronze. Height is a mere $2\frac{1}{2}$ ft in the first year.

I have used Sutton's early flowering 'Charm' chrysanthemums, which they now call 'Suncharm', for autumn bedding with pleasing results. The numerous single florets are carried on dwarf, bushy plants.

*GR:* Feverfew, now correctly called *Tanacetum parthenium*, has also been given some attention by plant-breeders recently. 'Santana' is an especially interesting one, as it was bred as a pot plant to resemble an anemone-flowered pot chrysanthemum. It is also day-neutral, which means that it will flower at any time of the year and it will also take up flower dyes well. (Heaven help us!) Even if you don't want to grow it as a pot plant, in the garden it makes a flattish dome of a plant and can look good in a large pot.

## Cladanthus *(Compositae)*

*CL:* Also known as *Anthemis arabica*, this is a half hardy annual to return to with pleasure from time to time. Its habit of growth (similar to that of the thorn apple, *Datura stramonium*) is stylish. A pair of new flowering shoots [more often five or six – GR] is made from beneath each of its yellow daisies. As these shoots flower in their turn, they produce another pair so that you finally have a complex candelabrum, the faded flowers being concealed beneath new growth. The leaves are filigree and the plant has a long season. It reaches 15 in in height and as much across.

## Clarkia *(Onagraceae)*

*GR:* Clarkia has long been a favourite for borders and cutting, and is one of the few hardy annuals available in separate colours. Easy to raise for flowering outside by making an autumn or spring sowing where they are to flower and thinning out rigorously, you can have flowers for cutting all the year round if you have the facilities.

Clarkia forms flower stems only when the night temperature rises above 50°F, but unlike many plants is indifferent to day length. So by sowing in different months and increasing the heat at different times, flowers can be encouraged almost all the year round. Sadly, few of us have the necessary facilities and I have certainly never tried it.

Double clarkias (and most of those available are doubles) have loose, rather open carnation-like flowers in a wide range of reds, pinks and white. White, carmine, salmon and deep purple are usually available as separate colours, while the best mixtures have over a dozen colours.

One of the good things about clarkias is that in many situations they will make their normal, rather stiffly upright $2\frac{1}{2}$ ft of growth and not need staking. The mixture makes a wonderful combination with the shorter *Iberis* 'Flash Mixed' in front; although both include colours described as scarlet as well as other harsh-sounding shades, all have a certain softness that prevents their jarring, and they share more or less the same colour range.

## Clematis *(Ranunculaceae)*

*CL:* Clematis seed is best sown fresh and the pan allowed to freeze in winter weather. Some species, *C. tangutica* for example, germinate quickly and will even carry flowers in their first summer. Others, such as *C. flammula* and *C. campaniflora*, germinate mainly in the second spring from sowing.

The large-flowered and other hybrids give very variable results. 'Minuet', a viticella hybrid, is one of the most prolific. Germination may be slow, and it is worth waiting two or three years if, indeed, it is worth growing the hybrids from seed at all. The offspring are seldom as good as their parents, but the doting gardener invariably mistakes his geese for swans and fails to make proper use of the rubbish heap. A planned programme of hybridization is quite another matter. We could do with more of that.

## Cleome *(Capparidaceae)*

*CL:* Because it enjoys hot summers, the spider flower *Cleome spinosa* (*C. pungens*), is used much more on the Continent than in the UK. It will do well in most summers in the south of England, however, provided the plants are brought on reasonably early (a March sowing is quite soon enough) and never allowed to starve. They should be given individual treatment at the pricking-out stage and, ideally, be planted out in May from 5-in or 6-in pots.

This is a handsome plant with a widely branching, shrub-like struc-ture, and it should grow 4 ft tall in a season. The plant has a slightly disagreeable odour when handled, but a more important point to bear in mind is the pair of hooked green spines on the stem at the base of each leaf.

The flowers comprise a substantial inflorescence and the long, extruded stamens give it its common name. The seed-pods are like long, thin sausages and are quite a feature. Plants of the spider flower seem capable of growing and flowering indefinitely so long as the weather remains warm. There are separate colour strains in deep mauve, pink and white (the white 'Helen Campbell' contrasts well with orange *Tithonia rotundifolia* 'Torch'), or in a pleasing mixture, 'Colour Foun-tain'.

## Clianthus *(Leguminosae)*

GR · If you grow Sturt's desert pea (*Clianthus formosus*), be sure to keep the smelling salts handy. Unsuspecting visitors are apt to need reviving after catching even a glimpse of this startling plant. Its flamboyant red and black flowers are simply breathtaking; elderly relatives of a nervous disposition should be kept well clear.

But, as these venerables are apt to explain (sometimes all too tediously), everything worth having demands a little hard work. Of course this is rubbish – courting could hardly be called a chore. But you certainly need to put a little effort and lavish a little care if you want to grow Sturt's desert pea.

It grows naturally in desert areas where rains fall only rarely; but when it does rain it comes in torrents. So the seed germinates when the rains come but as the plant grows the soil becomes drier and drier. These are not easy conditions to emulate, for as the sand dries out, the roots search more and more deeply for the ever-retreating moisture. Pots are too small to accommodate such questing.

One solution is to grow them in a chimney-pot or drainpipe filled with a very well-drained compost. John Innes or a peat-based compost mixed with equal quantities of grit seems to work well. It may even be worth trying almost pure grit with regular weak liquid feeding.

Sow the seed in the top of the drainpipe, keep it in a temperature of about 60°F, and thin the seedlings down to one. Alternatively they can be sown in any sort of bottomless pot and set in the top of the chimney-pot or drainpipe when still quite small. Disturbing the roots is fatal.

The plants should be kept in an unheated but well-ventilated greenhouse all summer. Should they thrive, the plants will reach about 12 in in height and spread widely, trailing over the sides of the container.

There is another method. Seedlings can be grafted on to roots of that interesting but ultimately rather tedious shrub, the bladder senna (*Colutea arborescens*). This can be a tricky method for the inexperienced but worth trying if all else fails. If you succeed make sure you have the St John's Ambulance Brigade on hand when the hordes come to view.

### Cobaea *(Polemoniaceae)*

*CL:* A fast-growing, half-hardy perennial climber, *Cobaea scandens* is a boon, treated as an annual for covering a large wall space quickly where the winter has killed its former occupant. It's good on trellises too.

Its substantial bell-flowers are well presented on long stalks. They are typically a murky purple (this is the kind of flower that is pollinated, in its native Mexico, by night-flying bats), and there is also a pale green form called 'Alba'. It is worth bringing your plants on fairly early, as their flowering otherwise gets under way too late in the autumn for comfort.

Bought seed may give poor germination, vitality being quickly lost. If you pick your own seed-pods, with a length of stalk, before they are frosted and ripen them (by January) in a glass of water on a windowsill, one pod will yield enough seedlings to supply an entire county.

*GR:* Seed is best sown on edge in individual 3-in pots, but you will probably need to pot the seedlings on and pinch and stake to prevent them taking over the greenhouse before they are planted out. Once they are growing well, keep them cool.

You may come across the variegated form, but it doesn't come true from seed and you need to root cuttings in late summer.

### Codonopsis *(Campanulaceae)*

*CL:* *Codon* means a bell and *opsis* means similar to. Many codonopsis are bell-flowered, though in some the flowers are star-shaped, like *Campanula isophylla*. They are hardy herbaceous perennials, the majority having a twining, climbing habit. Some, with green flowers and an invasive root stock, are too insignificant to be worth growing.

They make tubers and are easily increased this way, but are also quick from seed, which will often produce a flower in the same year from a spring sowing.

*GR:* Sow in a temperature of 50°F, or even in a propagator with the bedding. Prick out promptly into individual pots and grow on well protected in order to get first-year flowers.

*CL: C. clematidea* is the best-known species, beautifully marked inside the bell but with a strong foxy smell. *C. ovata*, pale blue, has beautifully flared bells. It shouldn't be difficult but I manage to lose it. Codonopsis seem to prefer Scotland to England. The one I grow for display in large pots outside my porch, where it climbs up pea-sticks and then into a cotoneaster, is *C. convolvulacea*, with blue, dished flowers. Forrest's form [sometimes known as *C. forrestii* – GR] has attractively patterned markings in the centre of the flower.

## Coleus *(Labiatae)*

*GR:* One of the sad things about the way coleus breeding has developed in recent years is that almost no attention has been paid to their use outside in the garden. A few years ago I tried about seven different varieties and by autumn there was still not one decent plant among them. [I have experienced the same disappointment – CL]. Having been developed as pot plants, they remained small and stunted. Even the brilliant yellow-edged red 'Scarlet Poncho', which was bred for hanging baskets, failed.

But as pot plants they are superb. There are a few single colours, like 'Molten Lava' with its purple-lobed foliage and pink centres, and the scarlet 'Red Monarch'. But this is a case where the mixtures have the edge. There is such variety, such stunning contrasts in the foliage, which almost always has two colours in the leaf and often three.

Treat the seed as a half-hardy annual, though it needs a temperature of 70–75°F to germinate well. Don't sow too early, however, as low light levels lead to poor growth and seedlings sometimes never recover. Better to leave sowing until March at the earliest and reap the benefit of the quicker-growing seedlings in the better light. Or you can leave it until May or later, which may be very convenient if the greenhouse is full of bedding seedlings earlier on.

'Sabre Mixed' is a very slow grower and was bred to be sold as a pot plant in small pots. 'Rainbow Strain' is a mixture of familiar, large-sized, nettle-leaved types in the widest range of colours. 'Fashion Parade' contains all the more unusual leaf forms – some lobed, some fringed, some long and narrow.

In my experience 'Scarlet Poncho', which was bred for hanging baskets, will succeed as a basket plant only if planted up in early May and kept in the greenhouse or conservatory for some weeks to ensure that it is well established before moving it outside to a warm, sheltered spot. Never allow the plants to dry out.

## Collinsia *(Scrophulariaceae)*

*GR:* Known in the Pacific States as Chinese houses, this name describes the whorls of flowers of *Collinsia bicolor* as they encircle the stem. The purple lower lip slanting outwards and the upper white lip being vertical, the whole cluster gives the appearance of a Chinese pagoda.

Reaching about 18 in, this is rather a floppy plant and demands discreet staking if it is to retain its natural upright character. A good shade plant in soil that doesn't dry out, a consistent moisture supply will ensure long flowering. It is also a very long-lasting cut flower.

The so-called blue lips from California, *C. grandiflora*, has a deep blue lower lip but is rarely found in catalogues.

Both are hardy annuals which can be sown in autumn or spring and set seed generously.

## Commelina *(Commelinaceae)*

*CL:* First cousin to the tradescantias, *Commelina coelestis* similarly flowers in the morning and goes to bed at noon. The strap leaves are moderately unprepossessing, but the flowers are an intense, dazzling peacock blue, with a shape not unlike a pea's. This is an exciting colour.

Plants are quickly raised from seed to flower, so you might as well treat it as a half-hardy annual, although its fleshy white roots can be lifted and over-wintered under frost-free glass. It's good in a moist, shady border.

## Convolvulus *(Convolvulaceae)*

*GR:* The bindweeds fall into three groups: the showy annual *Convolvulus tricolor*, the shrubby species such as *C. sabatius*, and the Mediterranean sprawlers such as *C. althaeoides*.

'Blue Ensign', or sometimes 'Royal Ensign', is the best variety of the annual species – rich blue trumpets with a ragged white centre and an orange-yellow eye. The plants are compact too, without being dumpy. Astonishingly, some seed companies list only a mixture of shades which includes feeble pinks and lilacs and eschew the radiant blue as a separate colour.

This annual convolvulus is also one of the best of all hoverfly plants, so is worth planting simply for the sake of the larvae which are prodigious aphid gobblers. Sow it outside in March or April where it is to flower. It prefers sun and a soil which is not too dry. Its rather lax habit hints that it might be a good hanging-basket plant, but its relatively unbranching habit demands some bushy cover, *Lobelia* 'White Cascade' perhaps.

Seed of few of the shrubby species is available, but *C. cantabricus* is occasionally found. This is more of a sub-shrub, with woody shoots at the base but top growth which often dies back. Sow the seed in spring, with the bedding plants, in the propagator in a light soil. No special treatment is necessary.

Unfortunately seed of the captivating Mediterranean sprawlers with their finely cut leaves and rich pink, blue or white flowers is rarely found in the familiar seed catalogues, although it does appear in the seed lists of specialist societies. Most need cold greenhouse conditions, where they make unusual trailers for large pots. If you should happen across some seed, sow this in spring in the propagator as well.


## Coreopsis *(Compositae)*

*GR:* There are just three varieties to mention here. *Coreopsis* 'Early Sunrise' was the first plant to be awarded a gold medal in the Fleuroselect European flower trials; it was also a gold medal winner in the All America Selections. Fleuroselect have now cynically changed their rules; gold, silver and bronze medals used to be awarded, but only 'Early Sunrise' won a gold in over twenty years and there were few silvers. Now silver and bronze awards have been abolished and plants of below gold medal standard are also awarded gold medals! Huh.

Treated as a half-hardy annual, 'Early Sunrise' will be flowering in June and will carry on for the rest of the summer throwing double orange-yellow flowers on 15-in stems. This is a really reliable new plant and in effect an earlier-flowering version of 'Sunray'.

But the good thing is that both 'Early Sunrise' and 'Sunray' are not only perfectly good perennials which will settle down to flowering from spring to autumn every year – they also have a very acceptable informal habit. At last the plant-breeders have created a new bedding plant that actually fits happily into a mixed border.

*CL:* I'm not quite so enthusiastic. 'Sunray' in its second year had smaller flowers on a less compact plant than in its first. 'Early Sunrise' has the vicious habit of not shedding its faded rays. They turn brown on the plant and need dead-heading every four days if the display is to be kept smart. Surely no gold medal qualification. And why confuse us by giving two such similar names to two coreopsis? I would not call their colour *orange*-yellow, Graham, but a very pure, penetrating yellow that stands out in just such a way (with abrasive arrogance, as you say elsewhere) as to make those who are frightened of this colour quail. Poor mutts.

*GR:* We'll have to agree to differ then. I see a definite orange tint to them; maybe there is more than one strain. But the mutts will still quail.

The name sea dahlia sounds a little weird, but such is the common name sometimes given to *C. maritima*, with its bright yellow flowers on 2-ft stems. Like many seaside plants the foliage is rather succulent, and in mild areas or in a frost-free greenhouse the plant forms a woody rootstock from which fresh shoots spring each year. But don't rely on this; grow it as an annual for the sheer brilliance of its display.

Finally, *C. tinctoria* and, in particular, 'Tiger Flower'. This neat little annual, about 9 in, with its masses of wiry stems, carries star-like flowers of around eight petals in almost pure crimson to almost pure gold with, in between, a range in which the petals are speckled and striped with both colours. A real treat for sunny beds and surprisingly long-flowering. The new 'Super Dwarf Gold' at around 6 in looks good too.

## Cosmos *(Compositae)*

*GR: Cosmos bipinnatus* is the most familiar of these easy annuals. It's a lovely cut flower and an amenable mixed border plant reaching around 3 ft, with finely-cut leaves and big single flowers in mixtures and separate colours.

The 3-in single daisies of the clean white 'Purity' make a fine blend in front of the almost greyish-lilac *Buddleia fallowiana*, and perhaps a group of the pinkish-lilac *Scabiosa graminifolia* in front might complete the trio. 'Sonata', at half the height, is good in tubs.

'Imperial Pink' is a very bright shade, while 'Gloria' is a rather softer rose with a dark central ring and 'Daydream' is the palest blush pink with a dark ring around the yellow disc.

The curious but pretty 'Sea Shells' has its ray florets rolled into tubes like shells, although it can be variable. A variety with a mass of shorter petals around the central disc is under development and should be available in the next few years.

A yellow-flowered variety, 'Yellow Garden', has recently appeared from Japan and this needs slightly different treatment. It's a short-day variety, so it won't usually flower until August or September. That means you can sow later, even as late as June, and it needs a sheltered spot so that harsh early frosts don't demolish it before it flowers. It would make a good conservatory plant too. Unfortunately some seed companies have changed its name, so exactly the same thing is also listed as 'Lemon Cream', 'Lemon Peel' and 'Butterkist'. I ask you!

Then there are the altogether more fiery shades – 'Sunny Gold' and 'Sunny Red'. Instead of the tall openly-branched plants of *C. bipinnatus*, these forms of *C. sulphureus* make neater, more rounded plants, bushier low down and with smaller flowers. 'Sunny Red' looks especially good behind the beetroot 'MacGregor's Favourite'.

*CL:* On my heavy soil, these yellow and orange cosmos go down to botrytis half-way through the season. I steer clear of them.

*GR:* Finally there are *C. atrosanguineus* and *C. diversifolius*. Both these tender perennials were once commonly raised from seed and treated as half-hardy annuals, but no longer. The first of these – chocolate-coloured and chocolate-scented – has recently resurfaced, but the clone in cultivation is sterile so there is no seed. The lilac or rosy-coloured flowers of the latter have not been seen, as far as I know, for many years.

## Cotula *(Compositae)*

*CL: Cotula barbata* is a 6-in tall, half-hardy annual that covers itself with yellow rayless buttons. Its season is too short for it to be of much value.

*GR:* This is rather hard on the poor cotulas. True, most of the more appealing, perennial ones from New Zealand are rarely listed in seed catalogues, but check out the society seed lists . . .
 Cotulas are among the best plants for gravel path edges, and all creep along flat with the soil and root at the nodes. Poor soil helps restrict their spread, which can be brisk. The leaves are tiny, pinnately divided and usually arranged in clusters about the nodes. The whole plant is usually less than $\frac{1}{2}$ in high.
 The flowers are small, less than 1 in, and are like daisies' eyes. *C. striata*, *C. potentilliana*, *C. sericea* and *C. squalida* are all worth growing. Their differences are not easy to explain clearly, but different they are.

## Crepis *(Compositae)*

*GR:* The pink hawkweed-like flowers of *Crepis incana*, which appear for many months, are set off attractively by grey foliage in this favourite alpine. It germinates quickly in a gritty compost without chilling, but sometimes as few as 25 per cent of the seeds are viable. Try it behind the little white daisies of *Helichrysum bellidioides* in a sunny, well-drained spot.
 The hardy annual *C. rubra* is a real gem, of upright habit and only 12–15 in in height, with the stiff stems arching upwards from the centre of the leafy rosette. The pink flowers appear for many, many weeks, and regular dead-heading will prolong the display even further. The white form, 'Snowplume', probably a straight renaming of the naturally occurring var. *alba*, is also worth a place, and two can be interplanted effectively. They are good at the front of borders and as long-lasting cut flowers. Sow in spring. I've not yet tried it as a winter annual.

## Crocosmia *(Iridaceae)*

*CL:* All the plants we knew as montbretias now belong here. Division is the obvious method of increase, but interesting variations and hybrids (with *Curtomus*) can be obtained from seed. I raised a red-flowered form ('Dixter Flame') of the normally orange *Crocosmia masonorum*, and I hope I am not being too partial in reckoning it to be a good plant. From Bressingham Gardens we have the excellent 'Lucifer' and others. There should be scope for further developments here.

*GR:* The new hybrid crocosmias set seed generously, and at 70°F they germinate in two to three weeks. There's no telling what their children will be like.

## Cucurbita *(Cucurbitaceae)*

*GR:* It was in February that I realized something was wrong with my gourds. The idea is that you cut them when they ripen in late summer, allow them to dry out and then spray them with lacquer to preserve them. I think I must have fallen down on step two, for I detected a curious smell and when I picked the first one up ... well, it was distinctly squashy and those in the bottom of the bowl were covered in sticky ooze. They had rotted inside.

So after picking, make sure you dry them off thoroughly before spraying. Since that sticky winter, I've taken care not only to dry them off on a windowsill, but then to move them into the airing cupboard until they lose their weight almost entirely and have become quite hard. Then I spray them.

*CL:* I don't think we've got to the bottom of the best gourd treatments yet. Weightless, dried-out gourds have lost their colour. It is while they are still lustrous and alive that they are most pleasurable, but how long they'll keep like this before either rotting or drying is something of a toss-up. I keep some in reserve to take the place of those that have prematurely given up.

I don't spray with lacquer, glamorous though the result may be. Gourds in their prime are still living, breathing objects. Lacquering them prevents respiration.

GR: Gourds can be raised like cucumbers or courgettes. Sow two seeds in a 3-in pot in a propagator in April. Remove the weaker seedling and plant out after the last frost. The vigorous plants can be allowed to trail along the ground or, better, to climb trellis. The fruits come in an entertaining range of shapes and colours and in generous quantities.

## Cuphea *(Lythraceae)*

CL: Best known in this genus is the half-hardy perennial *Cuphea ignea*, the Mexican cigar plant. The $\frac{3}{4}$-in-long tubular flowers are scarlet, with a dark rim as though charred from burning. In a bed, the plant is rather too leafy, the flowers not showing up enough.

Much more useful and effective is the cherry-red *C. miniata* 'Firefly', which makes a 9-in bushy plant with wide open flowers, the petals crimped. It blooms for months without tiring and ripens plenty of seed. This is a true annual. For a colour harmony I grow it with *Sedum* 'Ruby Glow' in front and *Hydrangea* 'Preziosa' behind.

GR: The newly arrived, rabbit-eared *C. viscosissima* has two large purple upper petals shading almost to black at the base, with four paler, much shorter petals below. Many other species were once grown from seed, and some of them sound very pretty. Next time the botanists mount an expedition going to South America, perhaps they can be persuaded to bring some back.

## Cyclamen *(Primulaceae)*

CL: There are seventeen principal species of cyclamen, several of them hardy in the average British garden, and there are some excellently marked and coloured leaf strains within the species, particularly of *C. hederifolium* (syn. *C. neapolitanum*) and *C. coum*. Cyclamen are self-fertile and are rarely insect-pollinated, which enables a strain to come 90 per cent true from seed after selection.

It is usually wise to sow the seed as soon as it is ripe, but it keeps well in a refrigerator if need be, as high as 80 per cent germination after five years being obtained. From seed to flowering, under cold glass, takes three years with the majority of species, all containers being topped with grit to discourage mosses, algae and liverwort. After this they can be planted out where they are unlikely to be disturbed. The tubers are remarkably like pebbles when dormant.

*GR:* You will find that the cross-pollinations that do occur in the garden lead to variation in foliage markings as well as flower colour. You can select for foliage colour, and even quite intricate, silvery leaf patterns can be fixed fairly well in time. It's a continuous process of choosing the appropriate seedlings and planting them together or, if they self-sow, of removing all but those of your chosen pattern from the site and replanting them somewhere else.

*CL:* A good way to start growing hardy cyclamen is to buy plants of the ones you fancy from a specialist like Tile Barn Nursery and then to save and sow your own seed.

*GR:* You can speed things up by soaking any but fresh seed for twenty-four hours before sowing in a good John Innes seed compost, giving them a little warmth. Space the seeds about 1 in apart, and after gritting, place the pots in a temperature of about 50–60°F. Germination will take anything from a few weeks to many months. After germination pot up the plants into John Innes No. 1 and place the pots in a partially shaded frame. With this extra heat, fresh seed of *C. coum* and *C. persicum* sown in winter can produce flowering plants in less than a year.

*CL:* Most species like shade and moisture, and there is never a month when some cyclamen is not in bloom, though they are least prolific in summer.

Everyone's favourite and the easiest species is *C. hederifolium*. Its pink or white flowers (there is a scented strain from Corfu) are borne from late July to November, but the beautifully patterned foliage is at its handsomest from autumn to spring. *C. cilicium*, September-flowering and with good leaf markings, is highly scented and hardy in most gardens.

*C. coum* is bright through the winter months from December and has many variants. It is typically magenta, but there are white forms. *C. trochopteranthum* is similar but with a propeller-like flower and well-marked ovate leaves, not round as in *C. coum*.

*C. repandum*, in a range of pink to magenta shades, wonderfully scented, is the main hardy spring-flowering species, but the larger-flowered, blush-white *C. libanoticum* has an undeserved reputation for being tender and is another spring flowerer.

In every case the foliage is of great beauty and interest.

*GR:* *Cyclamen persicum*, the ancestor of the florist's cyclamen that horrify most contemporary plantsmen, is a lovely plant. Small and dainty, with the flowers held above the prettily marked foliage and sweetly scented, the wild form is well worth growing in spite of the fact that it requires frost-free conditions. The swirling, twisted petals are usually white with a pink mouth, but in the wild they are very variable and can be all pink. This species flowers prolifically in a 4-in pot, and as many as 100 flowers can be carried on one plant in a single season.

## Cynara *(Compositae)*

*CL:* The globe artichoke, *Cynara scolymus*, and the cardoon, *C. cardunculus*, are closely related and may not even be distinguishable as species. In cultivation, the globe artichoke is shorter of stature (3–4 ft) and larger-headed; the cardoon is much more prickly, which is a handsome feature if you don't want to handle and eat the brute.

Globe artichokes for eating should never be raised from seed. You will do much better with selected, named clones. With cardoons, grown for ornament, seed is the best method of propagation, but your own plants will ripen it only after a hot, dry summer and early autumn. Thereafter it will store well for four to five years.

Cardoons are long-lived perennials and in forty years I have had no hardiness problems with my strain, but they vary a lot. The deeply-cut blue-grey leaves are a splendid feature in large borders. The branching candelabra of thistle-heads rise to 8 ft and need the stoutest stakes and the toughest string to control them. Their discs of lavender-blue flowers, loved by bees, open in August. The dead inflorescence retains a grotesque personality, especially when capped with snow.

Large plants can be brought on in the first year from a spring sowing but their hardiness will be greater when they have settled down to border life.

## Cynoglossum *(Boraginaceae)*

*CL:* Hound's-tongue, *Cynoglossum officinale*, is a perennial herb of waste land often seen (like elder) outside the mouth of rabbit-holes on the chalk downs. The leaves are tongue-shaped, the flowers a dingy maroon. Seed is available, to get you started, and it has been reputed to heal wounds, cure the bite of mad dogs and, more recently, to relieve piles. Most of us will be happy to leave it to the rabbits.

*GR:* Our native hound's-tongue has also found its way across to America, where it is known as gypsyflower and grows in fields and waste places from Canada to California. In Britain it was once used as a cure for stuttering.

*CL:* The perennial *C. nervosum* is of great merit in its early summer flowering season, with heads of deep blue forget-me-not flowers. In Scotland, where it flourishes so much better than in the south, it grows to 3 ft. Two ft is more normal with us, and it contrasts well with orange geums.

The annual or biennial *C. amabile* is commonest in seed strains called 'Firmament' and 'Blue Bird', between which there seems to be little difference nowadays. This is a startlingly intense light blue, pure and unadulterated by mauve. A patch of it in your garden will catch the attention of visitors who normally notice nothing less down to earth than the food on their plate.

The largest plants are obtained by treating it as a biennial from an August or (safer) September sowing. From a row, the seedlings can be transplanted to their flowering sites later in the autumn. A tough winter will kill them, but they will normally flower in May and the first half of June. They look spectacular with a pink flower like *Lychnis flos-jovis* or *L. viscaria*. Spring and summer sowings will flower in the same year.

*GR:* A variety of *C. amabile* called 'Blue Shower' has been developed, but it has not yet found its way into British catalogues. Bred as a cut flower, 'Blue Shower' is an unusually tall form reaching over 2 ft in height with large turquoise flowers. The English-language catalogue from Holland which lists it enthuses: 'it is ununderstandable, that this wonderful plant is not much better known'! I'd certainly grow it if British seed companies listed it.

## Dahlia *(Compositae)*

*CL:* With dahlia seed strains you have the great satisfaction of being able to dump your entire stock at the end of the season, instead of going through the worries of over-wintering tubers. On the other hand, any mixed seed strain will produce plants some of which you greatly prefer to others. So, if you do choose to mark your favourites, they can be saved and stored as tubers, so that in the next year you'll be growing a mixture of your own choice. Indeed, you can then take cuttings and work up stocks that will enable you to plan your own colour schemes. Thus, dahlias offer a good deal of flexibility.

It is really only in the field of dwarf bedding material that seed-raised dahlias are useful, and nearly all the seed strains are mixtures. The trouble here (as with antirrhinums) is that dahlias are almost too versatile. There are so many colours (only excluding blue), and some of them make pretty horrible bedfellows. The total effect, then, will be an unrefined and garbled hotch-potch, but still a lot of fun.

The breeders are being very clever (or so they think) in producing ever dwarfer seed strains, and are particularly proud of 'Figaro' in this respect and because it can be had in bloom at the point of sale by retailers. At 2 ft or less, the 'Early Bird' strain is quite dwarf enough.

Dahlia leaves are not very exciting as a rule (rather less handsome than a potato's), but in the 'Redskin' strain they are all suffused with purple. In the event, I didn't think this any help.

Most of the seed strains produce double, semi-double and single-flowered plants. The 'Coltness' hybrids are mainly singles and I like the single bloom myself, but it does seed heavily and even the doubles set a good deal of seed.

*GR:* It's certainly true that for quality of display the taller bedders such as 'Coltness', 'Sunburst' and 'Unwins Dwarf Hybrids' are more impressive. But when sowing cold, as described later, you need to shorten the time between sowing and flowering, and the newer, shorter varieties like 'Figaro' and 'Rigoletto' are definitely quicker.

The first F1 hybrid dahlias have recently appeared – the 'Sunny' series in pink, red and yellow. I've found they vary far more than we're used to in F1 hybrids, mainly because the genetic make-up of dahlias is very complicated. Flowers will vary from fully double, almost pom-pom forms to flat semi-doubles, and they vary noticeably in colour too.

Among my plants of 'Sunny Red' I've had plants of almost blood-red and also orange-red. You will find startling individuals among plants of each variety – and so you should with the price approaching that of F1 pelargoniums.

The arrival of dwarfer seed-raised open-pollinated dahlias in the form of 'Figaro White' ought to be more welcome than it is. Unfortunately this variety varies so much in height and in the flower power of individual plants that it cannot be relied upon. Previously 'Coltness Scarlet' was available as a separate colour, but this has now disappeared from lists.

Personally, for a bold and sparkling border of dahlias, I would choose the 'Unwins Dwarf Hybrids'; they include such a wide range of colours, over a dozen, with no duds, and what is more they look good together.

*CL:* Dead-heading is an essential chore with dahlias and needs to be repeated at frequent intervals, otherwise, as well as looking awful, the plants stop flowering. Some people have a dead-heading temperament and don't resent it. I don't myself, but you should always wear gloves when doing it otherwise you'll keep being stung by sleepy bumble-bees lurking in the flowers' centres. It is not good enough just to pull all the dead flower-heads off – that leaves a forest of stalks behind, which look hideous. You must cut away the stems as well, back to a leaf or strong young shoot, just as you would when doing the roses.

April is early enough to be sowing dahlia seed, with a view to planting out when the ground has warmed up properly in June. Seedlings that have to sit around in chilly weather turn yellow and look miserable. I find dahlias especially useful as a follow-on to June-flowering bedding, for example aquilegias, *Dianthus plumarius* seed strains, Canterbury bells, foxgloves or lupins (treated as biennials). An early May sowing under cold glass will be soon enough in that case, the seedlings being brought on to finish in 5-in pots so that by the time they're planted out, in early July, they're large plants ready to go straight into flowering for the next three months. For following sweet williams, dahlias need not be ready till late July, and a late May sowing will be early enough.

*GR:* This idea of sowing dahlias late and growing them cold is some-thing I have also discovered. This makes them especially useful for gardeners with no heated propagator or heated greenhouse, as the modern varieties like 'Figaro', 'Rigoletto' and the F1 'Sunny' series flower in double-quick time from a sowing without heat at the end of April. I have found that you can space-sow the seed in a 5-in pan, then prick out (when the plants are a little beyond normal pricking-out stage) straight into 5-in pots.

Not only that, they can even be sown outside in mid-May when they will grow quickly and come into flower when only a few inches high. But it is essential to use the more modern, quicker-flowering varieties for this treatment, as the older types just don't have the necessary pace.

## Datura *(Solanaceae)*

*GR:* Once wheeled out in tubs and plunged in beds for the summer, the perennial daturas are now reappearing in all those new conservatories which are sprouting on the backs of houses everywhere. In sheltered spots in the milder areas of the UK, the orange-flowered *Datura sanguinea* may survive outside for some years, as it does at Falmouth in Cornwall.

The seeds are big, and it pays to sow them individually in 3-in peat pots then move them on to 5-in pots as they grow. I've found that daturas need a high germination temperature, 70°F at least, but this is not always what is recommended. Eventually, after a few years of potting on, they may end up in pots as big as 18 in.

If you wish to use them in pots outside in their first summer and can maintain a temperature of at least 55°F after germination, sow them as early as January, so that when the plants go outside in early June they are already impressive.

The number of varieties available seems to be on the increase. All have large, rather sticky leaves and flared, tubular flowers hanging down from the spreading branches. *D. meteloides* is one of the hardier ones, and better suited to borders. The very slightly blue-tinted flowers are as much as 8 in long, and the wafting fragrance is astonishing.

*CL:* They open in the evening and are especially suitable for opera house gardens such as Glyndebourne, or near operatic substitutes.

*GR: D. sanguinea* has equally long flowers in orangy-red but may not flower in its first year. A new hybrid between *D. candida* and *D. aurea* is not only said to flower outside most reliably in its first year, but also comes in a range of colours including cream, white, pink and orange.

I here is also the thorn apple, *D. stramonium*, with its large, prickly but poisonous fruits on stout, widely branching plants. It's an interesting curiosity to grow as a hardy annual, but much despised in America as a weed. It's said that if you infuse two or three seeds in a glass of surgical spirit then shine a light through the glass, you can see a strong green fluorescence. I must try it.

*CL:* This appears as a weed in my garden, and makes a fine, branching candelabrum in hot summers. The skeleton is suitable for dried arrangements.

## Delphinium *(Ranunculaceae)*

*CL:* This genus includes not only the familiar border perennials but the annual larkspurs, *Delphinium ajacis* and *D. consolida*. I shall not soon forget the sight, on the plains of Hungary in early summer, of deep purple-blue larkspurs making a carpet as far as the eye could see, comprising the dominant cornfield weed.

As well as deep indigo and pale blue, larkspurs come in shades of pink and white and their branching inflorescences are excellent for cutting and for drying. They grow to 3–4 ft (the dwarf strains are less satisfactory) and need support. Like cornflowers, they make good pot plants from a September sowing, though there is some danger of the seedlings damping off in winter. Flowering starts quite early, in late May.

*GR:* In catalogues, larkspurs are confusingly named. Sometimes the names *D. ajacis* and *D. consolida* are used as if they were the same, and to make matters even more mysterious, *Flora Europaea* calls the former *Consolida ambigua* and the latter *C. regalis* subspecies *regalis*! Fortunately most catalogues avoid these difficulties by simply grouping all the annuals under larkspur.

Thankfully, separate colours are still available in larkspurs and this allows you the freedom to grow exactly what you like. No one colour seems to be more, or less, resistant to mildew, so adequate spacing to allow a good air-flow through the foliage is important. Autumn sowing, and therefore earlier flowering, will allow them to give their best before mildew strikes in mid-or late summer.

*CL:* Perennial delphiniums have proved such a success from seed that seed strains have largely replaced in popularity the named cultivars, which need to be propagated from cuttings.

Best known are the 'Pacific Giants', developed in California after the Second World War. It is wise to go for single colour strains in these – light or deep blue, purple, rosy mauve ('Astolat') and white with or without a dark central 'bee'. When they were first introduced, the 'Pacific Giants' were well selected and gave reasonably level results. Less so nowadays; you need to select the best plants from any batch.

Dwarfer seed strains like 'Blue Fountains' and 'Blue Springs' have become popular because they are more manageable. Those advertised as 2 ft, however, may reach 4 ft when established and may still need a little support. Actually, a heavy spike on a dwarf plant looks a bit stupid.

*GR:* There have also been some developments with the perennial types in recent years. Like so many new ideas in perennials, this has come about through breeding for the flourishing continental cut-flower business. The 'New Century' series has been developed in Holland, with help from some of the best British delphinium breeders. 'New Century' is derived from the best vegetatively propagated varieties, with cold hardiness as much in mind as flower and spike quality. They have taken ten years and twenty acres of trial crosses to produce. The result is a series of six groups of shades – white, blue, pink, lilac, deep purple, plus an eyeless group including greens, whites and blues, most of which are now available only in the mixture, also known as 'Dreaming Spires'. 'Pink Dream' is available separately and is a reasonably true colour; the others are all groups of more or less similar shades.

They reach 5 ft in height and should flower for the first time in mid-July from a March sowing in a propagator; cover the seed but lightly.

As you would expect, they make coveted cut flowers and for this use should be cut when most of the flowers on the spike are open. The flowers are very sensitive to ethylene gas, so they will deteriorate more quickly if displayed near bowls of ripening fruit.

An intriguing variant from the same breeder is the 'Camaraderie' strain, a mixture of veined and picotee types in pinks, lilacs, greys, creams and white with only a few blues. Surely there must be some among those worth propagating from cuttings.

Also worth a try is the quite different *D. cardinale*. In California this can reach 6 ft in height, with its open sprays of long-spurred tubular flowers, the two upper petals being yellow, the lower red. In cooler areas the height will be greatly reduced. Growing as it does on boggy areas near the coast, a moist soil in full sun suits this species best, and as it is often difficult to over-winter, growing fresh plants from seed each year is the ideal way to treat it. Fortunately it sets seed well and will flower in August from a March sowing. There's a pure yellow one too, 'Yellow Butterfly', although seed is difficult to find.

*CL:* It is essential, with delphiniums, that the seed should be fresh. Sown in March or April, seedlings that are pricked out at the cotyledon stage and then lined out for the summer will usually flower in September, but will be moved to their permanent positions in the following spring, which is traditional. You can move them in the autumn, though, if you take care to lift the fragile roots with a large ball of soil. Beware winter damage to dormant shoot buds by slugs. In their second year, delphinium seedlings will flower at the normal midsummer season.

Having much lighter, branching flower spikes, the single-flowered 'Belladonna' delphiniums grow no taller than 4 ft. 'Connecticut Yankees' belong here.

*D. grandiflorum*, usually listed as *D. chinense* 'Blue Butterfly', is grown as an annual, only 12–15 in tall, but with surprisingly large and rich blue single flowers for so small a plant. It has a branching habit with few-flowered spikes, and if you can bring it through the winter it makes a splendid show in its second year.

*GR:* 'Blue Butterfly' has now spawned a paler version, aptly named 'Sky Blue'. This was rightly selected as the most impressive of a number of very attractive seedlings by Dobies Seeds at their splendid trial ground in North Wales, now defunct.

## Dianthus *(Caryophyllaceae)*

*CL:* Pinks, carnations, sweet williams and hybrids between them all come under this heading, some annual, some biennial and some perennial. You can have a lot of fun and interest from the many seed strains available. They all like a sunny position, good drainage and a reasonably alkaline soil. Dianthus seed is flaky and brittle. It is sometimes packaged with sand to act as a buffer against damage.

Annual pinks derive from *D. chinensis*, and you need to pick your way among the F1 hybrids developed in recent years. Those that make very small, bushy plants, 6–9 in tall, put on a terrific show for a short season but are soon spent. Thus 'Baby Doll' seems a mistake to me, with large flowers on a squat plant; likewise 'Snow Fire' and the entire 'Magic Charms' series.

*GR:* According to the seed companies, 'Snow Fire' is the most popular of all seed-raised dianthus!

*CL:* 'Queens Court' and 'Telstar' are both excellent, long-flowering mixtures on sensibly sized plants up to 15 in tall that are capable of making new buds and flowers over a long season. Even better along these lines, I think (matters of opinion have to come into one's choice), are the 'Princess' series, especially the dazzling 'Princess White'. The plant looks so good, 12 in tall and as much across, the blossom borne at varying levels. There is even some scent. 'Princess Scarlet' is not unlike the older 'Queen of Hearts', a really fine, thrusting scarlet, pure and unadulterated.

*GR:* Improvements, real and imaginary, are constantly being introduced in this group by the breeders. Continuous flowering is the characteristic most in demand. As I write, my favourites are the following, though some may be superseded next season.

'Telstar Crimson', in a rich, deep blood-red, is one of the first to flower from a spring sowing, and unlike 'Crimson Charm' is not spotted by rain. Unlike many varieties which flower with a generous burst at first and then rest before flowering again, 'Telstar Crimson' keeps going all summer, even in hot spells. I'd prefer this shade with pure white rather than scarlet, but 'Telstar White' is not usually available except in a mixture. Same old problem.

The new 'Pink Flash' is an exquisite soft rose with similar long-lasting qualities, and I look forward to trying it with the darkest coleus of all, 'Roi des Noirs' (from cuttings I'm afraid), or perhaps the dark-leaved perilla. 'Colour Magician' has white, blush and deep rose flowers all at once.

*CL:* Spring sowings will give excellent results, but even finer plants will be obtained from sowings made in late August or early autumn. You may sometimes, as also with sweet williams, run into trouble with rust disease, which destroys the foliage but is well controlled by fungicide.

*D. deltoides* 'Brilliancy' is well named, quite dwarf and making a brilliant display of crimson-magenta blossom, the individual flowers small on a low plant so it is good as an edging. Again it is best from a late summer to autumn sowing, and so is my favourite, 'Rainbow Loveliness'. Favourite because its heavy scent carries so wonderfully on the air. The flowers, in a limited colour range from white through pinky-mauve to carmine, are heavily fringed. Their limited season is in early summer. Seed is ripe by late July and I sow it soon after. This is derived from the species *D. superbus*, which you find in alpine meadows in summer, and that also is available, its colour lilac-mauve.

There are many perennial pink seed strains, nearly all in mixtures (more's the pity) and most including a proportion of doubles, though the 'Highland Hybrids' are single with a dark central zone. All are scented. *D. arenarius* makes dense green cushions of needle leaves and has scented white flowers. These types can be treated as biennials and make a fine display in early summer if grown exactly like sweet williams. Sow in spring, line the seedlings out for the summer, bed them in the autumn and discard them (unless you want to save a few of the best) after they've flowered the following June. They can be followed by a quick-maturing, late-sown annual such as nasturtiums or by bedding dahlias.

Sweet williams (*D. barbatus*) deserve to be grown well. If sown too late, they'll flower at half-cock and reserve a good deal of their energies for the following year. Far better to sow under cold glass in April, prick off the seedlings, then line them out 12–15 in apart in their rows. Spray against rust at the same time as you're doing your tomatoes and potatoes against blight. When planting out in the autumn, plan a whole bed of them rather than dotting them about in a mixed border, cottage style. The latter method is pretty at the time, but your sweet williams look horrible from the second half of July onwards. They make a far stronger impression in a bed and are easily replaced by late summer and autumn bedding afterwards. I also interplant mine with tulips, which flower among the developing sweet williams and can be lifted and harvested when the sweet willies are being scrapped.

Double-flowered strains are good when well selected. Auricula-eyed types are intriguing at close range but look confused at a distance. 'Messenger' mixed are earlier flowering than the usual June–July strains but include too many boring magentas. If you grow a dark strain like 'Crimson Velvet' and a white strain separately, then mix them as you bed them out with one white plant to four deep red, the result is sumptuous. The assertiveness of white makes this about the right balance.

Dwarf sweet willies, double or single, make horribly dumpy little plants entirely without personality. [May the Powers protect us from the 5-in high 'Wee Willie'. – GR] Annual strains are not good yet. The stems are weak and floppy and many shoots fail to develop flower heads.

Carnations derive from *D. caryophyllus*. The seed strains of border carnations like 'Iron Stem' ('Tige de Fer' – quite floppy, actually) give best value if treated as biennials. From a spring sowing they'll flower in July the following year and need some support. The plants, with their glaucous foliage, are handsome long before they flower, and I like to make use of this asset by interplanting with bulbs, for example *Tulipa eichleri*, which has bluish leaves itself and red flowers.

Annual carnations tend not to start flowering till August. They germinate at quite low temperatures (42°F) and can be sown under cold glass in February. However, you get a stronger, slightly earlier-flowering plant by sowing and pricking off in the previous autumn, planting out in April.

The taller strains like 'Chabaud' need support. Dwarf, bushy kinds are much more easily managed, though their stems are exceedingly brittle at the joints. The F1 'Knight' series is outstanding, and within this, 'Crimson Knight' is streets ahead of any other, especially for its rich clove scent. If your plants still have plenty of unflowered shoots in the autumn, pot them up and overwinter them under well-ventilated glass. Given a mild winter, they'll survive outside and do another stint.

*GR:* 'Lillipot Scarlet' (its name alone would almost prevent me growing it) is my especial bane. Reaching 6 in at most and with very upright growth, you need battalions of them to fill even a small bed. And although they make less manageable pot plants, I agree that the 'Knight' series is superior in every way, especially the crimson; and cheaper.

But what about the superb 'Scarlet Luminette', given that you find scarlet carnations endearing, and not everyone does. Eighteen in high, self-supporting, early and long-flowering, good for cutting – an altogether excellent plant which will over-winter given half a chance.

Sometimes I think you need special training to sort out all the different groups of dianthus. For not only are there all the groups based on the species which Christopher has described, and more, but hybrids are now being developed between sweet williams and annual pinks, *D. barbatus* × *D. chinensis* ('Telstar' is one of these), and even sweet williams and carnations, *D. barbatus* × *D. caryophyllus*. These will doubtless be appearing soon.

Yet another intriguing development is a large, single-flowered F1 carnation with a strong scent and intense colours – scarlet, salmon, deep crimson, and pink. I've not seen them yet but they sound essential. Like 'Tige de Fer', these are treated as biennials.

Other curiosities include an F1 alpine pink (*D. alpinus*) called 'Cherry Beauty', described, I kid you not, as having 'candy-pink' flowers, and a seed-raised form of the old favourite 'Mrs Sinkins', split calyx and all.

In addition to all these border, bedding and cut-flower types there are also enough species to keep the alpine enthusiast occupied for some years. As alpines go, most dianthus are unusually undemanding – good viability, no chilling needed, prompt germination – and they can even be speeded up by a little warmth. Only the purplish-red *D. glacialis*, unspotted, unlike *D. alpinus*, requires chilling.

## Dicentra *(Fumariaceae)*

GR: For dicentras, chilling is necessary before germination can occur. In particular, the ferny-leaved *D. formosa*, with its rosy lockets in open sprays, seems to demand this treatment, and even so, germination may not be good. For the dainty, bluish *D. peregrina* fresh seed is vital.

So to take the best advantage of what seed is available (you may get only 10 seeds in a packet), the best policy for all species is probably to sow seed as soon as it is collected or arrives from the seed company, and leave the pots out in an open cold frame for the winter. Germination will take place in the spring and can usually be hastened by bringing the pots in for a little gentle warmth.

Once pricked out and grown on for a year, a cool site with well-drained, leafy soil seems to suit them all, although *D. peregrina* is usually best kept well observed in a cold greenhouse.

*CL:* A curious comment on *D. spectabilis* is that some clones in cultivation are sterile; others, including my own, ripen seed freely. I get plenty of self-sown seedlings.

## Dictamnus *(Rutaceae)*

*GR:* I must say that I have never seen it happen. The books all tell us that the volatile oils given off by this plant burst into flames if you approach with a lighted match on a hot, sunny summer day. I wait to be convinced. Fortunately *Dictamnus albus* has other charms, such as the distinctive spikes of white or veined purple flowers which last for many weeks, starting in early summer. The foliage is lemon-scented too.

This is another plant where a cold spell is necessary, this time a long one, to spark off germination. A British winter in the cold frame is usually long enough. For a permanent home it needs well-drained though fertile soil in full sun.

*CL:* I play the burning bush game on my dictamnus most years, and I must say it appeals to the child in me. Catch it when the sun has left your plants, in the early evening, so that the flames show up. It must be windless. Ethereal oil vapour surrounds the flanged seed-pods (a handsome feature). Hold your lighted match close to the lowest of these or to the stem itself (the seed-heads must still be fresh and green). Tongues of flame spurt up with a rushing noise. It's over in a second, leaving a nice smell on the air but no damage to the plant. This game appeals to all pyromaniacs and has no hideous results, like setting your pampas grass alight.

*GR:* I'll now take a box of matches to every garden I visit in summer, and will be setting dictamnus alight all over Britain!

## Dierama *(Iridaceae)*

*CL:* The wand-flowers or angels' fishing rods, as they are variously known, are quite unusual-looking plants. Their evergreen foliage is iris-like and not specially prepossessing. In July, *D. pulcherrimum*, the species we grow, makes 6-ft rods of great flexibility yet exceedingly tough. The weight of the narrow bell-like flowers, which hang in series near the top of the stem, arch it over into a parabola. The air is seldom still enough to stop all movement. The colouring is typically magenta, but pale pinky-mauves are frequent, there's a near white and, in a dwarfer strain, which gives variable results from seed, the flowers are salmon-pink.

Dieramas should be planted so that they stand high above surrounding plants. By the waterside looks good; they like free drainage and a not over-moist soil, but this will present no problem if the pond is lined. Again, they look fine as vertical (or parabolic) incidents in a paved area, where you may need to break the monotony of flatness.

*GR:* I would add only that you can create a startling effect by setting a good-sized plant by itself in a large earthenware pot. For not only does the parabolic fountain of flowers look singularly impressive, helped nicely by the fine foliage trickling over the sides, but in colder areas the pots can be moved indoors for the winter.

*CL:* The wand-flower makes chains of corms, one each year, much like some montbretias. The young roots are fleshy and dislike disturbance, but plants are easily raised from spring-sown seed, taking two to three years to reach flowering size. They are not entirely hardy, even in southern Britain, but near enough.

## Digitalis *(Scrophulariaceae)*

*CL:* Our native biennial foxglove, which springs up in woodland that has been cut or coppiced, the seed capable of remaining dormant for many years, while awaiting its moment, is *Digitalis purpurea.* Poisonous. Even rabbits seldom attack it, and slugs are unattracted.

Although we associate foxgloves with woodland, they also occur in perfectly open sites, especially in Scotland, and also on seaside shingles, as at Dungeness in Kent. The spikes are then only half length, much denser, and the colour more intense.

Colour is normally rosy-purple, a trifle muddy, and although it looks natural and right in the wild, in gardens we try to concentrate on cleaner or more interesting shades. The pure white albinos occur frequently in the wild. 'Apricot' is nearer peach, really; everyone admires it. I also like the mixed 'Giant Spotted' strain. The bells of a foxglove always face you and the back of the flower comes down lower than the front, so that you can look into them. In the 'Excelsior' hybrids this is made easier still because the blooms face horizontally outwards. Very showy but less graceful than the others.

There is always a tendency for self-sown seedlings to revert to the common pinky-purple. Some selection can be done at the seedling stage, since even as early as that, more pigment is noticeable in the leaf stalks of plants that will bear purplish flowers than in those that will be white or cream.

Self-sown foxgloves are often welcome, but for finest results seedlings should be raised as with sweet williams or Canterbury bells. Sow in a pot in April, prick off into a tray, then line out for the summer and plant out in a bed or a patch in a mixed border in the autumn. They can also, at this stage, be potted into large (10 or 12-in) pots for display in or outside the house.

Flowering is centred on June (in the south). By the time the last blooms are opening the spike looks like a demented green snake. Do dig the plants out betimes. They can be replaced with summer annuals, like cosmos or *Nicotiana sylvestris*.

*GR:* One of my all-time favourite plants is the white spotted foxglove. It has an entirely different air from the unspotted version, which seems to have rather a lost look. But the spotted white, as if the first bee to visit had stepped in maroon ink, is exquisite. Let it self-sow through north-facing borders and heave out, as Christopher suggests, any dark-petioled plants and any others in inconvenient spots. They may well insist on bursting through shrubs or rooting among bugles and pratias. Do not allow it.

I'm not a great fan of the 'Excelsior Hybrids', because although the flowers face you, they also face away from you and sideways, as they're carried all round the stem. This destroys the slight, graceful arch created by the weight of the flowers lined up along one side of the more natural forms. 'Foxy' is even worse, as it's only $2\frac{1}{2}$ ft high. Mind you, if we'd never seen a wild foxglove we'd probably rave over 'Foxy'.

A subspecies, *heywoodii*, has recently become more widely available. In this form, the greyish colouring usually restricted to the underside ot foxglove foliage covers the topsides too, and combined with the creamy-pink flowers creates a very dreamy spire.

*CL:* There are some pleasing perennial digitalis, though in all of these the colours tend to be subdued and to lack the panache of the typical foxglove. *D. grandiflora* (*D. ambigua*) for instance, is buff-yellow and reliable. *D.* x *mertonensis* is the hybrid between this and *D. purpurea*, rosy-mauve with buff thrown in, and about 2 ft tall. The semi-shrubby *D. obscura*, with amazing copper-brown and buff-yellow flowers, may justifiably get you excited, but it is not an easy plant. I've twice lost it before ever it flowered. Try it in full sun. The pale yellow flowers in *D. lutea* are quite tiny. For refinement, unexceptionable, but a bit of a yawn when it comes to it.

*GR:* I find the idea of *D. obscura* captivating – it remains to be seen if the plants live up to their description, for my plants are still small. It's a native of Spain, where it grows on rocky mountain slopes, and I suspect that Christopher's heavy soil is a little too much for it. I shall try it in a sunny, gritty raised bed. There are at least two colour forms around. As well as the rusty-orange, there is also a much yellower version.

I must also mention 'Temple Bells', a good perennial of rather stiff appearance, spreading slowly with neatly veined foliage and spikes of lemon-yellow flowers in July. It thrives in a north border with the eminently restrained *Lamium maculatum* 'Aureum', but would probably do better in the sun. Like most herbaceous foxgloves it lasts well in water. All should be stood vertically in a bucket straight after cutting. Like lupins, if you leave them lying in a trug or on a path the strongly directional light from above will cause the tips of the flower spikes to bend upwards. Cut the ends frequently to encourage them to last, and remove the lower flowers as they fade.

## Dipsacus *(Dipsacaceae)*

*CL:* Teasels are biennials. The fuller's teasel, *Dipsacus fullonum*, whose stiffly bristled whiskers (bracts) were used for napping cloth, is less attractive in the garden than our native wild teasel, subspecies *sylvestris*, found in woodland clearings and by stream and dyke sides.

It makes a stiffly statuesque and symmetrical plant to 6 ft. In the early summer of its second year, the soap-smooth yet prickle-covered leaves are borne in opposite, stem-clasping pairs and so readily condense moisture from the air that there is nearly always a pool at their base, even in dry weather. The small mauve flowers, popular with newly emerged peacock butterflies in July–August, first open in a band around the centre of an oval inflorescence, the band then dividing and moving upwards and downwards simultaneously. The seeds are beloved of goldfinches, the dark brown skeletons by flower arrangers.

*GR:* Do not be fooled by *D. inermis*. In spite of its name (literally 'unarmed' or without spines), this Himalayan species with scented, white flowers is ferociously prickly. And well worth growing.

*CL:* Once you have teasels you'll never be without them and will need only to remove unwanted seedlings. Even at the front of a border they are not out of place, because you can see through and past them. The foliage is subject to mildew in the second year, and is worth including in a spray programme.

## Doronicum *(Compositae)*

*CL:* Doronicums, also known as leopard's bane, are spring-flowering perennials with yellow daisies. The flowers bleach in strong sunlight, so this plant is best sited in damp, partially shaded borders. It makes a good spring bedding plant (try it with 'White Triumphator' lily-flowered tulips), in which case cut to the ground after flowering, lift, split as necessary and line out in a spare plot for the summer. It is also a good cut flower.

*GR: D. orientale* 'Magnificum' is a good form for bedding, as although it starts to flower before Christopher's white tulips, it will still be going strong when they're at their best. It can be treated as a biennial if that suits you better. An earlier-flowering orange tulip like 'Daydream' is an alternative companion.

*CL: D. pardalianches*, small-flowered and 3 ft tall, is widely naturalized in open woodland in northern England and southern Scotland. The seed strains on offer are shorter-stemmed and less suitable for this purpose.

## Ecballium *(Cucurbitaceae)*

*GR:* Most plants are grown in gardens because they're attractive or because they provide food or flavouring. But the squirting cucumber, *Ecballium elaterium*, is grown because it's rude.

A perennial which is normally grown as a half-hardy annual, it can be raised in the same way as a marrow or cucumber and planted out in late May. It forms rather a sprawling plant with rough, hairy, triangular leaves which make a very attractive, though widely spreading mound.

From summer onwards small, pretty, nodding yellow flowers appear, although they tend to be overshadowed by the leaves. It all seems very innocuous. Then the fruits form and the fun starts. The fruits are not large, a very unprepossessing 2 in, but nevertheless, when ripe, the slightest stroking sends a wet mush of seeds and jelly squirting out. 45 ft seems to be the record distance. Teenage girls and small boys seem to find it most amusing, but I've also seen straitlaced women of mature years rendered helpless with laughter and embarrassment at the sight of the plant performing in public by a Greek footpath.

You will see this plant growing by the roadside and in waste places from one end of the Mediterranean to the other. In the garden, plant it at the front of a sunny border in well-drained soil or let it trail over a low wall. And although it belongs to the cucumber family, don't be tempted to put the fruits in your mouth; the juice is a powerful purgative, so be warned.

My friend Frank, a chess and cricket authority of the first order, on hearing this name, rummaged in the remnants of his classical education and came up with this astonishing revelation. The name *Ecballium* is derived from the Greek meaning to fling out, while *elaterium* is derived from the Latin meaning ... to fling out. Well, the seeds do fly a long way.

## Eccremocarpus *(Bignoniaceae)*

*GR:* At last the Chilean glory flower, *Eccremocarpus scaber*, is getting the recognition it deserves. Clinging by tendrils, this climber of admittedly inelegant habit produces flowers in spikes which sometimes hang downwards and then arch up, sometimes stand up straight. These startling flowers are tubular, and the natural species is orange with a yellow lip.

Other colours were sometimes available – a golden-yellow and a dull red – and then Ralph Gould bred a mixture of pink, scarlet, crimson, yellow and orange called the 'Anglia Hybrids'. Subsequently another mixture appeared called 'Fireworks', bred by David Kerley of Unwins Seeds, which includes orange, golden yellow with a red lip, deep rose and yellow.

Now we have 'Mardi Gras', which I haven't seen but which is said to include orange, pink, red and yellow. And we also have 'Tresco', another new one I haven't had the chance to try, which apparently includes golden-yellow, carmine-rose and orange-scarlet only. A plant is more or less ignored for years and then all of a sudden we have 4 new mixtures. I wonder how different they really are.

This is an easy plant to raise as a half-hardy annual, but it pays not to start too early, or else to grow fairly cool after pricking out, otherwise the plant will grow so much as to become unmanageable. And as it is rather brittle, accidents must be accepted. Plant it on a south-facing wall or fence in a fertile but well-drained soil, or under a shrub sturdy enough to support it.

In the coldest areas eccremocarpus will be killed in its first winter. In most parts of the country it will survive three winters out of five, often being cut back slightly to older, woody growth from which new shoots spring in the first warm spells of the year. In mild areas it will flower almost all the year round. The fat pods contain large numbers of flat black seeds, and self-sown seedlings may well turn up underneath your original plant.

I prefer either the wild species, which looks surprisingly good through a summer ceanothus, or the golden form, 'Aureus'. But as they need plenty of room, don't be tempted to set out mixed plants in a row, for as a mixture they are less effective than individual plants set in different places.

## Echium *(Boraginaceae)*

*CL:* There are two quite distinct hardy biennial species of echium, *E. vulgare* and *E. plantagineum*, but they have unfortunately become confused in the seed lists. *E. vulgare* is the less garden-worthy, but is a fine plant to colonize in gravel; it grows wild in shingle near the sea. From a prickly first-year rosette, in the second year it sends up one rod-stiff inflorescence of blue flowers some 2 ft tall.

*E. plantagineum* is an altogether softer plant and bushy rather than erect, so that spacing can be as much as 18 in. You can treat it as a hardy annual. 'Blue Bedder' is the best selection, light blue in colour and contrasting well, for instance, as an edging or filler between bushes, with yellow roses. The 'Dwarf Hybrids' include blue-, pink- and white-flowered plants, and this is a pretty mixture. After a few weeks of flowering, the plants writhe like a tangled nest of vipers and should be pulled out, unless you wish to leave some to self-sow, which they readily do.

*GR:* Having now seen both *E. plantagineum* and the reddish *E. angustifolium* growing wild in Greece, where their vividness and attractive open habit is so appealing, I find them more exciting at home. Rich soil and poor drainage not only lessen the winter survival rate, but encourage lank, unappealing growth and make the vipers seem rather tired.

## Emilia *(Compositae)*

*GR:* This is a dainty half-hardy annual now making its mark as a cut flower after years as a third-division annual. *Emilia coccinea*, also known as *E. jauanica* and *Cacalia coccinea*, forms a dense rosette of foliage and from it throws up lithe stems about 2 ft high, each topped with an open head of small fluffy flowers, usually in an iridescent scarlet but sometimes in orange, gold or pink. Raise it in the greenhouse or sow outside in May.

The display is rather too open and sparse to make a strong group in the border, but a few plants in strategic spots can be very pretty. And as a cut flower it is delightful, flowering all summer if thinned to about

10 in and cut regularly. It makes a pretty posy with grasses and other delicate flowers.

### Eranthis *(Ranunculaceae)*

*CL:* The winter aconite is a woodland plant from southern Europe but frequently enjoys bright sunshine among deciduous plants, since all its growth is completed in the first four months of the year. Where suited, it self-sows freely and will make great drifts of yellow in January–February, beneath trees; lovely combined with the even more easily naturalized, mauve-flowered *Crocus tomasinianus*.

Winter aconites also combine well with undisturbed colonies of border plants. Thus at Wisley there is an old colony of hostas near the laboratory which is alive with yellow aconites in the New Year. Likewise a colony of romneya, the Californian tree poppy, is all the better for being cut to ground level in early winter, providing the opportunity for a separate act with winter aconites, crocuses, scillas, chionodoxas and early bulbous irises.

*GR:* Eranthis also associate well with many late winter plants. Recently they flowered among my pink *Bergenia* × *schmidtii*, whose early flowers are at aconite level. Among *Pulmonaria rubra*, also with flowers at the right level, they are just right, and in mild seasons when they coincide with the rich blue *P. angustifolia* they are sublime.

*CL:* Eranthis have small tuberous rhizomes and a ruff of three jagged leaves, which look like one and frame the single yellow flower. Seed ripens in May and can be collected in large quantities by the vigilant ('I have to watch them like a good cat,' as one correspondent and donor wrote me.) They can be scattered on bare or thinly colonized soil where you wish them to be. In the following year a single pair of shiny seed leaves is produced, soon dying away. The year after, there will be a small ruff of true leaves, and in the year after that, flowering should get under way.

*GR:* Buying rhizomes from the garden centre is often pointless – or worse. Few establish well, being dry and shrivelled, and many are

collected from the wild in Turkey, decimating natural stands. So seed
is the answer, both practically and morally.

*CL:* Winter aconites thrive on alkaline soils but they are choosy and
unexpectedly difficult to establish in some gardens, notably my own. I
keep trying.

## Eremurus *(Liliaceae)*

*CL:* Known as foxtail lilies (although eremurus is good enough for
most of us), these dramatic perennials throw spikes of star-shaped
blossom up to 8 ft tall (in *E. robustus*), flowering in May, June or
early July, after which they disappear completely. The fleshy roots are
arranged starfish-style around a central bud and do not increase at
speed, though increase is faster on light, open soils (including the
chalky) than on heavy.

Seed ripens readily and offers an alternative method, but only for the
patient. It may take six years for seedlings to build up to flowering size.

*GR:* With their shallow, spreading and rather fleshy roots, confining
eremurus to pots in the long term is something of a non-starter. Sow
in pots, over-winter in a cold frame, then bring them into the greenhouse to germinate. Prick them out into pots but do plant them out in
rows to grow on.

*CL: E. robustus* is blush-white, *E. himalaicus* pure white, *E. bungei*
yellow-orange, and the 'Shelford Hybrids' a range of pale yellow, soft
orange, pink and white shades.

*GR:* As cut flowers their very size is impressive, not to mention their
colour. Cut them when the bottom half of the spike is open and nip off
the flowers as they wilt; more will open. Re-cut the stems every day or
two and keep them away from strong heat or strong light.

## Eryngium *(Umbelliferae)*

*CL:* The common name, sea holly, is taken from our native *Eryngium maritimum*, a deep-rooted perennial of coastal sand dunes. All eryngiums have fleshy tap-roots and if grown on well-drained soils they are less likely to suffer from bacterial disease causing a smelly root rot. However, the perennial kinds are very long-lived, even on heavy ground, and seldom need to be disturbed.

They can be raised from seed, although root cuttings are the more generally accepted method. The evergreen, Central and South American species come well from seed, which should be sown under cold glass in the spring.

One of the most popular of all eryngiums is the monocarpic *E. giganteum* ('sometimes dies after flowering' is a euphemism in Thompson & Morgan's catalogue for 'always dies after flowering'), known as 'Miss Willmott's Ghost'. It appears to have been unknown in gardens until after the Second World War – at least, I've seen no references to it. A stiffly branching 3-footer, it flowers in July with ruffs of silvery bracts around a dome of sea-blue flowers which bees love. It dries well.

*GR:* I'm afraid Christopher's remark about 'Miss Willmott's Ghost' being unknown before the last war comes into the 'red-rag-to-a-bull' category. After rummaging about in my unpredictable archives I find that Gertrude Jekyll grew it at the turn of the century.

'If I had some long stretches of bare, unsightly heaps or ridges of sand,' she writes in *Home and Garden* as if she was the only gardener in the country to be denied such a feature, 'how I would plant the noble Eryngiums.' In addition to *E. giganteum*, Miss Jekyll suggests our native *E. maritimum* and the stunning rich blue *E. × oliverianum*. Bravely, she recommends *Elymus arenarius* as a companion. Elsewhere she suggests the eryngium as a plant for the blue garden and as a companion to silver foliage and white lilies, snapdragons and achilleas, plus lavender, and double pink godetias.

New as I write is a variety of *E. giganteum* collected by Martin Rix in Turkey. 'Silver Ghost' has bracts which open out flat rather than into a cup, and the individual bracts are narrower, creating a striking star-like effect.

*CL: E. giganteum* self-sows freely (too freely, sometimes) in garden borders once established, but takes time to settle in and you need to be able to recognize its seedlings, which may take several years to reach flowering size – only two years if the soil is good and there is not much competition.

To raise seedlings under controlled conditions, sow fresh seed in the autumn and allow frost to reach the container. Prick off the young seedlings in the spring and plant them out before the tap-root has developed significantly, otherwise growth will be inhibited and flowering will occur on a stunted plant.

*GR:* That otherwise impressive seed house, Thompson & Morgan, whose list has introduced so many gardeners to less common treasures, has something else to answer for I'm afraid. 'Delaroux' is an eryngium they list but this is none other than the steely blue *E. proteiflorum*. Why 'Delaroux'? It's a mistake for Delaroche which is actually the botanical authority for the Latin name and appears attached to it in scientific publications – *E. proteiflorum* Delaroche. Someone at T & M or their suppliers has got in a muddle and misread it into a variety name.

## Erysimum *(Cruciferae)*

*CL:* Most of the wallflowers have been or should be shunted into *Erysimum*. What's correct for the Siberian wallflower I do not know. Clearly it is a hybrid, though fertile, and it is usually listed as *Cheiranthus × allionii*. It has close affinities with *E. perofskianum*.

*GR:* At different times I have been given or found reference to three different methods of distinguishing the genera *Erysimum* and *Cheiranthus*. See what you think.

First theory (magnifier required): both have nectaries at the base of the stamens. In both *Erysimum* and *Cheiranthus* there is a ring of nectaries around the outer stamens. But in *Erysimum* there are additional nectaries located on the outside of the inner stamens. That's clear enough – if you have a powerful magnifying glass and you can recognize the nectaries and stamens.

Second theory (magnifier required again): in *Cheiranthus* the stigma is deeply lobed, in *Erysimum* the stigma is rounded, sometimes with a small notch making it slightly lobed. So all you have to do is work out the difference between slightly lobed and deeply lobed.

Third theory (no magnifier required!): open one of the long seed pods and you will find the seeds in one row in *Erysimum*. In *Cheiranthus* they will be in two rows – except that sometimes they may be in one row! And some varieties don't set any seed at all.

Unfortunately I am writing this in the middle of winter and although it's an exceptionally mild one, there are no wallflowers in flower on which I can test these theories.

*CL:* The Siberian wallflower is familiar enough, the most dazzling and pure shade of orange that I know. The scent is delicious, quite different from *Cheiranthus cheiri*, and its season is slightly later but still overlaps usefully with tulips in bedding schemes. Siberians can easily be overdone, theirs being such a staring colour, but you should on no account shun them out of fright. I saw a bedding scheme in front of a terracotta brick building at Bagatelle, in Paris, with blue myosotis, yellow pansies, soft orange and soft pink tulips and then, right in the centre, in front of the building's entrance, just a dozen or so Siberian wallflower plants. It was a great success. Siberians are perennial. Given the chance, they will seed themselves obligingly into paving cracks – a good use.

Most erysimums, such as 'Bowles' Mauve', are sterile hybrids propagated from cuttings, and that includes the soft yellow clone called 'Moonlight'. But there is a 'Moonlight' seed strain, also, rather smaller-flowered, its buds a darker brown. And a compact little number called 'Golden Bedder' or 'Golden Gem' – cheerfully plebeian, rather small-flowered. It will self-sow and is a worthy candidate for an area of gravel.

*Erysimum linifolium*, from Spain and Portugal, is an undeservedly neglected species which, with its deep mauve flowers on a 9-in plant, makes an excellent carpet for late orange or yellow tulips, such as 'Dillenburg', 'Mrs John Scheepers' or 'Texas Gold'. Like the Siberian wallflower, you treat it as a biennial, but don't sow too early or it'll flower too much in its first year. Late June or early July, in a row outside, is soon enough.

*GR:* There's only one other thing I want to say. There are around eighty species of *Erysimum* growing in Europe, the Himalayas and North America. Every one that I have ordered from a catalogue or seed list has been worth growing. So take a chance on some less common ones. And if they don't cross with each other you can raise fresh plants as soon as they are struck with virus – as they surely will be.

## Eschscholzia *(Papaveraceae)*

*CL:* This is the best known of several plants we call Californian poppy. In the wild it is bright orange or bright yellow, lovely to see as a wayside weed where it grows in drifts, often with pink clarkias. I can also recommend it, self-sowing, with annual ornamental grasses such as *Briza maxima*. [Along the edge of a gravel drive perhaps. – GR]

Breeding has given us a wide range of colours in this flower, including cream, copper and pink, as well as strains with semi-double blooms. These make an exciting change but, on self-sowing, they all quite quickly revert to the natural type which, I must say, I like best of all.

*GR:* The Californian poppy, *Eschscholzia californica*, is a sparkling hardy annual for sunny sites, flowering for many months in hot dry soils, especially if cut for the house (while still furled) or dead-headed; in mild seasons it can still be flowering at Christmas. The flowers circumspectly close on dull days to protect the pollen from rain, but the moment the sun shines they open. They self-sow enthusiastically and are easy to raise from a sowing outside at any time after March; you will then never be without them. However, the colours may tend to drift to orange if you start off with a mixture and to singles if you start off with doubles.

It's true that mixtures quickly revert to orange, which seems the dominant shade. The single colours available will retain their purity for longer, especially if you heave out the rogues the moment the flowers open. But like Christopher I find the white, purple and lipstick pink shades ... unsatisfactory, shall we say. The so-called doubles, with little more than an extra row of petals, likewise. And they drift to singles in just a few years if left to self-sow.

Grow the orange ones with blue lupins like *L. varius* or *L. subcarnosus*, or let the orange self-sow in gravel with the red and black 'Ladybird' poppies.

*CL:* On the light soils which are natural to them, eschscholzias reproduce freely. Their growth being thin, they do not cast much shade and are therefore excellent for prolonging the season of interest among beds of bearded irises without withholding too much light from the rhizomes of those sun-loving plants. If the winter is not severe, old plants survive and start flowering again in early May, continuing throughout the summer.

The tap root loathes disturbance, so direct sowing where they are to flower is normal.

For those whose nerves are easily jangled by strong colour, *E. caespitosa* is the answer, a mini-poppy with pale, almost primrose-yellow flowers. Only 6 in tall and quite bushy, it can be used for edging, if that's the kind of finish you like to a border.


## Eucomis *(Hyacinthaceae)*

*CL:* These are South African bulbs formerly in the lily family, whose beauty lies perhaps more in their handsome structure than in their colouring, which is predominantly pale green.

They come very late into growth, often not before June. From a basal rosette of broad strap leaves, the flowering stem rises to 12 or 30 in, according to the species, bearing a thick spike of slightly closed stars, these being crowned by a tuft of green bracts, in the style (but not the texture) of a pineapple.

*Eucomis bicolor* is one of the hardiest species, its green flowers margined in purple. Its pale form, 'Pallida', is lightest green throughout. *E. comosa* is somewhat less interesting and smells horrible, but is pretty tough. And there is quite a range of hybrids with more or less of a pink or purple suffusion in leaves, bracts and flowers.

All these are easily raised from seed, which can often be of your own saving, once you have purchased a few bulbs. Seedlings develop quite quickly and should flower in their third year from an initial spring sowing under glass.

The late summer to autumn flowering season is useful, and there is a notable combination, at Sissinghurst Castle, of a pale green eucomis next to a group of pink turkscap *Lilium speciosum*. A sunny, sheltered border should be chosen, as hardiness cannot be taken for granted.

## Euphorbia *(Euphorbiaceae)*

*CL:* The annual euphorbias which we can so much admire in southern Europe are a great disappointment in our climate. Thus the beautifully variegated *E. marginata*, which makes a handsome, branching bush wherein white and green are evenly distributed, when the climate suits it, never takes off here, forming a single, rather lank stem. Perhaps Graham has done better. Where it grows easily, this is a favourite cut flower.

*GR:* I think the trick is to sow early, prick out three seedlings to each 4-in pot, and plant out without disturbance in rich soil in a sunny spot. Although often listed simply under its species name, there are at least two distinct varieties. 'Snow on the Mountain' has white spotted bracts while in 'Summer Icicle' the bracts are streaked in white.

To ensure that cut stems last well, either recut them under water when the milky sap will coagulate quickly, or sear the ends in a flame for a few seconds.

*CL:* Likewise *E. heterophylla*, whose terminal bracts should colour to scarlet, like a poinsettia, just stays green or makes a feeble attempt. Of course you can grow either of these species as pot plants in the conservatory.

If you can get seed of the hardy herbaceous perennials *E. wallichii*, *E. longifolia* and *E. schillingii*, these all germinate well from a spring sowing under glass. They are excellent border plants, the last two especially valuable for their late, July to September, flowering. Protect the young seedlings from fungal disease.

Also successful from seed are the spring-flowering *E. myrsinites*, prostrate with glaucous evergreen foliage and terminal lime-green inflorescences, and *E. polychroma* (syn. *E. epithymoides*), which carries brilliant green-yellow flowers on foot-tall hummocks, good with white tulips.

*GR:* I've found the almost buttery *E. polychroma*, which looks splendid with grape hyacinths such as *Muscari* 'Blue Spike', a little fussy about germinating, as it has a hard seed coat which does not always admit water. Autumn sowing and a winter in the cold frame are required, and to ensure that the seeds take up water, soak them overnight before sowing. They should then germinate the following spring.

*CL:* The biennial caper spurge, *E. lathyrus,* is a handsomely architectural plant in its first year but can become something of an uncontrolled pest, seeding itself prominently in all the wrong places. It emphatically does *not* ward off moles. [I've seen a row of plants, set out as a barrier against moles by the chairman of an international seed company, simply upended by the little beasts. – *GR*] Another biennial, *E. stricta,* sows itself no less freely but is much more easily assimilated. It's delightful in paving cracks, with its red stems and clouds of lime-green flowers. Grow it through the feathery grey foliage of old man, *Artemisia abrotanum.*

The shrubby *E. characias* and its subspecies *wulfenii* generally give rise to an inferior product from seed. It is worth acquiring named or at least accredited clones that were reproduced from cuttings.

*GR:* I agree that clones are the best buy, but not everyone finds it easy to root cuttings of these plants or the more spreading but also rather tender *E. mellifera* once they've bought them. So, for many, raising seedlings is a practical alternative even if the results are unpredictable.

The rather fashionable, dark-eyed *E. characias* from the western Mediterranean, its equally trendy green-eyed subspecies *wulfenii* from the eastern Med, and *E. mellifera* from the Canaries are all easy to raise. But you may well find if you have a number of forms of the first two – and there are more than half-a-dozen, including a dwarf one – that the seedlings will prove quite variable. Outside an office block in a town near where I live there is a large bed in which these plants have self-sown for some years; there are hardly two plants the same.

It's a sensible precaution with *Euphorbia characias* and its relatives to sow fairly early in the year, to ensure that by the time winter comes the plants are large and tough enough to take a bad one. If you're forced to sow later, young plants are best protected in a frame over their first winter.

The seed is large enough simply to space out 1 in apart over the surface of John Innes seed compost. After the seed is covered, put the pot in a propagator (a temperature of 65°F is fine) and germination should take about three weeks.

Seed seems long-lived and germinates perfectly well after storage in the fridge. But there is a problem if you want to collect your own seed. On hot summer days the seemingly unripe pods suddenly start to snap open and fling the seed in all directions. The only answer is to tie a paper bag over the whole head the moment you hear the first one pop.

This group demands sunshine and a well-drained site, and indeed will thrive in almost pure gravel. Once you've seen the impoverished conditions in which they sometimes grow in the wild it is easier to realize that rich conditions are not necessary; although as long as the drainage is good they will tolerate heavier soils. But in cold areas and heavy or badly drained soils you must expect some losses in bad winters.

## Exacum *(Gentianaceae)*

*GR:* These pretty little pot-plants can be surprisingly awkward to raise. First the seed is smaller even than begonia seed, so is not easy to sow thinly. The compost both for seed-sowing and for potting needs to be better drained than many bought composts, so be prepared to add grit or perlite if necessary. Lastly, I have found, and I know commercial growers find too, that plants are sometimes susceptible to mysterious collapse owing to a root disease. Good drainage helps alleviate the problem, as does caution with the watering after pricking out. But watering with fungicides containing copper or benomyl is helpful.

Exacums are neat but characterless little plants, with their lavender-blue, white and now pink flowers, each with a blob of orange anthers in the centre. They need a temperature of at least 65°F for germination and grow best at a minimum of 60°F, which is rather high for most gardeners. At lower temperatures botrytis may strike – plants from early spring sowings are especially susceptible.

## Fatsia *(Araliaceae)*

*CL:* As a hardy foliage shrub, *Fatsia japonica* is unbeatable for the size and splendour of its glossy, fingered leaves. Happy in shade, a specimen will be the making of any courtyard. It can grow 9 ft tall by more across (good underplanted with ferns, hostas and snowdrops or, on a different tack, with impatiens), but if you have to cut it back it will take the insult cheerfully.

The umbels of white blossom are an unexpected bonus in November, and if the resultant berries are sown under glass *as soon as ripe,* the following April–May, the seed will germinate forthwith. Beware damping off and protect with fungicide.

## Felicia *(Compositae)*

*CL:* The best felicias are perpetuated from cuttings. *F. bergeriana,* the kingfisher daisy, is a rotten little annual, I regret to say. Six inches high, it flowers only in the mornings, and only on sunny mornings at that, blue rays and yellow disc. For the rest, its petals remain sulkily curled back on themselves.

*GR:* Well, that told you, didn't it! Far be it from me to add anything. Except that other species are occasionally offered by seed companies and that they may be worth trying.

## Ferula *(Umbelliferae)*

*CL:* Seed of the giant fennels, *Ferula communis* and nearly related species, is seldom offered, but plants are, and once your own has flowered it will seed. Sow it fresh and over-winter the container somewhere frosty. Germination will occur in early spring.

Because both genera are known as fennel, ferula is dreadfully confused with the aromatic herb *Foeniculum vulgare.* Ferula has scarcely any smell or culinary use. It has the largest leaf of any plant I grow except *Gunnera manicata,* but divided into such fine filigree that you are aware of a bright green undulating haze, rather than an individual leaf.

Growth starts in midwinter, and when a plant has built up sufficient energy, within a few years, it flowers at midsummer, suddenly throwing up a pale, lime-green inflorescence to 9 ft. After that the plant remains dormant till the next winter and will take a year or two recuperating before it flowers again.

*GR:* Plants of a variety called 'Giant Bronze' are occasionally listed, and if it really exists it sounds like an essential plant and should come reasonably true from seed. But I'm inclined to guess that this is another example of wishful thinking, or sloppy naming, getting the better of an enthusiastic nurseryman.

*CL:* If the leaves are bronze, I think this must be *Foeniculum*, not *Ferula*.

## Foeniculum *(Umbelliferae)*

*CL: Foeniculum vulgare,* of the aniseed aroma, is used to garnish fish dishes and salads (but dill is pleasanter and less coarsely-flavoured). It is found in seed lists in the herbs section. However, the purple-leaved fennel in particular is a handsome 5 ft plant with finely divided, mole-brown foliage. The yellow-green flower umbels are pleasing too. It is a good border perennial, coming true from seed, but unless you don't mind being overrun with its progeny, cut it down before the seeds ripen. [A veritable foam of new leaves will reward you. – GR] If you let it self-sow, you can plant the seedlings out in autumn to form a background for tulips, such as the pale yellow, May-flowering 'Niphetos'. This unlikely pairing was thought of by Brian Halliwell at Kew.

Easy to raise. Sow outside or in a cold frame in June. Thin to 3–4 in and plant out in the autumn.

*GR:* The dark-leaved version appears under four names – var. *purpureum,* 'Black Form', 'Giant Bronze' and 'Smokey', but I've never been able to work out if they're the same or not. I suspect they are. 'Smokey', from Holland, may be a little duskier, but without growing them all side by side it's impossible to tell; and seedlings will vary a little anyway. Root out any self-sown greens that appear. Either way, it also looks good with the pink 'Mary Rose', one of David Austin's excellent English roses, and with the blue grass *Elymus magellanicus*.

## Francoa *(Saxifragaceae)*

*CL:* Seed being offered as *Francoa ramosa* turns out to be our old friend *F. sonchifolia*. The evergreen leaves are lyre-shaped. A graceful inflorescence carries several spikes way above the foliage at 3 ft in June. The flowers are blush-pink stars with darker central stripes. The flowering season is rather on the short side. It's a perennial, and seed sown in spring makes strong flowering plants in the following year. It would be good to have the true, pure white *F. ramosa* in circulation again; it was beloved of Gertrude Jekyll for pot work.

*GR:* Quite why francoas have a reputation for being tender I don't know, although never having grown them in the Scottish Highlands this is perhaps a rash thing to say. Maybe it's because they are often grown in pots that people think they're tender, rather than the other way round.

## Gaillardia *(Compositae)*

*GR:* 'The native pride of Texans for their great state often causes considerable amusement among other Americans not so fortunate as to have been born in the Lone Star State. The claims of Texans for their state are often, one suspects, a bit exaggerated, but in regard to their native flora it would be difficult to exaggerate. The use of the strongest superlatives is justified in the descriptions of the vast fields of Texan wild flowers. Among the showiest of these are the blanket flowers, *Gaillardia*.' So says a former curator of the New York Botanic Garden.

There are both annual and perennial forms which create these sheets of colour, but in gardens it turns out to be the perennial that makes the best annual – if you see what I mean.

*Gaillardia aristata*, sometimes listed as *G. grandiflora*, is a perennial from the hills and prairies from Manitoba to New Mexico and has yellow-eyed, yellow daisies up to 4 in across. In the UK we grow it mainly as an annual, in several varieties from the deep wine 'Burgundy' to the sparkling yellow 'Goblin'.

The flowers of *G. pulchella* are a little smaller but have a purple disc, and the yellow petals tone to red at the base. These days, this is usually available in a double-flowered mixture.

Gaillardias are easy to raise from a spring sowing in the propagator or outside where they are to flower in May. They need sunshine above all. They will probably need staking, as the wind and rain beat on the flowers which are too hefty for the stems to support. For the house, cut them when the flowers are fully open.

The common name, blanket flower, is said to derive from the simi-
larity of their colours to those of the blankets made by Indians in the
south-west states. Said to . . .

## Galtonia *(Liliaceae)*

*GR:* Calling the galtonia the 'summer hyacinth' demands a bit of nerve.
The one most often seen, *G. candicans*, grows at least four times as tall,
has an elegance quite absent from its spring-flowering relations, is
entirely devoid of scent and can easily be raised from seed. Galtonias
come from South Africa, hyacinths from south-east Europe.

But we must not let the whims of gardeners past deflect us from
recognizing the value of galtonias. Mind you, in my garden they've
behaved rather strangely. Having started off as a planting of a dozen
bulbs they unaccountably faded away, in spite of regular feeding.
[Galtonias are subject to debilitating virus diseases, which are frequently
bought with the bulb and soon destroy it. – *CL*] However, before
finally vanishing they left seedlings scattered all along the border. These
seedlings have taken about three years to reach flowering size, and in
the younger stages the risk of digging them up or hoeing them off by
accident was always in the back of my mind. Fortunately a number
have survived, including one which is thoughtfully bursting through
my rich pink English rose, 'Mary Rose'.

If you don't want to trust to chance, the pods ripen in October and
you can collect your own seed. They should take only two years if
raised by sowing in the greenhouse in John Innes seed compost,
following the more urgent of the other spring sowings. After pricking
out into 3-in pots of John Innes No. 2, they can spend a year being
cosseted in a cold frame. After that they can either be lined out in the
garden where you can keep an eye on them, or potted on and left in
the frame. Watering regularly when they're in growth is important,
especially for frame-grown plants, and regular liquid feeding will
encourage them greatly.

*CL:* *G. princeps* makes as stout a plant and is as easy to raise and grow,
but is only half the height of *candicans* and has green flowers, plenty of
them, in a bold spike. Seeing that flowers are meant to be coloured and
only leaves green, I was surprised that *G. princeps* won an Award of

Merit when I took it to the RHS in August 1980. *G. viridiflora* is slightly less hardy, perhaps, but its pale green bells, which are flared at the rims, are particularly elegant.

## Gaura *(Onagraceae)*

*CL: Gaura lindheimeri* is an underrated perennial from the south-eastern United States. From a spring sowing it can make a rather weedy and disappointing plant that flowers too late, but if you get it going early, or over-winter your established plants (which, however, tend to be short-lived, like bedding penstemons), they will become quite bushy and cover themselves from July onwards with $2\frac{1}{2}$-ft clouds of white blossom like hovering insects. You'll have everyone asking what it is.

Easy though it is from seed, I have to admit that plants established from summer cuttings, over-wintered under cold glass and planted out in spring, give the most satisfactory results.

## Gazania *(Compositae)*

*CL:* As half-hardy flowers from seed, there are big developments happening in the gazania world, but they have a long way to go yet.

These are South African daisies with flowers in a great range of shades – typically orange or yellow, but including purple, crushed strawberry and murky pastel shades and, most intriguingly, flowers in which there is a central zone marked in different colours, sometimes with spots and eyes in rather incredible metallic green.

A dwarfish, tufted habit suits the gazania, and this you find in such as 'Mini-Star Tangerine' and 'Mini-Star Yellow'. 'Daybreak Bronze', with contrasting disc, is a lively, warming shade, the plant a convenient 9 in high. Single colours are to be preferred to mixtures, which include too many passengers. (Unless, of course, you like to choose your own winners from a mixture and keep them going from cuttings thereafter.)

Large-flowered gazanias can be exciting but they are borne on large, coarse plants – OTT, if you ask me.

*GR:* But 'Sundance' is a wonderful cut flower – the colours are unique: 4-inch flowers in orange, crimson, yellow, rusty and mahogany shades, most with contrasting stripes along each petal. They reach 15 in in height and open up well in a warm room. Outside, grow them surging through an undulating carpet of *Helichrysum petiolare*.

*CL:* Raise under slightly heated glass from a spring sowing and plant out in the sunniest spot you have. Gazanias open fully only in really warm weather, and even a three-quarters open gazania might just as well not be there. At their best they make you feel at your best.

*GR:* At their best, yes, but compared with some of the older, vegetatively propagated varieties, modern seed-raised gazanias can be something of a disappointment. In spite of the fact that plant-breeders have now succeeded in creating varieties whose flowers stay open when the sun is less bright and less warm, their dull foliage still lets them down.

The appeal of the old varieties was that although their flower colours were limited, the foliage of many was almost white and sometimes, as in 'Filigree', attractively divided. But although seed-raised strains have given us more colours, silver foliage is missing except in 'Silver Leaf Carnival' – though sadly this can only be described as grey, well, greyish.

It's sometimes suggested that you lift gazanias in the autumn and grow them cool all winter; if you have a heated greenhouse with space to spare you could try it, but I think there are better uses for the space – such as over-wintering some of the cuttings-raised old ones. Plant them all in the warmest place you have, but not in soil which is starved and parched.

### Gentiana *(Gentianaceae)*

*CL:* All gentian seed should be sown when ripe, and the containers stood where frost can reach them.

*GR:* Sorry to interrupt so soon, but research has shown that most gentian seed, including *G. asclepiadea* and *G. septemfida*, needs light to germinate; so don't cover the seed with compost. Perhaps the simplest way to ensure that seed does not dry out, yet is still open to the light, is to cover the compost with a shallow layer of lime-free grit. Then simply sow the seed on to the grit and water with a fine rose. The tiny seeds will lodge in crevices, where the grit will help ensure a damp atmosphere but enough light will still filter through.

Another point worth remembering is that although not all gentians dislike lime, some hate it; all, however, will grow happily in lime-free conditions. So if you're in any doubt, use a lime-free compost.

Finally, although most will germinate best after a winter outside, many, including *G. verna*, will also benefit from some extra warmth in the spring. So bring the pots into the greenhouse after the winter.

Oh, and prick them out when they're still small, as they can make a surprising amount of root in a very short time.

Now back to Christopher.

*CL:* Of the low-growing rock garden types, the least demanding is *G. septemfida*, with clustered heads of blue funnels on a 9-in, decumbent plant.

*G. asclepiadea*, the willow gentian, is a woodland plant, excellent with ferns in moist, shady places. It flowers in August all along the top side of many arching stems, typically blue. A real eye-catcher. The albino is rather a poor thing, but comes true from seed if not interfered with by blue neighbours. The roots of these perennials are deep and tough. They hate being moved, but will self-sow, even into lawns. [There is also a white available, plus a more difficult to find pink-flowered form. – GR]

*CL:* *G. lutea* is the giant of the genus, 4 ft tall, a plant of Swiss alpine meadows but rightly disregarded by cattle. From its roots is distilled the revolting liqueur Enzian, which turns you up just to smell it. Simenon said it was the last resort of alcoholics when all other stimulants had failed. The large, ribbed, plantain-like leaves are handsome, and so, in June, are the yellow flowers, borne in a series of whorls.

## Geranium *(Geraniaceae)*

*CL:* These are the true geraniums or hardy cranesbills (for the bedding 'geraniums', see *Pelargonium*). They are much in vogue among hardy-plant enthusiasts, and while I agree with their popularity as being deserved, it should not be forgotten that there is a good deal of rubbish among them, unworthy of any garden except the collector's. Some of the best are sterile hybrids, and of others seed is seldom offered since division offers a ready means of increase.

Several native species have become favourite garden plants, usually in selected clones. *G. sylvaticum*, 2 ft, has lavender flowers with a white eye and is good in light shade. Better, because cleaner looking, is its albino form 'Album', with pure white flowers and the pale green leaves characteristic of albinos. Flowering in May, it will come again if cut to the ground immediately the flowers are over.

The meadow cranesbill, *G. pratense*, is clear lavender-blue, easily raised from seed and admirable for colonizing in any meadow area as are its white and stripy and early-flowering 'Mrs Kendall Clark' forms.

The bloody cranesbill, *G. sanguineum*, generally found near the sea when wild, is one of our most stalwart front-of-border plants. Selected clones are to be preferred for flower size, shape and colour to random seedlings.

*GR:* There is a certain amount of variability in the germination habits of the hardy geraniums, but as most are pretty tough you can afford to sow the seed as soon as you collect or receive it and leave the seed-pots in a cold frame. Some will germinate fairly quickly, others will wait until spring. Curiously, the same species may produce seeds which behave in either way.

*CL:* Herb robert is an annual or biennial weed that needs no introducing (although I would if it weren't there). Its rosette of dissected foliage cheers us through the winter, while the pink flowers are borne from April on. I can recommend 'Album', a white-flowered strain that comes true from seed. There is plenty of dark pigment in the stems, calyx, etc.

*GR:* Confusion threatens with regard to this white form of herb robert. I collected a form in Scotland with very pale pink flowers and plenty of red pigment in the foliage. This, I find, should be called *Geranium robertianum* subspecies *celticum*. 'Album', as Christopher says, has white flowers and plenty of dark pigment. There is also one with white flowers and no dark pigment, giving very fresh, almost sparkling green colour to the foliage. This is called, I'm afraid, 'Celtic White'. Just to add to the range, 'Cygnus' has white flowers and some red pigment but not much! Fortunately, they are all almost entirely self-pollinating, so keeping more than one strain growing in your garden without them crossing with each other is not a problem.

*CL: G. rubescens* from Madeira is closely allied and behaves in just the same way, but is larger and more substantial in all its parts. It is particularly handsome in winter. Quite hardy and freely self-sowing, it is a first-rate filler. It has been known as *G. anemonifolium* in gardens, but so also has *G. palmatum*, another Madeiran. This last is a somewhat tender plant, but survives and self-sows in warm borders, making quite a large, stemless rosette and carrying plenty of sizeable purplish-pink blossom.

Allied to *G. palmatum* and often confused with it is the giant of the genus, the noble *G. maderense* (from guess where?). Alas, it is rarely hardy enough to survive a British winter, though it did that of 1987–8 with me in Sussex. In any case, its large, heavily dissected palmate leaves on long stalks make it worth growing as a foliage plant in sub-tropical bedding with cannas and the like. It develops quite a trunk. This will flower only if it has plenty of root space, so it is hardly the plant for a small greenhouse. When it does flower, it starts in March and carries masses of carmine blossom. After this the plant usually dies, but quantities of seed are set and this will keep under natural storage for at least five years. If it self-sows in the garden, you'll find seedlings coming up at quite a distance from the parent, which ejects the seeds with considerable force. This is undoubtedly one of life's gardening excitements and worth working at.

*GR:* I would only add a tip about growing the very large *G. maderense.* As the rosette gets larger the older leaf petioles fold back, rest on the ground and stiffen noticeably. They then play an active role in supporting the heavy rosette and it would be a sensible precaution to leave them in place rather than be tempted to remove them, particularly if you live in a milder area and have the plants outside.

*CL:* But if I could have only one cranesbill it would probably have to be *G. wallichianum*, in the strain called 'Buxton's Variety' (or 'Buxton's Blue'). And the only sensible way to propagate this is from its dark, sausage-shaped seeds. Sow them in April and they'll bloom for you the same year and increasingly as the years pass. This plant has a rambling habit that interweaves with other low-growing neighbours. The leaves are mottled in two shades of green. The saucer flowers begin their three-month-long season in July and are apt to be a slightly dirty mauve at first, while the weather is hot, but the colour steadily improves to near blue, the base of the petals white. This highlights the ten purple anthers at the flower's centre.

As *G. wallichianum* dies back to base at the end of the season and starts up late in spring, you can plant all around it with crocuses, windflowers, early-flowering alliums (I use *Allium acuminatum*) and the like.

## Geum *(Rosaceae)*

*GR:* Apart from the two old ladies, 'Mrs Bradshaw' and 'Lady Strath-eden', geums are not widely grown. Seed can be sown in a heated propagator in March and treated as you would seed of bedding plants, in which case they will flower in their first summer. But if your heated space is at a premium, as mine is, you will probably wait until May or June. Germination may take four weeks, even at 70°F. After pricking out, the seedlings can be lined out to grow on and will flower well the following year.

Both varieties are good cut flowers, and it is worth setting aside a few plants of each for this purpose. As it happens they look very well side by side. They are both tough and long-flowering in borders, although 'Lady Stratheden' is sometimes said to catch cold in bad winters, the poor dear. Both flower for long periods, and both are good doubles – especially in their recently reselected forms. The aristocrat comes in deep yellow, the commoner in brilliant scarlet.

Of the others available, I shall pick out only 'Borisii'. Neat, rather hairy foliage at ground level throws 12-in stems carrying warm orange flowers from May to August. A rather refined little plant in a welcome and unusual shade. Raise it in the same way, though germination may be poor – as it is in many others.

*CL:* In its principal May flowering, 'Borisii' contrasts compellingly with the purple of *Viola cornuta,* making a mat in front of it.

*G. montanum,* an alpine from the Carpathians, is early flowering after snowmelt; dwarf, with large yellow blooms followed by spidery seed-heads like a pulsatilla's. A good perennial.

## Gilia *(Polemoniaceae)*

*GR:* This is a surprisingly large group of annuals and biennials, though some are often found homes in *Leptosiphon, Linanthus* and *Ipomopsis.*

Christopher will doubtless enthuse about *Gilia rubra,* the astonishing Texas Plume or Spanish larkspur (neither name describes the plant evocatively). It's a very fine-leaved plant, a little like a conifer seedling when young, which climaxes in tall spikes of bright scarlet flowers. I'm afraid I managed to kill the only plant of it I was given – but in those days I didn't know how to look after it.

The hardy annual Queen Anne's thimbles, *G. capitata,* has fluffy heads of tiny blue flowers on 2-ft stems and is a good filler for cottagey borders – especially as this is a relatively uncommon colour among summer annuals. The white form does not seem to be available in the UK.

There are many other annual and biennial species growing wild in California and Texas, and many look worth growing. But only the hardy annual *G. tricolor,* with flowers attractively banded in three or four rings of colour – yellow at the centre to soft lilac blue at the rim – is generally available at present. A pretty little plant for peeping out among more substantial perennials, it generally self-sows in a sunny, well-drained site.

*CL: G. rubra* (syn. *G. coronopifolia*) is indeed a winner if sown in autumn and over-wintered under glass without grey mould destroying it. Usually single-stemmed to 3 ft, it needs loosely tying to a cane. The phlox-like flowers, arranged along an extended spike, are a beautiful soft shade of coral-red, discreetly speckled (*Penstemon isophyllus* has similar colouring).

*G. lutea* is generally marketed as *Leptosiphon* 'French Hybrids'. Again, this is vastly superior from an autumn sowing under cold glass. Spring-sown seedlings are apt to make miserable little plants. Only 6 in tall, and therefore commonly used as an edger (more subtle than alyssum and lobelia), it covers itself with tiny stars that open in the sun and are carried in succession throughout the summer. Flowers that stay closed in dull, damp weather may be a nuisance, but they give you a real oomph of joy when they do expand. There's nothing routine about them. The colour palette in *G. lutea* is an astonishing mixture of pink, orange, yellow, cream and carmine, such as might shock any sensitive gardener in a large flower but seems absolutely right and 100 per cent acceptable here.

The half-hardy annual listed as *Limanthus grandiflorus* is *G. liniflora*, and it comes well from spring sowings, making bushy 9-in-tall plants but with a lateish flowering season. It needs a good summer to do itself justice. The needle leaves are like a seedling pine's, and the open funnel flowers are white or palest mauve. Quite a charmer.

## Gillenia *(Rosaceae)*

*CL:* From the central and southern states of the USA, the hardy perennial *Gillenia trifoliata* was introduced in 1713 but has never become a general favourite. I think it probable that ease of propagation and, hence, availability are the reasons, for this is a most attractive plant – 3 ft high with a shimmer of narrow-petalled white blossom hovering over narrow, three-fingered foliage. Everything about the plant is light and airy. It flowers in June, perhaps for not quite as long as we might, greedily, wish.

Like most *Rosaceae,* even the herbaceous kinds, *G. trifoliata* has a woody rootstock which, *pace* the *RHS Dictionary*'s 'easily increased by division in spring', does not divide easily at all. Neither are cuttings easily rooted. Seed is the answer, but its October ripening is readily overlooked. Make a note in your diary to jog your memory. It can be sown immediately or the following spring with equal success, and takes two years to produce a flowering plant.

## Glaucium *(Papaveraceae)*

*GR:* The horned poppies are among my favourite members of the poppy family. In Britain the yellow-flowered *Glaucium flavum* is a seashore plant, growing in shingle and sand just above the high-water mark. This one species sometimes dominates vast tracts of shingle.

In the Greek islands the lovely deeper yellow, almost apricot-coloured *G. leiocarpum* behaves in the same way. Seeing it growing wild with fat bushes of the lilac-flowered *Matthiola tricuspidata* is a real treat – it beats bashing about in a pedalo any day.

The broadly divided foliage of the rosettes is a special feature of the

22. Lupins and onopordum.

23. A striking contrast in a damp border at Sissinghurst Castle of *Lobelia* 'Queen Victoria' and *Salvia patens* 'Cambridge Blue'.

24. Spring bedding at Dixter, with groups of tu behind blocks of wallflowers: 'Fire King', 'Ivc White' and 'Primrose Monarch'.

25. A self-sown tree lupin, *Lupinus arboreus*.

*Gilia rubra* is best from an autumn sowing but needs staking.

27. All the Dixter *Libertia formosa* are self-sown. They go well with *Euphorbia griffithii* 'Fireglow'.

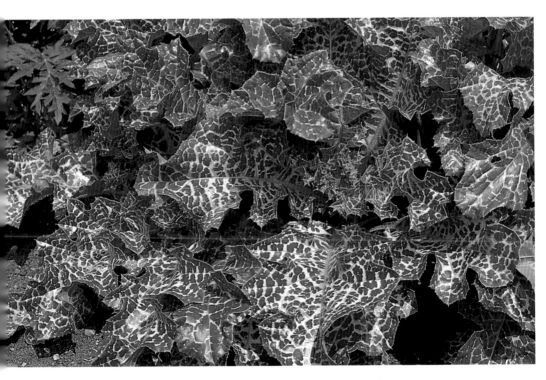

28. The white-veined foliage of the milk thistle, *Silybum marianum*.

29. Pink pomponette bellis daisies making a carpet and apron for 'China Pink' tulips.

30. *Helleborus orientalis abchassicus* comes reasonably true from seed if separated from close relations

Swiss chard with red verbenas, an unlikely but successful combination.

32. One of the best new developments in seed-raised perennials is *Lobelia* 'Compliment Scarlet'.

33. The felted rosettes of *Verbascum* 'Silver Lining' will not rush up to flower.

34. The dark leaves and white flowers of *Lavatera* 'Mont Blanc' sit well among *Centaurea rutifolia*.

35. An easy-going, open-pollinated strain of petunia, deliciously scented at night.

36. A self-sown colony of *Campanula lactiflora*.

Poppies, chrysanthemums and stocks growing wild on the island of Kos.

38. *Geum montanum* growing in the Carpathians, Czechoslovakia, soon after snowmelt.

Field poppies and *Sedum acre* growing wild in disturbed ground outside a Hungarian filling-station.

40, 41. The same border in different years: top, the white sweet rocket, *Hesperis matronalis*; bottom
*Verbascum olympicum*. Both are biennials, transplanted in autumn.

horned poppies. In some species the leaves are almost white with soft bristles, in others more grey. Either way, they are attractive at the front of sunny, well-drained borders for months before they flower.

The flowers themselves are typical poppy flowers, but the curved seed-pods can be 12 in long – hence the common name.

All are short-lived perennials which make a deep, rather gnarled woody rootstock up to 18 in long. From this it will be clear that moving established specimens is unlikely to be successful, and that they should be planted out as young seedlings if at all possible.

Raising them from seed seems to present no difficulties. Sow in spring or summer in a propagator or frost-free greenhouse. Prick out into individual pots rather than into trays, and plant out before they get pot-bound. What seems to happen if the plants stay in the pots for too long is that they remain relatively small after planting and the flower-stems are much reduced.

## Godetia *(Onagraceae)*

*GR:* This is another group where only one of many attractive species seems to be grown. But this one has been developed into one of the most popular hardy annuals for borders and cutting, and recent developments have kept them up with the times without destroying their style.

Sow them outside where they are to flower, thin them out (the final distance depending on their eventual height), and that's about all you need to do.

My favourites among the godetias are the almost salmon-pink and white 'Sybil Sherwood', the brilliant 'Crimson Fire' and the semi-double 'Rosy Morn'. The crimson and white 'Duke of York' now seems to be available only in the rest of Europe. Miss Jekyll grew doubles, and these are still sometimes listed.

Recently 'Grace Mixed' has appeared, an F1 hybrid intended to be grown for cutting. It reaches around 3 ft, with an upright habit, and comes in bright red, lilac, rose and a lovely pale shell-pink. The drawbacks to this strain are that the seed is expensive and that the plants do not flower for as long as the older types. But when they are flowering – well!

The good thing about all these plants is that although they have large flowers and are very colourful, they don't have that abrasive arrogance of many flamboyant flowers. So whether planted with perennials and shrubs in mixed borders, or in a row among the vegetables, they still look wonderful.

## Gomphrena *(Amaranthaceae)*

*CL:* Like celosia, the globe amaranth, *Gomphrena globosa*, really prefers a warmer summer than we can generally provide in England, let alone Scotland or Wales. It is a popular annual bedding plant in southern Europe.

It is an everlasting flower, with colourful papery bracts gathered into clover-like heads on a foot-tall plant. The colour generally ranges from white, through flesh-pink, to screaming magenta. [There's a new scarlet. – *GR*] This blazing colour is by far the most effective, and can be had by itself in the single colour strain 'Buddy' (tactfully described as red or royal purple in the seed lists). If used for drying, cut while still young.

Raise under heated glass from a March sowing and plant out in June. It helps to soak the seed in water for a few days before spreading it on the compost surface. Keep dark till germination in two weeks.

## Gunnera *(Gunneraceae)*

*CL:* The large-leaved gunneras, *G. manicata* and *G. tinctoria* (syn. *G. scabra, G. chilensis*), are exceedingly handsome waterside perennials, being the largest-leaved of any that we can grow as hardy plants. They can be increased by division, but for large numbers of new plants, seed is much the most productive method. Seed-heads should be collected before they are frosted in autumn, dried off, and the seeds sown under glass in spring where light can reach them. *G. tinctoria* germinates much the more freely and readily. *G. manicata*'s germination is uneven.

The two species are often confused. *G. manicata* is the larger. *G. tinctoria* has frillier, more indented leaves and notably upright inflorescences, narrower than in *G. manicata*. Their roots like to find water but the crowns will not stand being drowned for any length of time. Both leaf-stems and veins are covered with prickles, and the umbrella leaf itself, up to 6 ft across, is rough to the touch. Children and adults alike love to be photographed in front of or underneath these splendid plants.

*GR:* I seem to recall that Christopher once suggested gunnera as the ultimate ground cover plant, and recommended planting one on either side of the path up to the front door of a suburban semi!

*Gunnera magellanica* is quite the opposite of the waterside monsters, being a low, creeping, ground-cover plant for meandering among shrubs. Unfortunately seed is rarely available.

## Gypsophila *(Caryophyllaceae)*

*GR:* I'm not sure I'm the person to write about gypsophilas – I don't really like them. Even when cut from the garden and put into water quickly, the petals always seem to curl up. Maybe I glare at them too ferociously.

As well as the all too familiar white, there are unremarkable crimson and deep pink varieties of the annual *G. elegans.* These are best sown where they are to flower, at any time from March to May – I suppose.

The usual cut-flower variety is in fact the perennial *G. paniculata,* and special vegetatively propagated varieties ensure that shop gypsophila is a cut above the home-grown annual. There are seed-raised strains of this species, 'Baby's Breath' being the one usually listed. 'Double Snowflake' should produce 25 per cent double flowers, which will at least last longer.

## Helianthus *(Compositae)*

*GR:* Sunflowers are good fun. From the huge 'Russian Giant', which is the one to use if you want to get in the record books, to the almost bizarre 'Teddy Bear', with densely double flowers on plants only 2 ft high, all are entertaining.

Towering over the rest of the inhabitants in a mixed border, a few really tall sunflowers are well worth growing. The fully double 'Sungold' is a good alternative to the single ones, though the simplicity of the single-flowered variety takes a lot of beating. There are some lovely dark mahogany and bronze colours in the 'Autumn Beauty' mixture. 'Sunburst' is similar, but reaches only 4 ft, while the newer 'Velvet Queen' is supposed to be crimson with paler petal tips.

Perhaps the most startling recent development in sunflowers is 'Holiday' – a bushy sunflower. Developed as a cut flower and bred with good cutting qualities in mind, 'Holiday' makes a rounded bush about 4 ft high, each individual stem being about $3\frac{1}{2}$ ft long. From this you will deduce that it is strongly basal-branching. The 6-in single flowers have gold petals with a dark disc. Although intended as a cut flower, it makes quite an impact in a mixed or annual border. Some 'Black Prince' sweet peas trained through it might be interesting.

Tall varieties will need stout support, and *Thunbergia alata* will look good twining up both stake and sunflower stem. Plant them in front of a purple smoke bush, *Cotinus coggyria* 'Royal Purple', to set them off well.

You will hardly need telling that sunshine is a definite requirement, and sunflowers grow best in heavy soil. They can also perform a valuable service for gardeners weary of battling with their sticky clay. The deeply delving sunflower roots leave tunnels in the soil when they eventually rot, and these allow excess water to drain away more quickly.

There are two ways of raising sunflowers. Three seeds can be sown together in March where they are to flower, and two of the seedlings can then be removed, leaving one to grow on. Shorter varieties can be sown in rows and thinned. Alternatively the three seeds can be sown in a pot, thinned to one and grown on, potting on regularly. The plants can then be hardened off and planted out.

## Helichrysum *(Compositae)*

GR: *Helichrysum bracteatum* is an odd plant. For as well as including the familiar everlastings, ranging in size from tetraploid forms at around 5 ft high with huge flowers to neat little bedders at around 12 in, it also includes shrubs. 'Dargon Hill Monarch' and 'Skynet' are definitely shrubs, albeit tender ones; both widely branching, the former is a brilliant glittering yellow, the latter an unusual cream flushed with pink.

The annual kinds are now widely available in separate colours, and orange, scarlet, yellow and coppery shades are valuable constituents of fiery associations. Their everlasting qualities are as useful in the border as in the house. 'Hot Bikini' is a good dwarf form, with rounded rusty flowers on bushy plants about 12 in high.

A little different is *H. cassianum* 'Lichtrosa', a pretty everlasting with small pink single flowers each with a yellow eye, and long, very distinctive leafy bracts around each flower.

Seed of 'Skynet' is sometimes available, but my plants of 'Dargon Hill Monarch', showing themselves off nicely behind gazanias and orange tuberous begonias, produce clouds of fluff with not a fertile seed among it. Others are obviously luckier.

However, bought seed of 'Skynet' produced both yellow and whitish flowers, on stiffly upright plants – and without the greyish leaves. Very suspicious.

*CL:* I find that 'Dargon Hill Monarch' makes plenty of viable seed, but the seedlings are variable and not always as good as the prototype. The answer is cuttings, of course.

*GR:* Seed of annual types can be sown outside and thinned, or alternatively started off in warmth. The shrubby ones need more care, and a propagator is essential.

*CL:* With the tall everlastings used mainly for indoor winter decoration, I prefer sowing (in April) under glass, to obtain a more forward plant than is possible by sowing direct. Plants grow to 4 ft and take quite a while to start flowering. Separate colour strains are very welcome, and for drying purposes I recommend the golden-yellow, orange, bronze and deep red shades as holding their colour better than pink or pale yellow, which fade. White-flowered kinds get grubby indoors and you can't run the Hoover over them.

## Heliophila *(Cruciferae)*

*CL:* Within a family of mainly yellow- or white-flowered plants, *Heliophila longifolia* is the only member I have come across that is pure, intense blue (with a white eye). The flowers are borne on loose spikes above finely divided leaves on a $1\frac{1}{2}$-ft plant, and are followed by chains of articulated seed pods (like a radish's).

It is a not-quite-hardy annual. Sown in October, the seedlings can be pricked off three to a 5-in pot or five to a 6-in, and I then like to display them (supported discreetly with twigs) outside my porch at their May–June flowering. Or they can be sown in spring to make rather smaller, later-flowering plants in the garden. The colour is gripping. Everyone notices it but few can be bothered to grow it.

## Heliotrope *(Boraginaceae)*

*GR:* The problem with seed-raised heliotropes is that they just don't match up to the old cuttings-raised varieties. [Hear! Hear! – *CL*] The great qualities of heliotrope are the luscious scent and the burnished blue foliage – plus the flowers, of course. 'Marine', the most commonly grown seed-raised variety at present, has little scent and the leaf colour is very variable. The height of the plants is variable too – which is to its credit or detriment depending on your view – and the plants all start flowering at different times.

The newer 'Mini Marine' is a little bushier and shorter at about 15 in (38 cm); it's a good deep colour and a little more even. But the foliage colour, although better, doesn't have the deep lustre we really need for it to look good with *Plectranthus hirtus* 'Variegatus' arching among it. Better varieties are on the way.

Heliotropes should take about three weeks to germinate at about 70°F, and you can then take cuttings of your very best plants and over-winter them in frost-free conditions if you like.

*CL:* It is also quite useful to sow them late, in a cold frame, in early May and to bring the seedlings on, first pricking them out, then potting them individually, to use as replacements in July for sweet williams, Canterbury bells or Iceland poppies.

## Helipterum *(Compositae)*

*CL:* Commonly listed as acroclinium and rhodanthe, the helipterums are daisies, with papery, 'everlasting' bracts or rays, and might be likened to refined versions of *Helichrysum bracteatum*. But their colour range is limited to white and pink.

Best known is *H. roseum* (*Acroclinium roseum*), a smooth annual with narrow, stem-clasping foliage. Growing some 18 in tall, it is quite a suitable bedding plant with a long flowering season. In mixtures, white tends to dominate and this is rather boring. Better to concentrate on selected pink and deep pink strains; the colour is clean and bright.

*H. manglesii* (*Rhodanthe manglesii*) is of slighter build, very bushy; charming at its best but with a short flowering season. If it is to be used for drying, pull the entire plant while it is looking fresh.

Direct sow in a row outside in April.

## Helleborus *(Ranunculaceae)*

GR: Fashions in plants can be as bewildering as those of the High Street. I liked the nodding green flowers of *Helleborus cyclophyllus* from the day I first saw it, but I never dreamed that it would become a highly sought-after plant. The inky purple or densely spotted *orientalis* hybrids I can understand, but every hellebore now seems to be in demand.

Fortunately you only have to look underneath a mature *H. orientalis* in winter to discover how to deal with hellebore seed. In the garden the seed falls from the capsules in May or June, and germinates the following winter. So if you collect seed and sow it straight away, yours will germinate at the same time.

Use a good-quality John Innes seed compost and sow the seeds on the surface – they are large enough to be spaced out with the point of a pencil. Rather than covering them with compost, use $\frac{1}{4}$ in of grit and leave the pots outside.

As soon as they germinate, move the seed-pots to the shelter of a cold greenhouse, and when the first true leaf appears, prick them out into individual pots. Keep them growing well, give a liquid feed occasionally, and then plant out in summer and keep well watered and fed. They may flower the following spring and should certainly flower the spring after that.

Some species like *H. orientalis, H. foetidus* and *H. argutifolius,* are prolific self-sowers and you will never be short of seedlings; *H. niger* is much more shy. *H. lividus,* with its marbled foliage and pink-backed flowers, should be pollinated by hand. Its lack of hardiness requires it to be kept in a cold greenhouse, where there may be no bees and no breeze to dislodge the pollen for self-pollination.

## Heracleum *(Umbelliferae)*

*CL:* Our native hogweed, *Heracleum sphondylium,* with umbels of white or pale pink flowers in July and August, is a biennial, particularly common along roadside verges and in disturbed ground (in my garden, where badgers have been rootling in meadow areas, for example).

The introduced giant hogweed or cartwheel flower, *H. mantegazzianum,* is notorious for causing skin allergies resulting in painful, long-lasting blisters in many (by no means all) people. It should be handled with gloves on, and in dull, not sunny weather, as ultra-violet light activates any juices that may have touched you.

There is no disputing that this is a splendid-looking plant – 12 ft high, the huge, flat-topped umbels of white blossom in summer supported by large pinnate leaves. From seed it flowers in two to three years, then dies. Self-sowing is so prolific that it is wise to remove a flowered plant before its seed has ripened. If you dislike your neighbours, plant it against your dividing fence where it can seed into their garden. Of course, even more of it will seed into yours.

*GR:* This is indeed a magnificent plant. But not only will it seed into your garden and everyone else's, and so produce a barrage of complaint from irate mothers whose little pride and joy has been poisoned, but it will also spread into the wild. In Scotland it has become a menace, colonizing glens and rapidly shading out the natural vegetation.

To be fair, those who are susceptible to the rash can suffer very badly, especially children who use the hollow stems as blowpipes and develop horribly swollen lips, which can be very painful.

## Hesperis *(Cruciferae)*

*CL:* Sweet rocket, *Hesperis matronalis,* is a biennial or short-lived self-sowing perennial that is widely naturalized in the north, notably in Orkney. Together with rhubarb, it is often the last survivor of a deserted property. The typical cruciferous flowers, similar to those of honesty, are mauve or white, and sweetly night-scented. The plant may be anything from 3 to 7 ft tall, according to growing conditions; it flowers in May–June and is tolerant of shade.

I grow it from time to time as a bedding plant, and it makes a voluptuous early summer display. I prefer the white strain, which is available as a selection, and it shows up especially well in the gloaming, which is when its scent is switched on. Sow in a row outside in summer, thin the seedlings and plant them out in autumn. I follow with a late-sown annual. As a cottage garden plant it self-sows, and you merely need to weed out the unwanted seedlings.

## Hibiscus *(Malvaceae)*

*GR:* An intriguing hibiscus has been creeping into catalogues recently under the names of *H.* 'Coppertone' and *H. eetveldianus* – I'm sure it's the same thing. No fanfare and no fuss, it just seems to have appeared.

*CL:* There's yet a third name current for the same plant, *H. aceto-sella* × 'Red Shield'. It is a pity the EC does not insist on stand-ardization of ornamental plant names as it does of vegetables.

*GR:* That *would* be worth celebrating!
   This half-hardy perennial is intended as a bedding plant and makes an upright plant about 3 ft high. The special feature which makes it so useful is its dark, purplish-bronze, maple-shaped foliage, which is carried on long stems.
   For annual companions in the garden try it with dwarf white nico-tianas or with 'Red Seven Star' or other rusty marigolds. It should also look well in front of fiery crocosmias or behind the apricot *Hemerocallis* 'Stella d'Oro'.

*CL:* I liked it behind orange, red and yellow strains of 'Non-Stop' begonias. In a warm season, though the border was shady, it grew to 5 ft, following an April sowing in a cold-frame.

## Hosta *(Liliaceae)*

*GR:* Whether or not it's worth growing hostas from seed is open to debate. There are so many excellent varieties available which are raised by division or by micropropagation that raising them from seed may seem rather pointless. Seed-raised varieties are unlikely to be as good, and what's more, the results will be highly unpredictable as they hybridize promiscuously. They hybridize so much in the wild that even the botanists have trouble sorting them all out.

*CL:* I agree – there are far too many hostas around already and the Americans have gone mad, naming them in droves.

*GR:* But if you have a large space to fill with good ground cover and funds are restricted – for hosta plants can be expensive – then raising them from seed is worth trying.

A cool greenhouse or propagator with a minimum temperature of about 55°F is all you need, and the seed is large enough to space out in the seed-pot. The only other thing to remember is not to let the pots dry out. The seedlings will take some years to make good, ground covering plants.

## Humulus *(Cannabinaceae)*

*GR:* If you want to grow hops for home brewing then don't bother with seed, buy plants of the specially bred varieties. The only remaining member of the family is an equally rampant but variegated climber that is easy to raise when treated as a half-hardy annual.

The leaves of *Humulus japonicus* 'Variegatus' look rather like a cross between a maple and a horse-chestnut, but are flecked with a white variegation. Unfortunately the markings can be sparse, and then you're left with nothing more than a vast sheet of rough green leaves. If that's what you're after, to screen next door's tumbledown shed in a matter of weeks, fine.

*CL:* Three seedlings grown in a large pot up a tripod of sticks can make a handsome feature, but germination is often poor.

## Hunnemannia *(Papaveraceae)*

*CL: Hunnemannia fumariifolia,* the tulip poppy from Mexico, is often sold under the more palatable epithet 'Sunlite'. It is grown as a half-hardy annual, although it is perennial and will survive mild winters in the open. It is not the easiest of plants to grow well, but is worth working at.

Like other members of the poppy tribe, its roots loathe disturbance. Sow a couple of seeds in trays divided into small sections, or Propapaks, in gentle heat in March. The plants grow about a foot tall and flower through summer and autumn, never a blaze of colour but enough, seen against their delightfully fingered grey foliage, to be effective. The 3-in-wide poppies (closely allied to eschscholzias) are a singularly clear and lovely shade of yellow, and make a good contrast to the bright purple of *Verbena rigida* (*V. venosa*) or to the even more brilliant magenta *V. canadensis* (*V. aubletia*). Strong colour contrasts work particularly well and without causing indigestion where one of the partners – in this case the verbena – has tiny flowers.

## Hyoscyamus *(Solanaceae)*

*CL:* Henbane, *Hyoscyamus niger,* is a highly poisonous biennial herb and looks it. I cannot imagine anyone eating it by accident. Its aesthetic attraction resides partly in its wicked appearance, partly in its beautiful structure. The dried plant, which grows 3 ft tall, makes an unusual ingredient in winter 'flower' arrangements.

The growing plant is clammy, its grey-green leaves covered in long, soft hairs. In the second year it sends up sparsely branching stems which open their flowers in ones and twos over a long period. The flower is open-funnel-shaped, murky yellow – the colour of an advancing thundercloud – veined with purple, and is followed by a one-sided row along each stem of five-spiked seed-pods.

Small seeds are abundantly produced. I have never sown them deliberately. Their germination is exceedingly uncertain but they are long-lived and I can expect a few volunteer seedlings to appear in my garden every year. They should be left in situ, as they transplant badly. As a native, you find henbane most commonly in shingle near the seashore.

*GR:* Henbane also grows wild on old gravel workings.

There is a pale yellow-flowered species, *H. albus,* a Mediterranean plant, which is just as sticky and as angularly branched and which self-sows in just the same way. I seem to have this rather than the black version. And if you ever come across seed, try *H. aureus,* with its bright yellow flowers each with a dark purplish throat.

## Iberis *(Cruciferae)*

*GR:* Candytuft. There are two annual forms and a number of perennial species to raise from seed. The 'Fairy' type is the most familiar of the annuals, with its flat heads of flowers, mainly in lilacs and pinks. This is the childhood candytuft of cheap, cheerful packets, and it flowers in just a few weeks. What they never tell you when you're six is that if you cut the plants to the ground after flowering and water and feed them well, they'll bloom again.

Recently, after many happy years of unchanging pastels, bright red candytuft has appeared from Holland. Unfortunately 'Red Flash' is a very shy seeder, so you will get only a few red plants in 'Flash Mixed'. As a separate variety 'Red Flash' quickly disappeared, but its influence can be seen in the more vibrant shades in the mixture.

The other group is known as hyacinth-flowered, and the flowers form a cylinder instead of a flat head. Usually available only in a lovely pure white, there's also a mixture which is more difficult to come by. This form is sometimes grown as a cut flower, in which case it should be cut when the first flowers are open.

All candytufts are happy with the usual hardy annual treatment, but if you want good plants for cutting there's something you must bear in mind. Flowering is induced by high temperatures and long days, so if you sow too late the plants will attempt to flower while still small and may give you only short stems. The answer is to sow early in spring so that the plants have time to reach a good size before flowering starts, or to sow in autumn for the following year.

Both groups can be grown very effectively in front of mixed clarkia – the colours match and the forms contrast. I enjoy them along a gravel drive where they happily self-sow. As to the perennials . . .

*CL:* Sorry, I've no experience of raising these, but I see no problem. The dazzling white *Iberis sempervirens* is so good-natured that we are apt to take it for granted. One of mine was choked to death by aubrieta. A horrid fate.

## Impatiens *(Balsaminaceae)*

*GR:* In the 1960s tall, gangling busy lizzies were more often seen peering out of dark Victorian living-rooms than in the garden. But plant-breeding has transformed them into ideal bedding and tub plants, improving their growth habit and flowering capacity while introducing some exquisite colours. [Nevertheless, I wish the breeders weren't quite so hell-bent on dwarfness. – *CL*] The arrival of the rich velvety reds, soft liquid pastels, not to mention the more vibrant shades, has greatly increased the choice, especially for plants to grow in shade – for impatiens thrive in low light where few other plants will do well.

But nothing is that simple, and it has to be said that many people have trouble raising them. They do require a little more skill than the average marigold, but all you need to do is follow the rules.

The initial germination period is the most difficult; once pricked out, most of your problems are over. But if the germinating seeds or young seedlings are subjected to too much stress, they will probably fail.

Clean containers are essential to prevent damping-off disease, as is fresh, peat-based compost. Seed compost rather than that used for potting is also necessary, as imps like low nutrient levels in the early stages. Eschew even multipurpose composts if you can. Add a little drainage material if the compost seems to need it.

Sow the seed thinly. But then comes a dilemma. The seed needs light to germinate but must never dry out. I sieve enough fine compost on to the seeds after sowing to only just cover them, and I then cover the seed-pots with clingfilm to retain moisture. Newspaper over the top prevents them overheating. When germination begins, a little more compost can be sieved on to help the young roots take hold.

Alternatively, you can cover the seed with a fine layer of vermiculite which will keep the seed moist and just let enough light through.

The seeds need a temperature of 70–75°F for germination, but the thermostat in your propagator will probably be set at this temperature anyway. If they should need watering before pricking out, use warm water.

There's no need to prick out the seedlings the moment the leaves come through; leave them until the seedlings are about $\frac{1}{2}$ in high. They can go into trays, but you will probably need to pot them on later, so (if you have space) prick them out straight into 3-in pots where they can stay until planting out. Keep them protected from sunlight for a few weeks and grow them at about 65°F until established. They can then be moved to a cooler temperature of about 45°F minimum, and hardened off carefully before planting out.

This is the perfect regime. In the early stages it pays to try as hard as possible to stick to it and not to give them any shocks, but later they can often be persuaded to thrive in less than ideal conditions.

Almost every plant breeder across the world seems to have his own strain, but there are a few outstanding ones. The 'Super Elfin' strain is the best for its very wide colour range, and is noticeably stronger on soft pastel shades than its rivals. The plants are flat and spreading and do not get too tall and lank in shade. 'Accent' has fewer pastels and tends to draw up a little more in darker places. 'Blitz' is intentionally taller and more bushy and has huge flowers, but the colour range is limited, and out of the sun it can become so tall as to be unstable.

*CL:* I do not find that instability matters too much. If impatiens are knocked sideways by a strong wind, they'll turn up and right themselves within a day. It's the same with venidium.

*GR:* Here are my personal favourites. 'Super Elfin Blush', a lovely soft pink, is ideal with silver foliage and rich purple 'MacGregor's Favourite' beetroot. 'Super Elfin Pearl', in the softest lilac-blue, looks good with its 'Blush' cousin, with finely cut silver foliage such as *Artemisia* 'Powis Castle', or in a tub with the artemisia and *Melianthus major*. I've even seen 'Super Elfin Pearl' used under pink roses. 'Super Elfin White' is good with silvery *Helichrysum petiolare* and the upright spikes of *Salvia farinacea* 'White Porcelain'.

All the paler varieties, including white, are most welcome in dark courtyards and shady corners, and of course all will thrive in full sun as long as the soil is not too dry.

*CL:* It's all a matter of personal taste, of course, but I do like the strongest colours that this flower can produce. And the amazing thing is that you can mix magenta, pink, orange and scarlet and get away with it, thanks to their dark surrounding foliage. Clashes here can be triumphant.

*GR:* Just to complicate matters, when companies improve an existing variety they don't necessarily give it a new name. Both the 'Super Elfin' and its main rival the 'Accent' series are constantly being improved, so since I last compared them closely the 'Super Elfin' may have lost its lead.

There are also doubles which can be raised from seed, but the proportion of doubles to messy semi-doubles and singles is very low (about 25 per cent). So now that good doubles are available as plants grown from cuttings, I should forget growing them from seed. If you do risk it, give them partial shade, reasonable drainage, soil which doesn't dry out and no cold draughts – if you can find such a spot!

*CL:* The doubles are shy-flowering in the open and much better suited to the conservatory.

*GR:* You may see New Guinea types like 'Firelake' and 'Spectra', with variegated foliage and huge flowers, listed in catalogues as they slowly become available from seed. At present these are generally unsatisfactory and unreliable – though they will surely improve. Only the green-leaved, tangerine-coloured 'Sweet Sue', the more widely spreading 'Tangeglow' and the new 'Tango' are worth growing.


## Incarvillea *(Bignoniaceae)*

*CL:* These are exotic-looking but hardy perennials, throwing up a head of tubular flowers that expand at the mouth into a rotate disc. Although they start late into growth, they flower in May and June. The leaves are basal, pinnate. The fleshy roots are intolerant of poor drainage.

*Incarvillea delavayi* is the best-known species, 2 ft tall with flowers of a somewhat livid magenta that I find unattractive. Better is the clear pink *I. mairei grandiflora* ('Bees Pink' is similar), but its stems are so short when flowering commences that the flowers look disproportionately large. Matters improve after a few days.

It is easily raised from seed sown under cold glass in spring. The stump-rooted seedlings are among the easiest of any to prick off, and flowering can be expected in the third year.

Quite different is the sub-shrub *I. arguta* (syn. *I. olgae*), which grows like a bedding penstemon. It has pinnate leaves and panicles of slender pinky-mauve funnels in late summer, followed by long, thin seed-pods.

It is unreliably hardy, but easily perpetuated from cuttings. It also self-sows.

## Inula *(Compositae)*

*GR:* These yellow daisies vary in both stature and quality. The truly magnificent *Inula magnifica* is a big plant that needs plenty of elbow room to show off its large, rasping foliage and stout stems. The rich yellow flowers, about 6 in across, are on the same scale. The elecampane, *I. helenium,* is a smaller version which gains in elegance what it loses in stature.

*CL:* A miserable, weedy-looking plant, if you ask me. Always found in herb gardens, it's one good reason for not having a herb garden.

*GR:* At the opposite extreme is *I. ensifolia,* reaching only 12 in and a good front-of-border plant in equally rich yellow.
   All inulas seem to be tolerant plants as long as the soil they are given is not too dry. They are easy to raise from seed, require no chilling, and so can be sown in a propagator in spring if you have the space, or otherwise in a cold frame in early summer.

## Ionopsidium *(Cruciferae)*

*GR:* One of the tiniest of the plants we discuss in this book, the violet cress, *Ionopsidium acaule,* is a pretty little gem. Reaching only a few inches in height, the violet flowers fade to white as they age. Unlike other small annuals such as *Sedum caeruleum* and *Saxifraga cymbalaria,* the plants are neat and bushy and should appeal even to the alpine purist.
   They can be allowed to self-sow in gravel or raised beds, where they will flower in mild spells in winter, and I've even seen them used under *greigii* tulips in spring bedding; though they were rather patchy.

*CL:* Good in paving cracks too, and especially in shade. The flowers are sweetly scented, though you need to grovel on your stomach to savour this.

## Ipomoea *(Convolvulaceae)*

*GR:* At this point self-control could easily be abandoned. For the ipomoeas include the most exquisite and the most unpleasant of half-hardy climbers – indeed, 'Heavenly Blue' must be one of my all-time favourite plants. But having praised it beyond restraint in my annuals book and also vilified the variegated 'Roman Candy', perhaps a little sobriety is now in order.

These annual twiners, though superficially similar, are not as easy to raise as the annual convolvulus. They are noticeably irritable half-hardy annuals and so need a perceptive gardener to get the best from them.

In your excitement to start off these lovely plants, don't be tempted to sow too early. April is soon enough. Soak the seeds overnight in a saucer of water; chip any that don't swell up and soak those again. Then sow them individually in 3-in peat pots in a temperature of at least 70°F and preferably 75°F. Use a peat-based compost, but a well-drained one.

After germination, gradually reduce the temperature if you can and pot them on into 5-in pots when the roots penetrate the sides of the peat pots. Stake them, and pinch them if they get too tall. Harden them off carefully and gradually – dramatic changes of temperature cause the foliage to turn sickly.

Outside they need a site which is sheltered from cold winds, otherwise the foliage will look anaemic. The soil should be rich and not dry out, and even if the roots are in the shade, the tops need plenty of sun.

I've grown 'Heavenly Blue' up most things, from pea and bean netting to an over-wintered *Eucalyptus globulus,* and I rather fancy it growing through and peeping out of the white-edged foliage of *Pittosporum tenuifolium* 'Garnettii'.

The Japanese grow ipomoeas in a wide range of colours, only a very few of which are available outside Japan. In catalogues you'll usually find 'Scarlet O'Hara', in bright red, and the shorter-growing 'Scarlet Star' – which is not scarlet but a lurid pink with five white stripes in a star shape plus a white rim. Of 'Roman Candy', also known as 'Minibar Rose', I will say nothing.

*CL:* 'Heavenly Blue' is excellent grown throughout its life in 5-in or 6-in pots. The root restriction suits it, so it is convenient for training on trellis against a building with concrete footings.

## Iris *(Iridaceae)*

GR: This is another plant usually propagated vegetatively but which on occasions is worth growing from seed. But it's a huge genus, and many species and varieties are not worth attempting. Unfortunately their germination habits are rather varied, but help is at hand in the form of the British Iris Society, which produces a most helpful leaflet on growing irises from seed.

As a general rule, however, seed should be sown in John Innes seed compost during late autumn and winter and placed outside to get the frost. Many species will germinate in spring, although fresh seed may appear before winter.

Seedlings can be pricked out three to a 7-in pot of John Innes No. 1 (with extra grit). If you have only a small number of seedlings, the whole seed pot can simply be potted on to a larger size.

Of course seed from named varieties of flag and *sibirica* irises will not come true, but forms of *Iris foetidissima, I. chrysographes* and other species are more reliable.

And the recently introduced *I. versicolor* 'Blue Light' can be grown in the same way. This is like a smaller and more adaptable version of the yellow flag, happy in most soils. The blue flowers with their white falls appear in June and July.

## Jasione *(Campanulaceae)*

GR: The pretty sheepsbit scabious carries its dainty, rounded heads of sky-blue flowers in summer. Don't confuse it with the true scabious, most of which are lime-lovers. Grow the sheepsbit on well-drained, lime-free soil in a sunny spot. Germination is quick and thorough, without the necessity of the seed spending a winter outside.

CL: *J. perennis* is the species that I have raised from seed, and it does make a pretty puff of blue for a long time in late summer, with much more flower than leaf. Perhaps this is the reason for its being short-lived.

## Kniphofia *(Liliaceae)*

*CL:* Named after the eighteenth-century Professor Kniphof, the English make nonsense of this name. Speaking to Continentals you'll have to modify to Knip-hofia if you wish to be understood. It is a genus of mainly South and East African perennials, and I have seen it in Kenya making magnificent stands in marshy country. Here, kniphofias need good drainage to promote their uncertain hardiness.

They are known by the rather foolish name of red hot pokers, but are often yellow, white or coral. Seed of the hybrids produces mixed results, but they can be quite exciting if you will only be strong-minded enough to save the best-flowered seedlings and discard the rest. Sow under cool glass in spring and expect your first flowers in the second year.

## Kochia *(Chenopodiaceae)*

*CL:* Summer cypress seems the most appropriate of many popular names for this strange foliage annual. *Kochia scoparia trichophylla* forms a perfect cone, $2-2\frac{1}{2}$ ft high, of soft, narrow, pale green foliage that contrasts wonderfully with anything else you may grow, flowers or leaves. The freshness of its green is retained long after most greens have turned dark.

Gardeners have an irresistible urge to line it out in single file along a path, but it looks far better in small groups, contrasting, for instance, with dwarf orange or yellow *Tagetes signata pumila* alias *tenuifolia*.

In autumn the colour changes to magenta (the burning bush), which may not suit your colour schemes at all, but that happens quite late. In the past the variety called 'Childsii' remained green throughout, but what I bought as this turned magenta like the rest.

*GR:* Trust Christopher to want a burning bush that doesn't burn! Next he'll be after lethargic lizzies, love-on-a-clear-day, forget-me-please, sweet submarine, foul william, scrambled egg flower and sump oil plant! [Sow under glass in March. – *CL*]

Prick out your kochia seedlings into pots which can be easily spaced out to give evenly shaped plants. 'Acapulco Silver' has its foliage speckled with white. [Yes, I grew that one. It was the non-event of the summer. – *CL*]

## Lantana *(Verbenaceae)*

*GR:* Although this is a plant usually raised from cuttings, there is a good reason to grow it from seed.

Buying lantanas through the post is not easy, as they are so fragile; many nurseries simply refuse to send them. So unless you happen to live near enough to a nursery to go and collect them, it will be difficult to amass a collection in different colours.

Lantanas are wonderful bedders and tub plants, and are not difficult to train into standards. Only mixed colours are available from seed – some plants will carry flowers in just one shade, peachy-yellow perhaps, some in various bicolours. You can take cuttings from those you like best.

Soak the seed overnight and then treat in the same way as seed-raised pelargoniums. Once the seedlings start to grow, beware of whitefly – there can hardly be a plant on this planet that whitefly like more.

*CL:* In appearance, lantanas resemble a shrubby verbena with flat-headed corymbs. There is frequently a bicolour effect, the young flowers changing as they age from, say, yellow to orange or pale cream to deep pink. There is a wide colour range. The plants are spiny and emit a nasty little sour smell when bruised – but I love them. So do butterflies.

## Lapageria *(Liliaceae)*

*GR:* This is definitely one for the experts. The Chilean bell-flower, *Lapageria rosea,* is a highly sought-after twiner with pendulous waxy flowers in red, white or intermediate pinks; but it's one of the more difficult flowers to raise from seed. The first problem is that you will find it hard to persuade yourself to pay the asking price for the seed – you'll get one seed for about the price of a pint of beer. The second is that they take time and special conditions to germinate.

The seeds resemble nothing so closely as ants' eggs. For germination they need acid compost and a fairly long chilling period. Wrap them in a small polythene bag with a little moist peat and leave them in the bottom of the fridge for a couple of months.

The seeds will start to germinate in the fridge, and when the roots are $\frac{1}{2}$ in long they can be 'sown'. Use small pots of acid, peat-based compost with extra lime-free grit, and seal inside a polythene bag; keep them in a shady part of the greenhouse at about 55°F. Water with lime-free water as necessary.

The seedlings often sulk at first, but as they start to grow well, wean them from the polythene cover and eventually pot them on, standing them out in a cold frame for the summer.

Plant them in a well-drained (but not dry) acid, fertile soil in a sheltered spot; they will thrive on a west wall, on a partially shaded south wall or in a cold conservatory.

It sounds a lot of trouble – and it is. But it can be done, and it's worth it.


## Lapeirousia *(Iridaceae)*

*CL:* Also known as *Anomotheca, Lapeirousia laxa* is a South African corm akin to gladiolus but only 9–12 in tall. The perianth limbs open out flat and are in two cheerful shades of red. Flowering continues through summer and autumn and is as free in shade as in sun. There is an albino form, 'Alba', which comes true from seed. Self-sowing is generous and the species is generally hardy. The seeds are a deep, glistening red. Sow them in spring, not necessarily under glass and definitely in the light.


## Lathyrus *(Leguminosae)*

*GR:* Just for a change let's not launch into an overblown eulogy on the so-called 'queen of annuals', the sweet pea. This tired phrase still appears in print – as if simply reading those words will convince gardeners to grow them in vast quantities and, unquestioning, be delighted with the results.

This is a large genus, with around 130 species, and while none of the others quite match the range of colours available in the familiar sweet pea, there are some fine plants, unjustly neglected, simply waiting to be discovered. So let's start with the underdogs.

The delightful yellow flowered annual *Lathyrus chloranthus* is a real joy. It must be said that it is by no means as flamboyant as the familiar Spencer types, which derive from *L. odoratus,* and neither is it unique in its yellow flowers, but they're a good size and the slight greenish blush is more attractive than it sounds (it is *not* bilious). Indeed the flowers, which come in twos and threes, are an enchanting shade, the foliage is healthy and the plants are vigorous. Sadly it doesn't set seed well, so saving your own may not always be possible and seed companies can't always supply it.

*CL:* Yes, that is sad but I heartily endorse Graham's recommendation.

*GR:* However, if you are fortunate enough to acquire some seed, don't just treat it like any old sweet pea. The seed should be sown individually in small pots in spring and kept more moist than for Spencer sweet peas. They are very slow to germinate and grow, but once potted on and planted out they suddenly take a leap and flower well into November, by which time they may have reached 8 ft.

*CL:* They're nice rambling through a shrub like the purple-leaved cotinus.

*GR: L. tingitanus* is a large-flowered, purplish-red species which is easy to raise and which sets a lot of seed. But keep only one plant for seed; if you leave the pods to develop on all the plants, flowering will be fleeting, ceasing as the new seeds develop. There's a darkly streaked pink-flowered version too. Both are useful for training through winter- or spring-flowering shrubs. You may come across this species if you take a holiday in North Africa. [*Tingitanus* means of Tangier. – *CL*]

Sow it outside where it is to flower, choosing a sunny and well-drained spot, or raise it in pots in a cool greenhouse and plant out.

*CL:* I rub the seed between sandpaper before sowing to weaken the hard coat and allow moisture to reach the embryo.

*GR:* There has been some confusion about the origins of 'Lord Anson's Blue Pea', *L. nervosus,* and what exactly should be grown under that name, but the plant now correctly sold under the good Admiral's name is a perennial climber with lovely soft blue flowers and rounded, slightly fleshy leaves.

The first year I grew it, it didn't flower at all. The plants grew well, in a rich but well-drained soil in a sheltered spot in full sun, and reached about 5 ft but without a single bud. They still looked healthy at Christmas; six weeks later the tips were dying but new shoots were emerging a foot away from the crown. The following year there were flowers from spring, and seed set too. I've seen them with mildew in other gardens, I'm afraid, but the flowers really are special.

And so we come to sweet peas proper, the Spencers. It's such a huge subject that I'll simply tell you how I deal with them. Purists may cringe and my colleague on this memorable ride may have other ideas, but here we go.

Each year, I order most of the new varieties from the major seed companies together with the best from previous years. When they arrive I sit down with the seed packets, a nail file (safer than a knife), a glass of wine and a good play on the radio and file each seed until the pale flesh shows through the dark coat. Some people only file the dark-skinned types, but I file them all.

Then I sow six seeds to each 5-in pot. As to compost, a good John Innes seed compost is my first choice, followed by a bad John Innes, suitably improved with grit or peat as necessary – it needs to be well drained. I've also used commercial peat-based composts, usually with extra grit or perlite, and also my own peat/perlite mixture with Chempak base fertilizer added. The seeds are sown in October or November in holes $\frac{1}{2}$ in deep, made with the top of a pencil.

The pots are labelled and placed alongside the greenhouse on a gravel bed facing west – the frame is usually full of less tough plants. And there they stay until the spring. In very fierce weather they may be brought into the cold greenhouse, but very rarely. In colder areas than Northamptonshire it's true that they're better in a cold frame.

If you like you can space out the seed on damp kitchen paper in a warm place to sprout and sow it when the white fringed root first emerges. This will bring them on by about a week, but is it really necessary?

The time at which the young plants reach pinching stage depends entirely on the season, but I usually do mine when they have grown to about 3 in, in whichever month that happens to fall. Come the spring they're ready for planting out.

These days most of my sweet peas are either planted to climb through shrubs or grown up netting on a fence. Sometimes I grow a few for cutting. With this in mind I've occasionally grown them on cordons, the traditional method, and it really is a lot of unnecessary work unless you want to win prizes at shows. [I do so agree. – CL] More often I've grown them up plastic netting (the kind sold for peas and beans is ideal) and find it perfectly good. The soil must be very well-prepared, watering must be attended to regularly, and picking must *never* be neglected. Otherwise the stems will get shorter and then flower production will simply cease.

The number of flower stems a short length of row can produce is prodigious (I counted them once, 670 from twenty-one plants by the end of July!) so if necessary, when you've filled every vase in the house, carry on picking and give them away.

They can be sown in the early spring too, and if you're growing them for cutting, sow some late and plant them out in June to provide flowers later on in the season.

If grown through shrubs or up fences, good preparation is just as important to prevent competition from neighbouring plants being too destructive. And don't forget the regular dead-heading.

There are some varieties that I always try to grow, and though it's a very personal business, here are my favourite half dozen: 'Diamond Wedding' is a vigorous long-stemmed white with very strong scent. 'Lady Fairbairn' also has long stems and exceptional vigour, but with soft lilac-pink flowers and a reasonable scent. 'Midnight' is probably the darkest of all sweet peas, and has longer stems than 'Black Prince' – but no scent. 'Noel Sutton' is rich blue with a good scent and is an old favourite. 'North Shore' is a newish bicoloured variety, in dark purplish-blue combined with a softer blue. 'Southbourne' is another old favourite that has lasted, in soft pink.

*CL:* Flower size and brilliant colouring mean nothing to me in sweet peas. The only kind I'm interested in growing, simply to pick for the house, are the old-fashioned sweet-scented Grandiflora types that were current before the frilly Spencer sweet peas arrived on the scene, early in this century.

With this strain, excellent germination results without previous treatment of the seed-coat. I sow in the last week of March or the first ten days of April, spacing the seed in a 2½-in-deep tray and using John Innes No. 1 compost. The seedlings are potted off individually, stopped as Graham has described, then lined out in a picking row. They start flowering in early July, which is soon enough for me. The scent is terrific; much more pungent than in the Spencers.

## Lavandula *(Labiatae)*

*CL:* The whole lavender tribe germinates easily from seed, sown in spring, under cold glass, and this is the obvious way to propagate a species like *Lavandula stoechas,* the square-headed lavender from the Mediterranean with its flowers along the corners and a tuft of purple, flag-like bracts aloft.

The variable species *L. angustifolia* (long known as *L. spica*) produces lovely little plants from seed, but they will not be of uniform habit, colour or vigour. In a hedge, this might be undesirable, or you might welcome it. The point is to be aware of what will happen.

The rich purple *L. angustifolia* 'Hidcote' is probably the most popular of all lavenders, and there has been a tendency in the trade to raise it from seed, which gives fairly level results – more or less so, according to how much cross-pollination with other lavenders has occurred. In all events, the seedlings have no title to the name 'Hidcote', which is a clone and must, to remain correct, be propagated from cuttings. But it is a wicked world. Short cuts and popular misnomers are sometimes irresistible.

## Lavatera *(Malvaceae)*

*CL:* It is with the annual mallows, derived from *Lavatera trimestris,* that we are concerned here. The perennial, shrubby 'tree' mallows are apt to self-sow, but the results are nearly always inferior to selected clones. The variegated form of *L. arborea* does, however, come true from seed. This is essentially a foliage plant on the large scale. If only it were hardy.

Of the strains of *L. trimestris,* the two that have made news in the past ten years are the pink 'Silver Cup', with very large soft pink, dark-veined funnels, and the pure white 'Mont Blanc', whose flowers contrast with darkest green foliage. I seem to be alone in swooning over neither of them. 'Silver Cup' I find too heart-on-sleeve and simpering, the plant admittedly compact but ungraceful. 'Mont Blanc' is far too compact and congested, at 2 ft; fit for massing, but individual plants have no identity. These mallows go down like ninepins to a soil-borne fungus disease if grown in the same spot in successive years. [Some seed companies are now treating their seed against this disease. – GR]

The old strain called 'Loveliness' and the similar 'Tanagra' are typical mallow-pink in colour and they are still current, the best to grow as specimens in large pots from a late August sowing. Six feet tall and widely branching, they make stylish plants but need a stake per plant and a not too exposed position.

*L. trimestris* is a hardy annual and can be sown at times to suit yourself. I often wait till May and use it (or malope) as a follow-on to June-flowering biennials or perennials treated as biennials (aquilegias, sweet rocket, lupins). The seedlings dislike root disturbance and should be pricked off into pots when quite small.

*GR:* A newer variety is called, with stunning originality, 'Pink Beauty'. Christopher may appreciate this rather more, as it is altogether less strident in colour than 'Silver Cup', having the palest pink petals with darker veins. Latest to appear is 'Ruby Regis', in deep reddish pink.

Some gardeners like to mix the pink and white varieties together, but with their different heights 'Silver Cup' and 'Mont Blanc' are not ideal companions. Look out for the less often grown 'Mont Rose' as a partner for 'Mont Blanc'.

I find that when treated as half-hardy annuals and planted out as good-sized plants in May, these lavateras often grow strongly, flower heroically but are reduced to brown twigs by August. Fine if you have replacements to hand – alarming if not.

## Layia *(Compositae)*

*CL: Layia elegans* is a foot-tall hardy annual and carries yellow daisies, shading to white at the ray tips, on a straggling, unprepossessing plant. I can do without this in my garden but should like to see it in the wilds of its native California.

## Libertia *(Iridaceae)*

*CL:* The libertias are hardy or nearly hardy perennials, with strong, evergreen, iris-like leaves and small white flowers that make a triangular impression.

Best known and the tallest is *L. formosa* (*formosa* means beautiful), 3 ft high, May-flowering. It makes a good show and self-sows freely yet without becoming a nuisance – rather pleasing in the risers of steps or the not-too-narrow cracks in paving. Old plants become tatty with unshed brown foliage. If you cut them back to tidy them up, they'll recover but look pretty awful even then. I'm inclined to dig out older plants and allow young self-sowns to replace them.

*L. formosa* comes from Chile. *L. ixioides* and *L. peregrinans* are New Zealanders. The former is a neat little plant, 9 in tall, that makes a lovely fresh display with its white blossom followed by globular orange fruits. In *L. peregrinans* the flowers tend to be swallowed up by its foliage, but this is the plant's main asset, being bronzy, especially along the midrib, and brightest in winter. Not much more than a foot tall and with a suckering habit, so that it forms a colony.

*GR:* All germinate well if sown in a heated propagator in spring.

## Lilium *(Liliaceae)*

*CL:* There is a great satisfaction in raising your own lilies from seed, and it has the material advantage (besides being cheaper than buying bulbs) of starting you off with virus-free stock. Virus diseases are the bane of lily-growing. Nevertheless, it is untrue to say of lilies that, like turkeys, they have only one ambition in life: namely, to die.

Some lilies, for instance *Lilium auratum* and *L. speciosum*, will germinate within two to three weeks of sowing, at 50°F, if the seed is fresh. You are unlikely to be able to buy fresh seed, but you can save your own. *L. formosanum*, sown in September, will flower a year later. I delay sowing till the following spring, as no special arrangements need then be made to raise the necessary temperature. Flowering then starts in the following year. *L. regale*, sown in spring, will often produce its first bloom in the summer of the year after. *L. auratum* usually flowers for the first time in its third year.

*GR.* I have tried to flower *L. formosanum* from a spring sowing, and having started the seed off in the propagator in January, about half the bulbs flowered in the autumn of the same year. But the stems were so short, about 6–8 in, and the flowers so large, almost as big as *L. regale*, that they looked very silly. I won't be trying again.

*CL:* There are some lilies, notably the European kinds that are base-rooting only (no stem roots), which do not put up their first leaf until two springs after sowing. Such are *L. martagon* and *L. szovitsianum*. In the first year they make a bulbil below the soil and no activity is visible.

Matters can be speeded up by conning them that two winters have elapsed whereas they have actually passed through only one. Sow in the autumn or early winter, topping the compost with grit or chippings, and plunge the pots outside under a north wall. In January or February, bring the containers into warmth at 50°F. Some species will then germinate fairly soon. Those that don't should again be plunged outside for a further cold period. Top growth will appear in spring. Of course, if you're not in a hurry you can wait the extra year.

The disturbance of pricking lilies out does them no good and checks their growth. Better to sow six to eight seeds in a $3\frac{1}{2}$-in pot, and when the seedlings are growing strongly, transfer the whole thing to a 6-in pot. This will usually be in the middle of the first summer after sowing. Keep them in these pots for another year. Then, in the early autumn, divide and plant them out.

*GR:* It is sometimes suggested that the speediest method of all is this one. Put the seed in a polythene bag containing moist vermiculite and keep it in a warm place – about 70°F. After about three months tiny bulbs will have formed alongside the seed. The seeds/bulbs can then be sown individually in small pots, or spaced out in larger pots and given six weeks at just above freezing, say about 40°F. A cold frame or cold greenhouse is suitable. This will prompt leaf growth, and from an autumn sowing you will have growing seedlings in spring.

LILIES THAT GERMINATE QUICKLY

*brownii*

*candidum*

*cernuum*

*formosanum*
*henryi*
*lankongense*
*leitchlinii*
*longiflorum*
*pumilum*
*pyrenaicum*
*regale*

## LILIES THAT NEED A COOL PERIOD

*auratum*
*bulbiferum*
*canadense*
*hansonii*
*japonicum*
*kesselringianum*
*martagon*
*monodelphum*
*speciosum*
*szovitsianum*
*tsingtauense*

## Limnanthes *(Limnanthaceae)*

*CL:* Inelegantly popularized as the poached-egg or fried-egg flower, the message is that *Limnanthes douglasii* is yellow at the centre and white on the outside. There is also a pure yellow form which I find tends to dominate when close to the yellow and white. The all-white I have not seen.

*GR:* There was also once a very pale pink-flowered form with darker veins, but this has not been listed for many years.

*CL:* This is one of the freshest and most gladdening of hardy annuals, with bright yellow-green, pinnate foliage, almost succulent in substance. It flowers at 6–9 in and is a good bee plant.

Its primary season is May, overlapping into June. After that, let it seed, then immediately clear away the remains, scratch over the soil surface and, if you like (and I do), plant something else there for late summer flowering. Meantime the next batch of limnanthes seedlings will appear, and by the autumn it will be flowering again, spasmodically but enough to be worthwhile. If the winter is mild, sporadic flowering will continue throughout – nice to pick for indoor enjoyment. The main rush of blossom will follow in the spring.

Once you have this flower you are unlikely to lose it. Just thin out the seedlings to give those that remain a chance. Initially, broadcast a direct sowing in autumn or early spring.

*GR:* It's stunning popping up through trailing mats of *Tropaeolum polyphyllum.*


## Limonium *(Plumbaginaceae)*

*GR:* Prized for drying and good in the border too, statice (*Limonium sinuatum*) has improved greatly in recent years. This improvement lies mainly in the more manageable growth of newer varieties, especially the relatively new 'Fortress' strain, whose stems may be shorter but are still quite long enough for cutting. The colours are also especially vivid and include some unusual pastel shades. More new varieties in new shades are on the way.

Statice can be treated as a half-hardy annual and raised in a propagator by sowing in March or April, or alternatively by sowing outside in rows in May. Now that single colours are available, you might consider it for the mixed border. Although the actual petals may be fleeting, it's the calyces which provide the long-lasting colour; and this is valuable in the border as much as in the living-room.


## Linaria *(Scrophulariaceae)*

*GR:* Linarias are much underrated. The common yellow toadflax, *L. vulgaris*, may be rather too rampageous for beds and borders, but its sparkling yellow flowers and glaucous foliage should encourage gardeners to investigate other members of the genus.

This investigation will quickly reveal at least four good hardy perennials: *L. dalmatica*, *L. macedonica*, *L. triornithophora* and *L. purpurea*.

The first two are variants of our native toadflax. *L. dalmatica* reaches 3 ft and is a little floppy, but the long spikes of sparkling yellow flowers appear for many weeks. *L. macedonica* may be shorter, the leaves and flowers may be smaller, but the flower spikes are upright and gathered into heads like exploding fireworks. They both run, but not excessively. Either looks wonderful in front of fiery crocosmias.

Rather more subtle, *L. triornithophora* is also taller and more demanding of well-drained soil. The flowers, instead of running all the way up the spikes, are gathered in whorls of three or four. The individual flowers are purple with a yellow lip and a purple-streaked white spur. There is a rare yellow-flowered form. This is by no means as showy a plant as the yellow-flowered species, but the individual flowers are lovely.

Then there's *L. purpurea*, a tall, slender species. The small glaucous leaves have a purplish tint and the tiny purple flowers are carried in long spikes filling the top third of the 4-ft stems. The unbranching stems surge up directly from ground level, giving the plant a very distinctive appearance. It is easy to raise from seed and will self-sow once you have it, sometimes finding a home in stone walls. 'Canon Went' is a lovely pink-flowered form which will throw a few purples if left to self-sow.

Seed of all these species seems to germinate promptly without chilling, and seedlings grow quickly.

*CL:* The most popular annual toadflax is *L. maroccana*. It makes a bushy, foot-tall plant and seethes with spikelets of small flowers in a wide range of colour (almost too wide, for general effect). Hardy, best sown in spring.

*GR:* There are also a number of intriguing alpine species requiring sharply drained conditions or even alpine house treatment. Look out in particular for *L. tristis* 'Toubkal', a small greyish plant with astonishing purple, yellow and grey streaked flowers.

## Linum *(Linaceae)*

GR. There are perennial and annual linums. The hardy annual *L. grandiflorum* is a slender, narrow-leaved plant about a foot tall, with almost disproportionately large flowers in a lovely shimmering blood-red. It flourishes in most soils and sunny spots. A variety called 'Bright Eyes', with a deep red centre and wide white rim, was lost for some years but was rediscovered in a seed bank and is now available again. At twice the height, *L. usitatissimum* is more willowy, with wafts of small sky-blue flowers.

The perennials – *L. perenne* and *L. narbonense* – are all generally rather similar: about 18 in in height, with slightly glaucous leaves, upright habit and clouds of sky-blue or white flowers. The exceptions are 'White Diamond', which is a little shorter and pure white, and 'Blue Saphyr', which grows only about 8 in tall.

Seed is easy to raise. The annuals can be sown where they are to flower in spring, the perennials in a propagator for planting out in July (*perenne* is quicker than *narbonense*) or in a cold greenhouse or seed-bed in early summer.

*CL:* What I particularly like about *L. grandiflorum* is its tremendously long flowering season. Also the thin dark pencil line near the centre of the flower and the radiating rays, like a sunburst, within this. Own saved seed has given me far better germination than seed I have bought.

## Lobelia *(Lobeliaceae)*

*GR:* The first thing to remember about lobelias is that all the ones we usually grow are actually perennials, as are many of our most prolific bedding plants – geraniums, petunias, begonias, ageratums, verbenas, salvias, violas, impatiens. True annuals like alyssum and calendula rarely reach the autumn in full flower; usually only perennials have the stamina.

So, in spite of the fact that we raise bedding lobelias from seed, one look at the base of the shoots at the end of the season will show a mass of fine white roots seeking out the dampness. The double-flowered 'Kathleen Mallard' can be kept going only from cuttings taken of these shoots.

Lobelias have almost invisible seed, and this poses problems. We've described ways of dealing with fine seed in the introductory section (page 16). Lobelia is usually pricked out in patches of a few seedlings together. With mixtures this can lead to an especially speckled planting rather than individual plants of different colours.

Unfortunately, with white varieties, pricking out in patches leads to a curious effect. It's genetically impossible to produce pure white lobelia – 10 per cent of all the plants will be blue. So pricking out in patches ensures that the blues are thoroughly mixed in with the whites – inseparable. If you can be bothered, sow white lobelia early, prick the seedlings out individually and the plants should flower in time for you to plant out only the white. (Or you could grow them from cuttings – sorry, heresy in this book.)

The bushy bedders and the trailers are all varieties of *L. erinus*. The blues are the most effective, and the white. The newer murky reds and pinks are hardly comparable. Don't be blinkered into always using the bushy ones in borders and the trailers in baskets. A mass planting of 'Blue Cascade' makes a lovely foamy billow, while in the warmth of a sheltered porch or a sun-room the trailers get too long and sparse – the bushy types are just right.

Other species are also grown. *L. valida*, sometimes reaching 18 in, is stiffer, more upright, with narrower, rather fleshy, brighter green leaves and large flowers. A lovely plant, looking perfect with *Diascia fet-cairniensis* and *Elymus magellanicus*, it's less tolerant of inhospitable situations – good soil, sun and a little shelter are required. *L. tenuior* 'Blue Wings' also appreciates a little shelter. It makes sinuous stems topped with large, brilliant blue flowers. Both make a welcome change in habit from the familiar types.

Then there are those that we always think of as perennials. I wouldn't bother growing *L. cardinalis* or *L. fulgens* from seed; better varieties are raised vegetatively. But 'Compliment Scarlet' is different. Initially bred in Canada by the man who gave us 'Cherry Ripe' and 'Dark Crusader', it was 'finished off' in Europe. Treated as a half-hardy annual, it can produce as many as four spikes towards the end of its first summer. In its second year, my first four plants produced forty spikes between them. Plants of 'Bees Flame' raised from leaf bud cuttings at about the same time managed only one or two half-hearted spikes each.

'Compliment Scarlet' reaches about 4 ft, with green leaves and brilliant, intense red flowers on unbranched stems. The newer 'Fan

'Cinnabar Rose' is a narrow-petalled, pink-flowered version.

For the best first-year flower spikes, sow in January at about 65°F, covering with vermiculite or not at all. The seedlings should appear in a couple of weeks when they can be pricked out into small pots. Feed well and plant out from mid-April onwards, as the young plants tolerate light frost. They should flower for two to three months in their first season. Alternatively, treat them as a biennial by sowing in May.

'Compliment Scarlet' has been quite hardy with me in the two winters that I've had it, but in cold areas both these varieties may need protection from the worst of the weather in winter.

There is also 'Pink Flamingo', in a range of warm pink tones which derives from a seedling found in a New Zealand garden – other varieties will be appearing soon.

*CL: L × vedrariensis* is a good late-flowering perennial, 3 ft tall, with spikes of rich purple flowers that contrast well with the numerous yellow daisies of autumn, for instance *Rudbeckia* 'Goldsturm'. Easy from seed, and quite ready to self-sow.

## Lupinus *(Leguminosae)*

*GR:* There are about 150 species of lupins growing in a variety of habitats around the world, so you would expect them to be something of a mixture.

I'm especially partial to annual lupins, so will concentrate on these and allow Christopher full range with the herbaceous perennials and tree lupins.

There is one annual which stands out above all the others, *Lupinus varius*. Growing wild in Israel and the eastern Mediterranean, this is a rather variable plant, the Israeli form being the most flamboyant and the one usually listed.

The seeds are huge, about the size of a large fingernail, and rock-hard. I used to hit them with a hammer to crack them before soaking, but a few moments' work with a coarse file seems to do the trick just as well. You're wasting your time with a pocket-knife or nail-file. If they don't plump up after a day or two in soak, you haven't filed them enough.

After soaking, sow them individually about $\frac{1}{2}$ in down in 3-in pots of John Innes seed compost and place in a cool greenhouse. They soon surge through the soil and produce two fat seed-leaves, followed quickly by small lupin leaves edged with silver hairs. When they have three or four true leaves, pot them on carefully into 5-in pots. You will find most of the yellow roots at the bottom of the pots, so you need to be careful. Growth is quick and the rate depends on the temperature, but they will eventually need larger pots unless planted out.

I've sown them in late autumn, late winter and spring, and sowing them in autumn and treating them as winter annuals gives the best plants. Spring-sown plants simply shoot up to about 12 in on a single stem and then start to flower, although in a really hot spot with well-drained soil they will then bush out if watered well. But by August they will probably still be shrivelled.

When they flower they should be about 2 ft high, rounded in habit, with beautiful silvery leaves and fat spikes made up of whorls of large rich blue flowers. When the flowers open, each has a white eye, but this changes to almost black as the flowers age, hence *L. varius*. You will often have 12 in of flowers all open at once.

They make splendid specimens in large pots which can be moved outside in May, or you can plant them from their 5-in pots in a hot, well-drained, but not parched, site.

The Texas blue bonnet, *L. subcarnosus*, the state flower of Texas, is altogether smaller than its Israeli cousin, with a white or yellow eye, but exceptionally pretty. This is more suitable for spring sowing outdoors, but can also be given the winter annual treatment.

Yellow annual lupins are impressive too, and *L. luteus*, from Spain, is the one usually listed. 'Yellow Javelin' is a form with longer spikes of flowers. This too can be spring-sown.

The one problem with these annual lupins is that the flower spikes are not usually produced evenly over the plant. Although the plant itself may seem uniform, you will often find that the branching structure is irregular and the flower spikes sometimes seem to lurch out here and there. But then we'd be fools to expect a garden to be orderly.

Alpine lupins like *Lupinus ornatus* are generally a little difficult to grow, needing perfect drainage and protection from winter wet. The seedlings also require special treatment. In particular they need pricking out when they are very small, just as the cotyledons are opening. This is because the seedlings develop a deep tap root at an astonishing rate and may die if this is damaged.

Now the perennials.

*GL:* The perennial herbaceous lupin was derived from *L. polyphyllus*, and older seed strains made 4 to 5-ft plants with long, narrow spikes, in pink, purple, pale yellow and blue but with a strong tendency, when self-seeding, which they freely did, to revert to blue. Although later despised by gardeners, these lupins are wonderful for colonizing waste places on acid soil (they detest lime) and are still a thrilling sight where they have gone wild, as at the mouth of the River Dee, in eastern Scotland.

With the advent of the Russell lupin we had a far showier plant, with thicker, denser spikes and the bicolour effect (not to everyone's taste) of two contrasting or harmonizing colours in the top and lower petals. Seed strains are nowadays so good that it hardly seems worthwhile to keep many named varieties going from cuttings.

There are many named seed strains, 'Band of Nobles' being one of the tallest at 4 ft, and it is also obtainable in separate colours. Dwarfer strains claim to be a mere 2 ft, but this is wishful thinking. [I've found 'Dwarf Gallery' to be reliably short. – *GR*] In windy sites it would certainly be convenient. However, by the time lupins are flowering in late May and June, there's a fair chance of respite from high winds and I hope to get away with no staking. Often I'm lucky.

Before sowing seed in pots or trays in April, rub it briskly between sandpaper to weaken the seed-coat, otherwise germination will be patchy and uneven. Seedlings can be moved straight to the open ground to grow on in a row. They'll flower a bit the first year, and you can throw out those you think worthless.

Plant into their flowering positions in the autumn – I interplant them with tulips to give earlier interest. The lupin foliage gives the tulips a good background.

After they have flowered, lupin plants look pretty terrible, no matter what you do to them. You can't just cut them right to the ground, as you can with oriental poppies or delphiniums; they need their foliage, but this invariably goes grey with powdery mildew.

For this reason I treat lupins as biennials, throwing them out in early July at the latest (harvesting the tulip bulbs) and replacing them with zinnias, tithonias, malopes, petunias, rudbeckias (not all in the same year!) or whatever else I fancy and have raised from a late sowing.

In the autumn, back go the lupins and the tulips.

The tree lupin, *Lupinus arboreus*, is an evergreen shrub and slightly tender. It is particularly happy near the sea. The bright, evergreen foliage is a great asset in winter.

Typically the flowers, which open in May, are pale yellow, which I like best, but seed strains include white and skimmed-milk blue. As with all lupins, the flowers are arranged in whorls along the spike, but there is a distinct gap between whorls in this species which produces the contrasting effect of vertical (the spike) and horizontal (the whorl). Very good it looks. The scent is deliciously sweet on the air (more peppery in the herbaceous lupin).

Tree lupins grow fast from seed. Having a tap root, seedlings should be planted out as young as possible. They soon damp off in a pot. Plants are in their prime when two years old, after which they tend to break up, but they are easily replaced (often from self-sown seedlings).

A pest imported from America, the lupin aphis, has afflicted tree and herbaceous lupins of recent years. It is large and extremely waxy – not easily controlled, but you must, if your plants are not to be ruined.

*GR:* In mild winters these huge beasts over-winter on tree lupins and piptanthus, ready to invade first the young shoots of perennial types in early spring and then the annuals. They multiply very quickly, sometimes completely coating 6 in of shoot, but one thorough spray of Rapid (*Pirimicarb*) sorts them out in a matter of minutes.

### Lychnis *(Caryophyllaceae)*

*CL:* Brilliant scarlet border plants are none too numerous, so we are particularly beholden to the long-lived *Lychnis chalcedonica*, which carries domed heads of scarlet flowers on a stiff, $3\frac{1}{2}$-ft plant in July. It should be divorced from pink flowers but looks well with purple *Salvia nemorosa* 'Superba', bronze *Helenium* 'Moerheim Beauty' and yellow *Thalictrum speciosissimum*. It's a shame that it flowers for only two weeks. From seed it flowers in its second year.

The hybrids *L. × arkwrightii* and *L. × haageana* are longer flowering, only 12–18 in tall, and not very strong in the stem. They include softer shades, but scarlet is what we look for from them and it is found particularly in *L. × arkwrightii* 'Vesuvius'. These are front-of-border plants that can be – and best are – treated as annuals since they are short-lived anyway.

GR: The way to get these to flower well in their first year is to sow them singly in divided trays in February in as warm a temperature as you can manage, move them on to $3\frac{1}{2}$ in pots before the roots get too twisted, and keep them growing frost-free at least. Plant them out in June and they should flower from July to the frosts.

CL: Also short-lived is *L. coronaria*, the rose campion, best discarded after two flowering seasons in favour of its generously self-sown seedlings. They flower in their second year. Its disc-shaped flowers, borne at 3 ft above grey stems and foliage, are a wonderfully vital shade of brilliant magenta. This may be a dangerous colour and to be handled with care, but I must admit that when some of my self-sowns flowered among the brick-red *Crocosmia* 'Lucifer', I was not displeased. The height of its flowering season, which is quite prolonged, centres on July. There is a white-flowered seed strain and another (which comes true from seed, if isolated from other colour forms) called 'Oculata'. This starts white but then develops a pink central zone.

GR: I've often wondered why there was no blush-pink version – but now there's 'Angel's Blush' (what a name!) which is exactly that and should satisfy everyone who likes silver and pink together. This and the others do surprisingly well in a north-facing border as long as it is not overhung.

CL: *L. flos-jovis* carries heads of clear pink flowers on a foot-tall plant with greyish leaves. It is quite long-lived but easy to raise from seed. Flowering in May–June, it makes a stunning foreground to the blue-flowered *Cynoglossum amabile*.

## Malcolmia *(Cruciferae)*

GR: Virginia stocks were once much prized and available in many separate colours, including the yellow now sadly absent from modern mixtures. I suppose it would be a labour of love rather than a commercial proposition to reselect these separate colours.

I like to see Virginia stocks scattered or raked into gravel or left to self-sow. I like a few in raised beds too, where although the purists may look down on them – simply because they're annuals, I'm afraid – they are still very pretty.

Just an aside: if you ever come across seed of *Malcolmia littorea*, give it a try. It has narrow grey leaves on a rather floppy plant with large pink flowers.

## Malope *(Malvaceae)*

*CL:* Closely allied to *Lavatera*, *Malope trifida* is my favourite annual mallow. Time was when Sutton's offered it in separated red, pink and white selections as well as mixed; now, not at all. The process of streamlining has cut their range of species, and that of other seed houses, to the bone. Thompson & Morgan and Chiltern Seeds are the major exceptions. They offer *M. trifida* 'Grandiflora' and 'Vulcan', which are as good as any with crimson red funnels. At the base of these, the petals narrow revealing green, translucent slits (the calyx), which shine like slivers of stained glass when the light is behind them.

*GR:* The white form does still exist – it's called 'White Queen'. But its flowers are so much smaller than those of 'Vulcan' that nobody bothers to list it any more. In France a pink is still to be had.

*CL:* Plants grow to 3 ft and need a stake apiece. From a May sowing (I follow lupins with them), they'll flower till November if the autumn remains open. Prick the seedlings off into pots to minimize root disturbance.

## Malva *(Malvaceae)*

*CL:* The common mallow, *Malva sylvestris*, a true perennial, looks exciting in the run up to flowering but then disappoints, the flowers themselves being small and in need of being sent to the laundry. *M.s. mauritanicus* (*mauritiana*) has much more personality. Treat it as a hardy annual, though some plants will do a second year. A sparsely branching plant, it quickly runs up to 6 ft or more and needs a strong stake. The rounded leaves, on long stalks, are coarse but the flowers are exciting – semi-double and densely clustered in the leaf axils, their colouring blackcurrant-purple, with a six-week flowering season. This doesn't quite add up to a first-class plant (no malva does), but it is different.

*GR:* This is one of the very best of recent annual introductions and why more seedsmen are not listing it I can't imagine. It's an astonishing plant, whose darkly veined flowers are as much as 2 in across and carried in unbelievably dense clusters.

It will over-winter well if grown in well-drained soil and cut down by at least half in autumn to prevent wind rock loosening the roots.

There seems a little confusion over the name of this plant. Some say it is actually *Lavatera cretica*, while others deny the validity of the *mauritanicus* bit and subsume it into straight *M. sylvestris*. This last idea is especially ludicrous.

Two more worth a mention are 'Zebrinus', which is much more like straight *M. sylvestris* except that the flowers are paler than usual with petals striped in a darker colour. Then there's 'Brave Heart', discovered at the side of the gravel drive at the Dower House, Boughton House by Sir David Scott and introduced after his death by his widow, Valerie Finnis. The petals are unusually large, though far from approaching *mauritanicus*, and deeply notched, giving a strikingly heart-shaped appearance.

*CL:* The deep-rooting perennial *M. alcea fastigiata* is a reliable border plant. It runs up to 5 or 6 ft, needs staking, and has mallow-pink flowers over a long period. Self-sowing is free and a bit of a nuisance.

The same applies to *M. moschata*, the musk mallow. Preferable to the pinkish-flowered type plant is 'Alba', white with a faint pink flush at the centre and nice cut leaves. Only $2\frac{1}{2}$ ft tall and self-supporting. Pretty, but you'd get bored with a lot of it.

## Matthiola *(Cruciferae)*

*CL:* This is the genus of the stock, which is an abbreviation for stock-gillyflower. Stock means stick, stem or trunk, and the longer-lived stocks do develop quite a trunk. The European *Matthiola incana* and our own native sea stock, *M. sinuata*, enter into the parentage of stocks, which have long been among the most popular of cottage garden annuals and biennials. They are less popular now, probably because the seedlings lack appeal at the selling centres. If flowering at that stage, the plants are already ruined through flowering prematurely and before they have had the chance to make decent-sized plants. Starving and overcrowding must never be allowed. The seedlings need to be kept on the move and always with plenty of space, until planted out.

Stocks have a deliciously warm fragrance, that is common to them all (but if you are using them as cut flowers you should always put a few drops of a disinfectant such as Hibitane in the water, to prevent the stems becoming an evil-smelling slime). The difference between single- and double-flowered plants is spectacular, and has to be the exception for those (one keeps stumbling against them) who declare that they always prefer the single, natural flower to gross man-made doubles (they have a point, admittedly).

Various ingeniously devised seed strains have been developed to take care of this preference, so that singles and doubles may be distinguished at the seedling stage. In some strains, doubles make the larger seedlings but are distinguished from the singles mainly by their paler leaves. For this difference to show up clearly, the seedlings, following sowing at 55 or 60°F, need to have the temperature dropped to 50°F or lower, and it is easiest to do your selecting under a grey sky, not in sunlight. In other strains, a notch at the side of the leaf (both in seed leaves and in true leaves) distinguishes the double-flowered plant.

Stocks may be divided into three categories:

(1) For summer bedding.

(2) For cut flowers.

(3) Biennials.

For summer bedding, the dwarfest strains have far less staying power than those of 15 in or more in height. I would avoid dwarf ten-week and dwarf park stocks. On the other hand Beauty of Nice stocks flower for two months at least. They make big, bushy plants and are useful for cutting.

The principal stocks raised as cut flowers for the trade are non-branching column stocks, and these are usually grown under glass. However, it is worth sowing a row, April–May, in the open ground for your own use.

Of biennial stocks, the Bromptons are sown in June–July. It is generally safest to pot them off and over-winter them under cold glass, though botrytis is a danger. I find they need regular protective sprayings with fungicides. East Lothians are a little less hardy and are sown in heat, early in the year. If sown too late, so that they develop in warm weather, quite a lot of the plants will fail to flower. There is an exceptionally good mixed strain of East Lothians called 'Tartan', recently released on the retail market, which should be watched for. Sown in January, it produces bushy, heavily flowered plants in an excellent colour range and, without selection, very few of them are singles. Flowering is from July.

Bromptons sown the previous summer flower in June or even earlier. These are the stocks which sometimes, on light soils and especially in maritime districts like East Lothian itself, make quite long-lived perennials, though they are apt to be weakened by virus disease. This shows up most obviously in streaking of the flower, with a bicolour effect.

The night-scented stock, *M. bicornis*, is a hardy annual nearly always direct-sown in some key spot near which you'll sit and sniff its almond scent after sunset. Its flowers are single, pinky-mauve, and are in a state of collapse by day. It should be smelt but not seen.

*GR:* If you ever get seed, the wild species and single-flowered types which Christopher rightly dismisses for bedding work are valuable in raised beds and sunny, dry gardens. You may be able to collect a little seed while holidaying in the Med. *M. fruticulosa*, *M. tricuspidata* and *M. sinuata* are the ones you're most likely to come across, and all three are good garden plants.

*M. fruticulosa* makes a dense, rounded plant about 15 in high with the usual stock foliage springing from a short, stout, woody trunk. In late spring the plant erupts into spikes of scented pinkish-purple flowers. All these wild stocks are best in sharply drained soil in full sun, and make well-branched plants which usually survive for two to three years. A great deal of seed is usually produced, so it's easy to raise new plants. In the more subdued setting of a dry raised bed, these wild species are perfect.

## Matricaria *(Compositae)*

*GR:* The botanists have been bringing order to what seemed perfectly orderly already by redistributing some of the plants formerly listed under *Matricaria* to other genera. And although most of those grown are now, correctly, *Tanacetum parthenium*, we intend to cover here those with neat pompoms of flowers on aromatic foliage – whatever they're called.

Breeders have got to work on matricarias in recent years, and new longer-flowering varieties in different flower forms, intended for cutting, are available to the trade and would make useful plants for the home gardener – but no seed company has yet seen fit to make them available. The dumpy, hummocky ones are a different matter, but why should it be assumed that all gardeners want is buns?

'Golden Ball', with small yellow poms all summer on plants around a foot high, has little character; the white version, 'White Ball', has a cleaner look. But there's also a white-flowered one with a neat row of petals around a white domed centre, variously known as 'Tom Thumb White Stars' or 'White Gem', and this is very pretty. Planted in a mass, it makes an interesting undulating carpet and needs something stiff and surging to rocket through it – *Lobelia* 'Queen Victoria', perhaps.

*CL:* Better than 'White Stars', I thought, seeing them both at Wisley in their formal garden for bedding out, was the slightly taller (12 in) 'Snow Puffs'. Very neat, pure white poms.

*GR:* A newcomer that looks better than most is 'Santana Lemon', which grows to only about 6 in but spreads out like an alyssum. The flowers are creamy with a yellow centre, and last longer than alyssum.

All are easy to raise as April-sown half-hardy annuals, needing a cooler temperature than most half-hardys to start them off.

## Maurandya *(Scrophulariaceae)*

*GR:* Once again we come to a plant which has migrated from genus to genus according to the unnecessary wilfulness or improved taxonomic understanding (depending upon your prejudice) of botanists: *Maurandya* is often found in *Asarina*.

Unlike the creeping *Asarina procumbens*, this is a half-hardy perennial climber reaching 6–7 ft, usually treated as an annual. Three are usually listed, all with slightly downy leaves and penstemon-like, rather than asarina-like flowers. There's the deep purple *M. lophospermum*, the rosy pink *M. barclaiana* and *M. erubescens*, which comes in a mixture of colours including white, pink and purple.

All need an early start, a high germination temperature and a steady growing period. Plant them out at the end of May in a sunny site in good soil. They are all twiners so need netting or trellis, but I've not found them too successful when encouraged to grow through shrubs.

## Meconopsis *(Papaveraceae)*

*GR:* You might well be in for some surprises if you raise meconopsis from seed; they are such promiscuous devils that you could be faced with a great deal of variation when your seedlings flower. It all depends on the parents from which seed is gathered and the extent to which they are grown in isolation.

Meconopsis have a reputation for being difficult to raise, but research at the National Collection in Durham and by James Cobb, who explains his findings in his essential book on meconopsis, has shown the way. The best compost to use is a peat-based one, though added grit is helpful, especially below the top $\frac{1}{2}$ in of the mix. After sowing the seed finely, dust the surface with just a little sifted compost to keep the seed moist, but not so much that the light the seed needs is excluded.

Sowing should be done no later than February, and the seed-pots should be put in a propagator which will give a night-time minimum of 45°F. The compost must never dry out. Germination should take place in three weeks. Seedlings can be pricked out into deep boxes, using a peat-based compost, when they have two true leaves. Growth is usually rapid, and the plants can be put out later in spring, giving them a long season of growth.

This system will suit species such as *M. betonicifolia*, which is the toughest. Some of the more difficult ones need more careful treatment, and a compost incorporating sphagnum moss has proved successful.

One thing you have to watch with monocarpic species and perennials is that they sometimes rush up to produce a feeble flower and then promptly die on you. Starting them off early to give them time to develop into stout plants by the first winter certainly helps. But cutting out any premature flower stems as soon as they start to emerge is not always successful. James Cobb explains it all.

Once established, *M. betonicifolia* makes a splendid border plant, but most of the others have more specific requirements – acid soil and a humid atmosphere in particular.

## Mentzelia *(Loasaceae)*

*GR:* The flowers look like poppies, but are not. You may find it in catalogues under *Bartonia aurea*, but don't be deceived. *Mentzelia lindleyi* it is, and it's a fine plant for full sun. And unlike most members of its family, it does not sting.

A true annual, it is one of the first to flower from a spring sowing outdoors, sprinting up to about 18 in and bursting into a dashing splash of brilliant yellow. This is the moment to prepare for action, and when the flowers are past their best it's out with the shears and the courage for a sharp haircut is in order. Cut back to about 2 in.

Have the watering can ready too, and the liquid feed, otherwise all you'll have for the rest of the season is a patch of sticks. But if fed and watered, new shoots will appear and it will flower for you again, even if on rather shorter sizes.

## Mesembryanthemum *(Azoaceae)*

*CL:* The popular Livingstone daisy, *Mesembryanthemum criniflorum*, is certainly incorrectly named; it should, perhaps, be *Dorotheanthus belli-diformis*, but will always remain mesembryanthemum in common parlance, this being a rhythmic word (like *Ionopsidium* and *Pentapterygium*) and a pleasure to say. It isn't a real daisy at all, but looks it.

The flowers, on a foot-wide, prostrate plant, stay obstinately shut in dull or wet weather, but when they open to the sun, heaven is let loose. There is no more gladdening sight, and they are readier to please than gazanias.

The colours from a mixed packet include pink, salmon, carmine, yellow, apricot and white, and all look well together. When the plants are well grown, they can be spaced a foot apart and each will make its mark. In a poorly selected mixture, magenta tends to dominate.

Although a succulent, this plant should not be starved or over-crowded. A sunny site is its chief requirement. Flowering is not prolonged, a month at most, and even if you go to the trouble of dead-heading spent blooms, it makes no difference. When using mesembryanthemums I would therefore recommend planting them out in early June, after the wallflowers or other spring bedding, scrapping them in July, and following up with a late-sown annual like heliotrope or with bedding dahlias sown in early May,

The pale yellow 'Lunette' is delightful, and has a bronze-red eye to offset its gleaming rays.

You cannot grow this flower in the same ground for long without running into fungal disease, which suddenly wipes plants out while at the height of their glory.

## Mimulus *(Scrophulariaceae)*

*GR:* Blood-drop emlet, *Mimulus luteus*, with blood-splashed yellow flowers, is from Chile but is now naturalized in Britain, as are one or two others. It's a pretty waterside perennial. But now that plant-breeders and plant-collectors have turned their attention to this genus, we have some especially good forms available.

Recent breeding has led to a number of varieties becoming available for bedding, including, in descending order of size, 'Viva', 'Calypso' and 'Malibu'. Well known for their vibrant red, orange or yellow flowers, they are excellent in shade and in dampish positions generally, but need watering in dry soils and are useless in tubs and baskets unless kept constantly moist. One of their great advantages is that they germinate and flower very quickly, especially if given some warmth and a peat-based compost, though they seem determined to germinate even in the gravel on the greenhouse bench, and can also be sown outside.

These mimulus are good emergency gap-fillers, and given the right site they will persist from year to year.

A plant-collecting trip to South America led by John Watson has given us 'Andean Nymph'. 'It was wallowing in the waters and spray of a classic rock pool and waterfall half-way up the pass,' he writes. 'Indeed one would not have been surprised had a Grecian nymph or two been posing there for an artist ...' But instead of painting this nymph, our ever-so-British explorers dined on cheese, onion and cucumber sandwiches! A most extraordinary picnic for a Chilean mountainside.

'Andean Nymph', in reality probably a new undescribed species, is small and creeping with soft pink flowers, each with a creamy throat. A real beauty, and it comes true from seed if grown in isolation. Perhaps it is this plant that has led to the addition of bicolours to the 'Malibu' mixture.

## Mirabilis *(Nyctaginaceae)*

*GR:* I suppose the marvel of Peru, *Mirabilis jalapa*, is something of a marvel. It has tuberous roots not unlike those of a dahlia, though a little less tender. The tough, woody stems carry large, privet-like leaves and long-tubed, fragrant flowers which open in the afternoon, giving it its other name – the four o'clock plant. The flowers can be magenta, yellow or pink, sometimes white or red. 'Not very marvellous,' you mutter. Fair enough.

But what if I tell you that flowers in two or even three different colours can often be found on the same plant and that individual flowers can even be striped with different colours, or that different shades may colour opposite halves of the same flower? A little more marvellous, I think you'll agree.

Treat as a half-hardy annual. You can lift the tubers in autumn and store them like dahlias.

## Moluccella *(Labiatae)*

*GR:* Bells of Ireland, *Moluccella laevis*, is an unusual and attractive annual flower for drying, with huge, green, papery calyces attractively veined in white. The little pinkish flowers within are of little significance. Generally reaching about 2–3 ft, there is a form known as 'Long Spike' with longer than usual flowering spikes, which received the Award of Merit in 1989, but this form is never identified in catalogues.

Seed germination can be erratic. Winter storage in a cold temperature is sometimes recommended, and a relatively modest germination temperature of 55–60°F seems to work reasonably well. The seed can also be sown outside in rows, where it can be slow, though germination is usually good in the end.

The much taller *M. spinosa* from southern Europe and Syria, with its reddish stems and long spikes of white flowers inside two-lipped calyces, looks well worth introducing.

## Monarda *(Labiatae)*

*GR:* Weeding around plants of sweet bergamot, *Monarda didyma*, is a pleasure even in early spring, when the slightest brushing of the creeping mats of foliage releases their penetrating scent. But, sadly, the flowers from most of the seed-raised varieties lack the purity of the named varieties propagated by division.

And those curious whorls of flowers (fooling the uninitiated into believing them daisies) need to avoid the rather murky shades of some of the seed-raised strains.

The ones we grow are derived from the red *M. didyma*, which prefers a damp soil, and the purple *M. fistulosa*, which is happier in dryer conditions. Both like full sun.

'Cambridge Scarlet' is the famous, sparkling red, and seed is available which will produce a high proportion of good plants. Line them out first and choose the best; even so, to follow the rules to the letter, they shouldn't really carry the 'Cambridge Scarlet' name. Many of the other colours available are rather dingy lilacs and pinks. A strain called 'Panorama' contains scarlet, bright pink, soft pink, salmon and crimson.

Sow in a peat-based compost at any time from March to June, cover the seed very lightly, and put the pots in a propagator at 70°F; germination should take about three weeks.

## Morina *(Morinaceae)*

*GR:* The prickly basal rosette of *Morina longifolia* is reminiscent of a thistle, a teasel or, more accurately, an eryngium. [The crushed leaf gives off a deliciously fresh scent. – *CL*] It throws up slightly spiny stems carrying tiers of white tubular flowers which darken to pink with age. Not entirely hardy, a well-drained but not dry soil in a sunny spot suits it best.

The slightly fleshy roots resent disturbance, so space the seeds widely when sowing so that the roots don't intertwine, or sow individually in small pots. The temperature need not be high, about 55°F, and germination will take up to two months. If you've sown in trays, prick the seedlings out when still small into individual pots to minimize the shock when planting out.

*CL:* From seeing how it thrives in a horribly cold Perthshire garden, I should hazard that this plant *was* hardy. I wish that *M. coulteri*, from Kashmir, with primrose-yellow flowers, could be brought into cultivation.

## Nemesia *(Scrophulariaceae)*

*GR:* A genus with a great potential which is only just beginning to be realized.

Change is coming on two fronts. First, in the annuals, single colours are again appearing. This is coming about as a result of selecting colours out of the current mixtures, selecting the rare new colour in a field-grown seed crop for bulking up, and also by deliberate crossing.

*CL:* It is ironic that in 1927 Suttons were already offering nemesias in twelve selected colours. We have gone mixture-mad of recent years, and are now regretting it.

*GR:* There is plenty of inherent variability in nemesias, and even in the existing mixtures there are some delightful shades that could be worked on. The startling raspberry-red and white 'Mello' was the first of the more recent, and was said to have been developed from a single plant in the seed crop of a mixture. However, what seems to be the same variety, then called 'Aurora', was highly commended in RHS trials in 1951, having been sent by Sluis and Groot from Holland.

It then transpired that what was probably the same thing was grown about the turn of the century as 'National Ensign', and this name has now been resurrected by another company. What seems to be the same thing is grown in Germany as 'Helvetia'; 'Royal Ensign' is a name which is also now used, and yet another company calls it 'St George'. Such completely unnecessary confusion! What's more, there are now two slightly different strains, one a little more compact than the other. But these are never distinguished.

In the same trial 'Orange Prince', with orange flowers and purple marks, was also highly commended; this variety has also now been reintroduced.

'Tapestry' includes some lovely bicolours in lilac and white, and blue and white, together with soft yellows; 'Carnival' has some good fiery shades including a sharp yellow with a red eye.

'Carnival' and 'Funfair' concentrate on fiery shades and are probably the same; 'Tapestry' and 'Pastel' feature paler shades and *are* the same. 'Fire King' is scarlet. 'Mello' is raspberry and white, 'Mello White' (= 'Snow Princess') is white, and 'Blue Bird' is blue – all with small flowers.

The one extra quality that needs breeding in is resistance to drought and hot sun, for while nemesias are wonderful long-lasting plants in the cooler parts of Britain, in the south they can burn out in mid-summer.

Treated as half-hardy annuals, nemesias are easy to raise in a peat-based compost; they are fast-growing and bush out quickly, given the space. Pricking out into small pots rather than trays, or moving them on from trays to 3-in pots, gives them space to develop into good plants before setting out.

They are at their best in damper spots, though they hate water-logging, and provide a spectacular show in north-facing borders or courtyards shaded by walls rather than trees. They are good cut flowers too, though 'Ali Baba', the tetraploid strain bred for cutting, is difficult to get in the UK. 'Jingle Bells' at 14 in will do.

There are also developments on another front: perennial nemesias are beginning to appear from South Africa and could well be developed into a range of hardier seed-raised strains. Look out for them in the late 1990s.

*CL:* Accepting that nemesias may have a short life but are still worth growing, they can be raised from a late March sowing, planted to follow the spring bedding, scrapped in July, when running to seed, and can themselves be followed by an annual or by bedding dahlias, sown in May. High-maintenance gardening this may be, but why not? In these days when so many plots are far smaller than we should like them to be, intensive rotations make sense.

## Nemophila *(Hydrophyllaceae)*

*CL:* Two excellent, low-growing Californian annuals here, both hardy. *Nemophila menziesii* (*N. insignis*) is the better known – as baby blue eyes. Baby white eyes would be more accurate. Most of the flower is true sky-blue, and that's a colour we can't have too much of.

*N. maculata*, the five spot, has white, slightly purple-veined, cup-shaped flowers with a violet purple blotch at the tip of each of its five petals. I usually sow it in September, over-winter the seedlings under cold glass, and plant them out into my mixed border (the plants are 6–8 in tall) in early spring. It then flowers in May, and the public adore it, though they are annoyed to find it's 'only an annual' (I could strangle them). It can be sown in spring to flower a little later, and also self-sows. It does not enjoy root disturbance.

*GR:* Both these species demand a soil which does not dry out. In a dry spell they vanish.

Occasionally a plant with pure white flowers may turn up among a patch of *N. menziesii*. Collect seed from it, or even root a few cuttings, and you can keep it going – which is well worthwhile.

Unusual variants of *N. maculata* also appear occasionally. I've had plants with smaller but completely purple flowers, and also one with white flowers completely covered in tiny purple dots – demure but very pretty.

## Nepeta *(Labiatae)*

*CL:* The popular mauve edging plant *Nepeta mussinii* (often synonymous with *N. × faassenii*), can be grown from seed sown in spring under glass (though it is more often grown from cuttings), and is reliably perennial if the soil is well drained. For my money I would prefer *N. nervosa*, which I have seen more frequently in Scotland than in England. It has upright blue spikes, no more than a foot tall. It is excellent from seed, flowering in its first year, and makes a good contrast as a foreground to crimson roses.

*N. govaniana* is a very different plant, 2 – 3 ft tall and rather preferring moist shade. Its flowers are pale yellow, in loose sprays. Sometimes I like it; sometimes I feel it's slightly lacking in personality. It needs to be strengthened with a brighter flower near by. It can be treated as an annual – in fact, the plants often fade out in winter.

## Nicotiana *(Solanaceae)*

*GR:* If the greenhouse effect continues to raise our winter temperatures ... [Come off it, Graham; have you forgotten the three consecutive dire and destructive winters of 1984/5, 1985/6 and 1986/7? – *CL*] Not at all! In the gravelly, well-drained soil of my previous garden, nicotianas over-wintered in two out of those three years. But they wouldn't on Christopher's clay, or the heavier soil in my present garden. Where was I? Oh yes. If our winters continue to become generally warmer, tobacco plants will soon be treated as hardy perennials. After all, they *are* perennial and I've found them hardy in the east Midlands in maybe three winters out of five. The plants make fat, fleshy, yellow-coloured roots which often regrow even if cut up while forking through the border.

But I digress; this is a book about raising plants from seed ...

Nicotianas are easy to raise from a March sowing in a peat-based compost at about 70°F as long as the seed is very lightly covered. They will be through in a fortnight. The smaller varieties can be pricked out into trays, while the larger ones, such as *N. alata* 'Grandiflora', are best moved on to pots before planting out.

The standard bedding variety is now the F1 hybrid 'Domino', a significant improvement, with the face of the flowers turned upward to give a better show when one is looking down on the plants. 'Roulette' is a cheaper F2 version. Unfortunately not only is there no scent, but the popular 'Lime Green' colour is rather poor compared with good strains of the taller variety, known simply as 'Lime Green'.

The much taller 'Sensation' is scented and has a very wide range of colours, including peachy and apricot shades, many with darker shades on the backs of the petals. The flowers are sometimes so large that the petals flop under their own weight.

The best scent comes from the tall, pure white *N. alata* 'Grandiflora' and from the tight white heads of *N. sylvestris*. The former is in the standard tobacco plant form, but in the latter the long-tubed, white flowers are clustered together in dense heads and hang down elegantly. Both can reach 4–5 ft.

*CL:* N. *sylvestris* has much the sturdier and more architectural habit, its large, bright green paddle leaves quite a feature in themselves. Its flowers do not collapse nearly so markedly during the day and its night scent is creamier, less rough than *alata*'s, delicious though that is. It looks good with cannas.

*GR:* Finally the delightful N. *langsdorffii*, the one which brings the green to 'Lime Green'. The flowers are like small bells with a constriction at the top – like a woman in a crinoline perhaps; they are carried well spaced out along slender branches. The colour is deep apple green and they look wonderful with *Salvia patens* 'Cambridge Blue'.

'Domino White' looks good with silvery *Senecio cineraria* 'Cirrus' and with a soft pink geranium like 'Appleblossom Orbit'. 'Lime Green' is good with the yellow flowers and filamentous foliage of *Bidens ferulifolia*, or with the lemony-lime foliage of *Helichrysum petiolare* 'Limelight'. N. *alata* is a fine mixed border plant, and shows up brightly in front of a purple-leaved smoke bush.

*CL:* There is strong evidence that, after a number of years in the same piece of ground, nicotianas suffer from replant disease, like polyanthus, lilies and roses. Take the hint and change the site (or the soil).

## Nierembergia *(Solanaceae)*

*CL: Nierembergia hippomanica*, from the south of South America, makes a bushy, fine-leaved plant about a foot tall and covers itself with cup-shaped flowers, about 1 in across, over a long season and until frosts intervene. In the wild its colouring is generally weak and pale, but the selection 'Purple Robe' is rich violet and comes pretty true from seed.

It should be sown early, in a heated propagator in January–February, if you can keep the plants happy and growing until planted out in late May or June. With our cool summers, the plant's chief trouble is in developing sufficiently to flower well in its first year (it does a lot better in New England). However, the plant is perennial and is well worth lifting and potting up, in autumn, and over-wintering under glass. Indeed, if the winter is mild, it will survive comfortably outside and perform much better in its second year.

## Nigella *(Ranunculaceae)*

*CL:* The traditional love-in-a-mist (or devil-in-a-bush, if we're speaking of its seed-heads) is *Nigella damascena*, and the blue strain named after Miss Jekyll is still going strong. The flowers open pale, but mature to an intense pure shade of sky-blue such as we all find irresistible. The leaves are fine filigree. It is a hardy, self-sowing annual (but resentful of transplanting) and grows about 18 in tall. It looks charming with the red flax, *Linum grandiflorum* 'Rubrum', or indeed with almost any flower of any colour; not with another blue flower, though – blue is a colour that benefits from contrast.

'Miss Jekyll' is so good that I have never introduced any other strain of *N. damascena* to my garden for fear of contamination, but the others are good in their own way, including the 'Persian Jewels' mixture.

Do, as a change, try *N. hispanica*, another hardy species with great personality: bluish petals and a wonderful pattern of stamens, red anthers and dark centre. The seed-pods are handsome and are worth drying for winter decoration.

Nigellas should be sown direct by broadcasting seed in autumn or spring.

*GR:* The ghastly 'Dwarf Moody Blue', a horribly dumpy thing reaching only about 6 in, should be avoided at all costs.


## Nolana *(Nolanaceae)*

*GR:* Only the pretty trailing varieties of nolana are usually grown, and at present only one of them seems to be listed in catalogues. *N. paradoxa* 'Blue Bird' is a broadly-spreading trailer with blue flowers rather like a convolvulus, each with a white eye and a broad yellow throat. The flowers look a little like pale versions of *Convolvulus minor* 'Blue Ensign'. They stay closed on dull, chilly days.

Raise them as half-hardy annuals. The seed is quite large and easy to handle, presenting no special problems; the seedlings should emerge after about ten days at 70°F. When planted out they make a wide, low mat with the trumpet-shaped flowers facing up towards you. Thriving on most soils, in hot dry sites they make more compact plants but tend to fizzle out before the end of summer – perhaps because they're impossible to dead-head. They certainly set a lot of seed.

Try them planted under the glaucous foliage and yellow flowers of *Linaria genistifolia* or among *Artemisia* 'Valerie Finnis'. Alternatively, allow them to ramble through *Verbena* 'Silver Anne'.

Interestingly, many seed companies had both this variety and 'Lavender Gown' on trial a few years back, but no one bothered to introduce the lavender-flowered variety.


## Ocimum *(Labiatae)*

*GR:* Basil, *Ocimum basilicum*, may not seem an especially ornamental plant, but there are three varieties which are worth growing for their foliage. They are all rather delicate plants, needing half-hardy annual treatment, careful hardening off and special consideration as to their summer homes. Being tropical plants from Africa and the Pacific islands, the basils need sun and shelter and should not be put outside too early – the middle or the end of June is soon enough. A light but rich soil is best.

*CL:* On my heavy soil, I have never made a success of them. I grow my pot of basil under glass.

*GR:* The three varieties worth considering from the ornamental point of view are 'Dark Opal', 'Purple Ruffles' and 'Green Ruffles', although others such as anise basil and neapolitana basil are quite pretty.

'Dark Opal' has large purple leaves and pink flowers and is by far the best of the three. The ruffled types have heavily crimped and fringed leaves – one in green, the other in purple. I've found these two even more delicate than 'Dark Opal'.

Try 'Dark Opal' in front of rue, among silvery gazanias or with *Tanacetum parthenium* 'Golden Ball'.


## Oenothera *(Onagraceae)*

*CL:* Pronounced Eenothera, as the first two letters are a diphthong.

These are loosely classified as evening primroses, though some open by day and close by night. The two best-known night-flowering species are sweetly scented, and these are the ones we always grow from seed, generally treating them as biennials, though *Oenothera stricta* may do a second term. It is very like *O. biennis*, but occurs in a pale primrose-yellow form as well as the usual bright yellow, which makes a change. It grows to $2\frac{1}{2}$–3 ft.

*O. erythrosepala* (*O. lamarckiana*) is built on the grand scale, rising to 7 ft in its second year and making a branching candelabrum (good if dried, at the end of the year) whereon large, bowl-shaped yellow blooms open at dusk over a long summer season. As it is tap-rooted, you should either sow direct or transplant young. These evening primroses will self-sow. [Sometimes too enthusiastically, I'm afraid. – GR] The flowers open at dusk, almost too late to be enjoyed by the average, hard-working gardener, but they persist into the following morning, especially if this is dull.

Although night-flowering, the perennial *O. missouriensis* (the synonym *O. macrocarpa* highlights its large, flanged seed-pods) persists through most of the day. It is a prostrate ground cover plant of spidery habit, with large yellow blooms. The seed germinates easily but damps off equally easily if not protected by fungicide.

*GR:* Many of the lower-growing American species are now being listed more regularly. These tend to be sprawling in habit, some with flowers up to 3 in across. They may be pink flowers, or white ageing to pink, and are usually biennials or short-lived perennials. *O. albicaulis*, *O. pallida* and *O. texensis* look especially good, and I suggest trying them whenever you see them listed.

## Omphalodes *(Boraginaceae)*

*CL:* The annual *Omphalodes linifolia* is a charmer and far too little known, one reason being that for quite a few years no one was offering it. But it is available again. This is a hardy, self-sowing annual, with grey leaves and loose spikes of white flowers not unlike a gypsophila's but a whole lot better. From autumn seedlings, flowering is in May–June. The plant is no more than a foot tall, upright-growing, and looks fresh and cheering near to cushions of yellow helianthemums (sun roses). Spring sowings flower later. On heavy soils like mine, this navelwort tends to die out and need renewing, but it is self-perpetuating on lighter fare.

*GR:* Although a prolific self-sower in light soils, *O. linifolia* rarely smothers its neighbours, and if it spreads rather more than you wish, you can pull it out easily. It looks good with so many plants which are likely to share its love of good drainage that you can allow it to find its own home. I'd be inclined to set a pinch around helianthemums as Christopher recommends – try the grey-leaved, pink-flowered 'Rhodanthe Carneum' and the double red 'Mrs C.W. Earle', as well as a yellow such as 'Golden Queen' or 'Boughton Double Primrose'. I'd also suggest scattering a few among maiden pinks and to soften magenta penstemons.

*CL:* The hardy perennial *O. cappadocica* is one of our finest shade-loving perennials for spring flowering. Its rich blue, forget-me-not flowers are in bloom for two months. It self-sows quite readily, or you can collect seed.

## Onopordum *(Compositae)*

*GR:* Well, you either love them or you don't; personally I think they're wonderful. Huge candelabras covered in silvery down (not to mention nasty spines), surging up from big spiny rosettes, create a genuinely awesome effect – at least for those who have not seen them before.

And they are big. The Scotch cotton thistle, *Onopordum acanthium*, reaches about 4–6 ft, but the Mediterranean *O. arabicum*, which is really the one to grow (except for patriotic reasons), may reach as much as 8–9 ft.

The problem with plants of such gigantic proportions is that they elbow everything else out of the way. What starts off as a little silvery rosette soon reaches 2 ft across, smothering everything within reach. Then when the flower stem starts to grow and to spread, its widely branching habit becomes a danger to even more plants. Finally, when, in spite of the most conscientious staking, a rainstorm blows the soaring monster over, most of the border, not to mention the shed and greenhouse, is in danger.

Grow it, without neighbours, against a dark background like a yew hedge which will show it off well, but beware of self-sown seedlings whose rosettes can expand uncomfortably quickly in choice alpine cushions. An ideal plant for a new garden or a huge tub.

*CL:* Despite presents of seed from kind friends, I have managed to avoid growing this biennial in my garden so far. I enjoy seeing it in yours, where I don't have to handle it. When running to seed it looks horribly tarnished and is seldom extracted in time.

## Osteospermum *(Compositae)*

*GR:* Botanists have had their fun with *Osteospermum*, *Tripteris* and *Dimorphotheca* over the years – lumping, splitting and redistributing species – so there's no telling where you'll find them in catalogues.

We can definitely say that *Tripteris* rightly belongs here under *Osteospermum* while this and *Dimorphotheca* contain both annuals and biennials. In case you're interested, the difference is that in the former the disc florets set no seed, while in the latter both disc and ray florets set seed. (Now the next time you visit Dixter you'd better not be caught on your hands and knees pulling seed-heads to bits to check what Christopher is growing.)

The perennials are fast becoming very popular, and new forms are turning up all the time. The finest are raised from cuttings, and the best of the seed-raised perennials, 'Starshine', though a good variety, lacks a certain refinement. Bred in Britain by veteran plant breeder Ralph Gould and with hardiness much in mind, the plants also spread well, as much as 18 in in good soil and a sunny site. The 2-in daisies are restricted in colour to a range of pinks plus white.

They are easy enough to raise, germinating in about a fortnight at 70°F. Once planted, they are generally very tolerant – though sunshine is essential. This is a case when raising as many plants as you can, planting out a big group on a sunny bank and then rooting cuttings of your favourite forms is probably a good plan.

*CL: Osteospermum (Tripteris) hyoseroides* is one of my favourite annuals, and I like to have some every year, mixed up with grey-leaved *Ballota pseudodictamnus*, *Briza maxima*, and the blue of *Cynoglossum amabile* or of a biennial campanula like rampion, *C. rapunculus*. Give it half-hardy treatment and plant out before it gets drawn. Even then, I prefer to give each plant a little support. It grows 18 in tall and produces a long succession of the brightest, freshest-looking orange daisies with dark centres. Around noon, the rays roll back and the display is over till the next morning. Often listed as 'Gaiety'.

## Paeonia *(Paeoniaceae)*

*CL:* Although peonies have now been hived off into their own family, they belong far more obviously where they always were, to *Ranunculaceae*.

If you have to pay a lot of money for a choice species such as the yellow *Paeonia mlokosewitschii*, or the white, purple-leaved *P. obovata alba*, consider that it has certainly been raised from seed and that it takes about five years to obtain a flowering plant.

Since peony seeds are fleshy and rather soft, they need to be sown fresh and before they have shrivelled. This is easy enough when collected from your own garden, but explains why marketed peony seed so often fails through having been kept hanging around.

Peony seed needs no coddling. Leave the container where it is sown, in a plunge bed outside. The first year produces no signs of activity but in fact a root is put out. In the second year, the first leaf appears.

The showy, June-flowering *lactiflora* peonies quite often ripen seed, and you can raise some pleasing hybrids of your own in this way. The large, shining black seeds are anyway irresistible. Something must be done with them.

*GR:* Tree peonies can also be raised from seed, as you will realize if you look at undisturbed ground under a mature plant. But they too have a dormancy problem. Roots will often grow fairly promptly, but before a shoot will develop a cold spell and then a warm spell are needed.

This is a case where the salad box and the vermiculite are perhaps the necessary equipment (see page 13).

The yellow-flowered *P. lutea* and *P. ludlowii* have now been reduced to subspecies of the blood-red *P. delavayi*, which may account for the fact that the yellow and the red hybridize if grown together; you can help them of course. You may get a brighter, more cheerful red, or an orange yellow with red picotee.

## Papaver *(Papaveraceae)*

*GR:* The delightful simplicity and elegance of a poppy is always a pleasure, from the tightly furled bud to the opening of the crimped and crinkled petals and finally the stunningly effective yet simple seed-pots. The valves at the top allow the wind to shake the seed out only when it's strong enough to blow it a good distance, and that seed can survive buried for at least 100 years, only to burst into growth when suddenly brought to the surface.

Annual poppies are the easiest thing in the world to raise, in spite of their small seed. Choose a sunny spot in fertile, but not rich, soil. Have none of this sadistic notion that they like spartan conditions. Sow them outside in spring where they are to flower, and thin them out conscientiously, keeping in mind the eventual size and scale of full-grown plants. Dead simple!

The three annual species that you're most likely to meet in catalogues are *Papaver commutatum, P. rhoeas* and *P. somniferum.*

The first of these is a large-flowered standard red poppy which is characterized by a bold black blotch at the base of each petal. The variety 'Ladybird' is the one usually met with.

Our native corn poppy, *P. rhoeas,* has given rise to many different forms over the years. Those raised by the Reverend Wilkes at Shirley in Surrey were once pre-eminent in gardens. Unfortunately it's now impossible to be sure that what you ask for is what you get.

The 'Reverend Wilkes Strain' was once a mixture of semi-double and single flowers but now is often all single. It should also be restricted to reds, pinks and white and include picotees and bicolours, but these two forms are sometimes rather sparsely represented. Some of the picotees – white with a carmine edging, for example – are delightful.

The last time I grew these I simply flung the seed in a wide arc across a mixed border and left it all to its own devices. It would have made a wonderful show had there been far more pinks and far fewer bright reds. Poppy red is fine in the right place, but not all the way through a mixed border. This preponderance of reds is due, quite simply, to bad roguing by the seed supplier. It's infuriating. One of my too many retirement projects is to select out the most beautiful colours from this and the following poppy mixture so that they will be available separately. Christopher will think I'm potty.

*CL:* Not in the least – dead sane on this occasion (chalk it up). *P. rhoeas* will always have a tendency to revert to the single scarlet wild type, as *P. somniferum* will to the single wan mauve. We need constantly to fight to retain the wider range in flower form and colour.

*GR:* The good clergyman's 'Shirley' strain should be double-flowered, but often contains only a few doubles, and originally contained no reds at all; reds usually now turn up. Hmmm.

The most recent mixture to become widely available is 'Mother of Pearl', formerly (incorrectly) known as 'Fairy Wings'. This originated with Sir Cedric Morris, who was an inspiration to many. It was a purely pastel mixture, and Sir Cedric ruthlessly pulled up any that reverted to poppy-red. Seed passed to another great plantsperson, Valerie Finnis, and from her into the seed trade. There's an astonishing dove grey, a dusty pink, delicate lilac – grow it yourself and see how many soft shades you find. It will self-sow, so do pull out any reds as there should be none. This does not stop some seed-suppliers ensuring that reds are present, presumably under the philistine impression that the widest possible range of shades is always the best. We've still got a lot of work to do, Christopher.

I'm sure scattering them through the border is the way to grow all these poppy mixtures. Sow a few seeds here and there (or in a grand sweep) and allow them to flower where they fall. Pull out those you don't like and leave those you do. With so many shades you will get some lovely associations – and some ghastly ones!

Finally, there's the opium poppy, *P. somniferum*. The wild species is good in its distinctive pink with its glaucous foliage, but there are also some lovely varieties. 'Peony Flowered Mixed' contains some astonishing shades, with a dense double peony flower form. They were once available separately, but now only the salmon and the white are listed. I especially liked the dark velvety maroon which was almost black, the almost gold and the deep red.

There are also forms with especially large pods (not for illicit purposes but for flower-arranging), and a hen-and-chickens form too.

'Summer Breeze' is different from all these. Derived from perennials but grown as a bedder, the orange, yellow or white flowers really shimmer.

And now over to Christopher for the biennials and perennials.

*CL:* The Iceland poppy, *P. nudicaule* (which you won't find in Iceland) is generally treated as a biennial in this country, where it is a popular cut flower. At the Van Duesen show gardens in Vancouver, however, it lasts for three or four years at least and makes a grandly garish display in June with yellow *Allium moly* and carmine ixias.

Seed is very small, and should be sown in spring under glass on a peat-based compost and not covered; it must have light to germinate. No poppy enjoys root disturbance, so prick off into individual peat pots before planting out.

Orange is the natural Iceland poppy colour, with yellow and white as close runners-up. These you'll find in the 'Garden Gnome' mixture, whose foot-short stems are the answer to a tendency in Iceland poppies to blow sideways. 'Oregon Rainbows' includes a wide range of carmine, pink and apricot, as well as the usual shades. Valerie Finnis developed a particularly large-flowered strain called 'Constance Finnis', but I have my doubts as to whether this extra size is a practical advantage.

The early summer-flowering oriental poppies are now receiving attention from the breeders of seed strains. In a recent RHS trial, a blood-red-flowered strain called 'Beauty of Livermore', similar in appearance to *P. orientale bracteatum*, was voted an Award of Merit. Mixed seed strains are still very mixed. For example, 'Allegro' gives rise to a great many worthless plants, though you could segregate the few that seemed worthwhile. From seed sown under glass in spring, a good flowering will be obtained in the following year.

*P. spicatum* (syn. *P. heldreichii*) is a lovely perennial species with softly furry grey foliage. It flowers at $2\frac{1}{2}$ ft, the top bloom opening first, followed by a succession, in groups of three, down the length of most of the stem. The colour is apricot, and the flowers are not small but they shatter at midday, like a cistus's. Easy from seed, flowering in year two.

## Pelargonium *(Geraniaceae)*

*GR:* Any seed company which can persuade gardeners to pay more for a single seed than for a growing plant is clearly not heading for bankruptcy. So 'geraniums', as we shall continue to call them, should keep them solvent for many years yet.

'Summer Showers' is an ivy-leaved geranium mixture of, to put it charitably, mediocre quality. A single seed will cost you more than a sturdy rooted cutting of any one of the best vegetatively propagated varieties. And if, as sometimes happens, only one or two seeds from a packet of six actually germinate (and they then have to be raised to planting-out size), seed-raised plants become very expensive indeed.

But, almost in spite of ourselves, we have been seduced by the seed companies into raising geraniums from seed. So every year we (although probably not Christopher) scan the glossy pages in the catalogues for the new varieties.

To be fair, there are some good ones. Most of these have been developed relatively recently and make good outdoor bedders, with a tendency to produce more flower-heads than old cuttings-raised varieties and to recover better after bad weather.

Forget old names like 'Sprinter' and 'Double Steady Red'; we can trip off a few more promising names – 'Pinto', 'Diamond', 'Sensation', 'Multibloom' – and these will all produce exceptionally colourful plants. The British-bred 'Sensation' is one of the best. The plants are bushy and spreading, covered with flower-heads all summer, and they recover rapidly after a thunderstorm. The florets are not densely crowded, so are very rarely plagued with botrytis after rain.

The only problem with using these plants for bedding is that they are very uniform, while cuttings-raised plants often develop a slightly uneven shape which I find rather appealing.

As with petunias, marigolds and impatiens, there are too many geranium varieties. And to be honest, I'm becoming rather tired of the constant succession of 'better than ever before' varieties. All come in series with supposedly encouraging names and up to fourteen colours; and all more or less the same. 'Century', 'Ringo', 'Sundance', 'Orbit', 'Hollywood' – most gardeners can't tell them apart and it doesn't really matter. At least in Britain we've raised some which are genuinely different, while the Dutch and American breeders plod on in the same old way.

So let me help by recommending some I have grown and by picking out others to avoid at all costs. I'm sure that it's no coincidence that the best for Britain are *bred* in Britain.

As I write, 'Sensation' is only to be had as a mixture of five colours, although the separate colours will soon be available. This variety, with more wild species in its blood than most, represents something of a departure from the traditional bedding type, as does 'Scarlet Diamond', from East Germany. This is a fine traditional scarlet, but with spreading growth and many flower-heads, and to thrive it needs good soil, watering in hot summers and regular dead-heading. 'Scarlet Diamond' has already started to slip from catalogues but is the best for growing with silver foliage – if you like that sort of thing.

'Gala' is a more traditional type in as many shades as you can possibly want, but does not end up as leafy and large as most.

'Video' and 'Breakaway' are quite different again. 'Video' is poor in a mixed border except in a small confined space – it is just too resolutely compact and so easily smothered. But it makes a good container plant and has character; its foliage is especially dark.

'Breakaway' has an exceptionally flat and spreading habit. One plant can reach 2 ft across, and although it is intended for hanging baskets, I grow it in the mixed border, where its unusual habit and narrow-petalled flowers help it fit in much better. Unfortunately, it comes in only two colours – red and salmon.

If you are especially keen on dark leaf-zoning, the salmon pink 'Chérie' is the best, while the scarlet-flowered 'Ringo Deep Scarlet' and 'Mustang' are also good. No whites are zoned.

Now a few that should never make the starting line. Growing 'Summer Showers' is pointless, as cuttings-raised varieties are so much better. 'Sprinter' may have been in the lead once, but is now a tail-ender, slow to start flowering and with the most foliage relative to the number of flowers. None of the doubles are worth growing at all; they end up as very tall leafy bushes with only the occasional flower. 'Red Élite' may flower early but is poor later.

With one exception, only the F1 hybrids are worth growing, so forget all the others, which tend to tall and leafy growth at the expense of flowers. 'Lucky Break' is the exception, and is similar to the 'Diamond' varieties but includes the very unusual white with a pink eye – which you can keep going from cuttings. But it needs good growing conditions.

I've tended to grow geraniums in mixed containers with at least some foliage plants, for as the garden is not formal, opportunities in borders are few. So, in a carefully planned variant of the old red, white and blue, you could choose 'Sensation Scarlet', 'Scarlet Diamond' or 'Ringo Deep Scarlet' geraniums with lobelia 'Crystal Palace' in very

Late season annuals following lupins: zinnias (front), *Rudbeckia* 'Irish Eyes' and *Tithonia rotundifolia* 'Torch' (back).

43. The wild Californian poppy, *Eschscholtzia californica*, has an attractive simplicity.

44. The sultry red flowers of the 'Empress of India' nasturtium look well set against its blue-tinted foliage.

45. *Gazania* 'Sundance' comes in a fiery mixture of colours.

A sparkling poppy for summer bedding, 'Summer Breeze' was developed using carefully selected wild species.

A June evening in the Long Border, Dixter. White *Allium neapolitanum*, *A. christophii*, foxgloves and golden elm.

48. In a broad but bold mixture of colours, the 'Beauty' strain of *Phlox drummondii* flowers over a long season.

49. An old variety, but still one of the best: *God* 'Unwin's Dwarf Mixed'.

50. The 'Florestan' carnation strain is best treated as biennial. It is seen here with *Phlox* 'Mia Ruy' and *Geranium* 'Russell Prichard'.

51. Silky *Salvia argentea* is a self-sowing biennial for sunny, well-drained spots.

The Swan River daisy, *Brachycome iberidifolia* 'Purple Splendour', infiltrated by *Helichrysum petiolare*.

53. An F1 strain of zinnia, 'Pacific Yellow'.

54. A yew background for the foxtail lily, *Eremu robustus*, which is slow to mature from seed.

55. The bright green of *Kochia tricophylla* 'Childsii' with the yellow daisies of *Bidens ferulifolia* at K

56. *Smyrnium perfoliatum* lights up shady places in late spring and self-sows reliably.

Never happier nor hardier than in a wall, antirrhinums become perennial. These were photographed in Northumberland.

58. Pots of seed-raised *Lilium formosanum* flowering in late September.

59. The wand-flower, *Dierama pulcherrimum*, as a tall feature in paving, with the Mexican daisy, *Er* *karvinskianus*. Both self-sow.

deep blue with dark foliage. Add an occasional loose mound of the grey-leaved *Pleiostachys serpyllifolius* (from cuttings).

Starting with the best of the whites, 'Gala White', add the greyish *Verbena* 'Polaris', planted widely so as not to block out the white. The shining red foliage of the beetroot 'MacGregor's Favourite' makes a surprisingly effective addition.

'Breakaway Red' will hold its own against the creeping *Artemisia* 'Valerie Finnis', and the dark leaves of 'Video Blush' set off the shoots of the blue-grey *Acaena affinis*. Other good foliage companions might be silvered helichrysums, cinerarias or artemisias, yellow *Helichrysum petiolare* 'Limelight', parsley, and variegated plectranthus.

Always choose varieties in separate colours, or sow sufficiently early to ensure that you can identify the colours before you plant them out.

Many pages could be written on how to raise geraniums from seed – I've done it myself in my annuals book. But it can all be conveniently reduced to a few crucial points. Do not sow too late, especially if you have to grow them cool; mid-February to mid-March is about right. Keep the temperature constant and high, at least 70°F, during germination, and prick out into individual pots while the seedlings are still small. Keep growing well until planting. Geraniums are not difficult to raise, but it's particularly important to keep the temperature high early on.

Geraniums inspire strong feelings – sheets of scarlet in seaside parks do not inspire the plantsman. But like so many plants, careful choice of colours and imaginative selection of companion plants can bring out their best qualities.

## Penstemon *(Scrophulariaceae)*

GR: The resurgence of enthusiasm for penstemons has been based mainly around the older cuttings-raised varieties, and some newer varieties in the same mould. Seed of some of the wild species is sometimes available from specialists, and the seed lists usually list a number of alpine species. But most of those available are mixtures of one sort or another, intended for bedding out.

These penstemons are easy to raise as half-hardy annuals but will also survive mild winters outside, especially in well-drained soil.

To be honest, I quite like a big flashy bedful of 'Hyacinth Flowered Mixed' (also known as 'Skyline'). They combine brilliant colouring – in reds, pinks, purple and deep blue, most with white throats – with an elegance that the plant breeders have not succeeded in removing. True, the plants are short in habit and the flowers are carried all round the stems. But while this has ruined foxgloves, penstemons seem to have stood it well. Plant them in a group, backed by evergreens or spring-flowered shrubs.

In warmer areas, where they'll probably survive for some years, you can discard the ones you don't like and fill the gaps with plants raised from cuttings taken from the best.

*CL:* The great advantage in a batch of mixed penstemons is that none of the colours clash – all are in the pink, carmine, mauve and purple range. Another good point, when used for bedding, is that they have a later flowering season than most seeds that we treat as biennials. For this purpose, sow in early August and over-winter under cold glass, planting out the following spring. The large-flowered gloxinia types are rather splendid.

## Perilla *(Labiatae)*

*CL:* Grown as half-hardy annuals, the purple-leaved forms of *P. fru-tescens* were once popular foliage plants and should still be, in my opinion. [In mine too. – GR] Growing about 2 ft tall, their rich colouring handsomely offsets an orange- or lemon-yellow-flowered African marigold, for instance. I prefer the plain, heart-shaped leaf, but you more often come across heavily frilled strains ('Crispa', 'Laciniata', 'Nankinensis').

Even these have dropped out of the principal seed lists and must be sought from specialists in herb seeds. Perilla leaves are pleasant to nibble. These are short-day plants, not flowering till autumn. The flowers have no merit anyway, but in our climate seed is never set in time before autumn's end and so it always has to be imported.

*GR:* Apparently perilla is an unpredictable seeder, and the unaccountable failure of seed crops is the reason for its irritating absence from seed lists. 'Many forms are listed in catalogues' (no longer, alas), a book from the 1950s tells me – including one with white-spotted foliage which presumably has the look of a hypoestes about it; hmmm.

'Shiso Red' is the one you are likely to find now, in the Suffolk Herbs list at least, but this is a crisped variety. Try it with marigold 'Red Seven Star' in front or *Tithonia* 'Torch' behind. *Lobelia* 'Compliment Scarlet', *Cladanthus arabicus, Lobelia valida* and variegated chlorophytum all make good companions – though perhaps not all together.

Sow in a pot under heated glass in March–April.

## Petunia *(Solanaceae)*

*GR:* The first rule to remember about petunias is this: be selective. There are such a vast number of varieties – some are impressively unpleasant, most are cheerful bedders for containers or sheltered beds, a few are exquisite – that a little thoughtful catalogue-browsing really does pay. One commercial seedsman offers 118 varieties, one mail order company thirty-one.

Not only are there so many varieties, but they come and go with such bewildering speed that in a few years you may not be able to find the ones we recommend.

In general, however, the very palest lilacs, blues and blush pinks, together with whites, are the most successful – 'Supercascade Lilac', 'Chiffon Magic' and 'Supermagic White'. The powerful startling colours can be more difficult to use except in the most flamboyant bedding schemes, but if you like them, the white-edged 'Red Picotee' and 'Blue Picotee' are dazzling. Yellows are a complete wash-out.

For planting in mixed borders or in informal bedding schemes, the smaller-flowered multiflora types are generally the most suitable. These are fine in containers too, but you also have the option of the larger-flowered grandifloras, for which shelter and warmth are more important. All are pathetic in cool wet weather; doubles are suitable only for conservatories or greenhouses – if you can bear to look at them at all.

Raising petunias is something that many people find tricky, and if you would rather not try you don't have to; seedlings are available from most of the mail order seed companies.

Sow the seed in March on the surface of a peat-based seed compost, but don't cover it, as some varieties need light to germinate. Cover the pots with clingfilm to keep the seed moist, and put brown paper over the top; enough light will penetrate. Keep at a temperature of 65–70°F.

When the seed has started to germinate, sift on a little fine compost to help the new roots take hold. Remove the polythene as soon as the seed-leaves have opened.

Prick out the seedlings into trays as soon as they are large enough to handle, and reduce the temperature a little. When they are established they can be grown even cooler, about 45°F; bushiness is encouraged at cooler temperatures. The best plants are grown by moving the plants into 3-in pots for their last few weeks in the greenhouse.

Damping off is often a problem with petunias, and clean pots and trays are essential. The effective fungicides that commercial growers use to prevent disease are not available to home gardeners, so copper fungicides and benlate (both, alternately – not just one, continually) should be used regularly from seed-sowing time until pricked-out seedlings are growing well.

Don't forget that if you can't face this every year, cuttings can be over-wintered with the fuchsias and geraniums.

Does all this sound off-putting? It's intended to be realistic both in terms of what to grow and how to grow it. For petunias can be delightful: the white-edged scarlet 'Red Picotee' with beetroot 'Mac-Gregor's Favourite' or in front of *Artemisia* 'Valerie Finnis'; 'Super-cascade Lilac' in front of artemisias or silver cinerarias, or under pink or white shrub roses.

*CL:* In our climate, weather resistance is the most important factor in petunia-growing, and your troubles are compounded if you garden on a heavy soil (I write with feeling). The horrid but all too familiar situation arrives where a heavy rain or hail shower batters every flower to pulp. This is followed by a long sulking period, during which botrytis may afflict the damaged crop to such a degree that it never recovers. Or it may recover. Much depends on the variety grown, as Graham has pointed out. Reds are the worst. There is a link between colour and weather resistance under adverse conditions.

Given our climate, I feel that the petunia has been too highly developed for its own good. It has become a neurotic. Which is why I annually save my own seed from open-pollinated petunias in a strain that I originally had from friends in Hungary, where annuals have not received the benefit of intensive breeding. The colour range is narrow, but the plants have tremendous vigour and their sweet scent on the evening air is terrific.

## Phacelia *(Hydrophyllaceae)*

*CL:* The best-known species is *Phacelia campanularia*, a nearly hardy annual from California. Its sizeable, upward-facing bells are true deep blue, on a compact plant no more than 9 in tall. It is a pity that its dusky leaves make a slightly sooty impression. It dislikes being transplanted and is generally sown direct where it is to flower, which it will do in seven to eight weeks from a spring sowing. In mild areas autumn sowing is on.

*GR:* After the main burst of flowering is tailing off, be brutal. Cut the plants off about an inch above ground level and give them a good soak with liquid feed. Without this stimulus there will be no second burst of flowers, only a twiggy bush of crisp dead foliage. Give *Mentzelia lindleyi* the same treatment – unless you follow Christopher's usual advice and whip them out to make room for something else. But not all of us have the facilities to bring on follow-ups.

*Phacelia tanacetifolia* is now being sold as a green manure plant, but its curled heads of dusky blue flowers, much loved by bees, and ferny foliage make it a good border plant too.

## Phlox *(Polemoniaceae)*

*CL:* The half-hardy annual *Phlox drummondii* is the only species that need concern us here, and it is a first-class bedder with a long flowering season.

The large-flowered kinds have the disadvantage of making sprawling, rangy plants that need pegging down to keep them in order.

The dwarf strains need not be too dwarf, and they make conveniently compact plants. Avoid those, like 'Twinkle', with fussed-up, variegated flowers. A solid, monochrome flower is far more effective, and you will find quite sufficient variety in the 'Beauty' strain mixed. Indeed, the range of colours is amazing – red, salmon, pink, pale yellow, biscuit, purple, pale mauve, white – and all go well together. This is a splendid strain for bedding, some 9 in tall. Sown in April under cold glass, flowering will continue from July to late October. A sunny site is best, and these annual phloxes tolerate dry conditions pretty well, if they must.

*GR:* I agree, the nasty bicolours with their small starry flowers simply look messy. If only some of the colours in the 'Beauty' mixture were available separately – the biscuit, the bluish-pink and the softest lilac-blue, for example. We live in hope.

## Platycodon *(Campanulaceae)*

*CL:* The balloon flower, *Platycodon grandiflorus*, actually has balloon-like buds, which open to wide, $2\frac{1}{2}$–3 in saucers with sharp marginal points. The colour is campanula blue, white or pale grey, and there is a pinkish-mauve shade of the same dirty colouring as 'pink' lavender. Flowering is in July–August and the most useful strain, 'Mariesii', only a foot tall and reasonably self-supporting, comes true enough from seed. Sown under cold glass in spring, each seedling will produce a single bloom in its first year and will be prolific thereafter.

The white roots are fleshy and need good drainage.

## Polemonium *(Polemoniaceae)*

*GR:* The fact that a number of polemoniums are apt to self-sow demonstrates how easy they are to raise. This is one of the first perennials that I raised from seed all those years ago and, knowing no better, I treated it like a bedding plant. I was delighted to find that it flowered, albeit feebly, in its first summer.

The Jacob's ladder, *P. caeruleum*, is an indispensable plant. The divided foliage is bright and useful even when the plant is not flowering, and the blue flowers are greatly enhanced by sharp yellow anthers. The white form is especially clean and lovely. The various forms in pinkish, pale and deep blue are not usually grown from seed because it's not available, but you can collect your own.

Sow early in a propagator, prick out into pots, and plant out in a nursery bed or quiet corner after hardening off. Once the colour is obvious and has been noted, cut the flower spikes down. Fresh flushes of foliage will help bulk up the plant for moving, carefully, to a border later.

This is a short-lived plant – it tends to die out in the centre after a year or two but can be rejuvenated by division. This is easy enough to manage, and stems that flop on the soil will help by rooting; seedlings will pop up all around – which is no bad thing – unless the dying flowers are cut down promptly.

I grew the blue form in a border slightly shaded by a raised bed from which tumbled *Alyssum saxatile* 'Citrinum', just behind the blue polemonium flowers. *Rosmarinus lavandulaceus* elbowed its way in alongside. Around the base of the polemonium, in the partial shade, a rather darker seedling of the alyssum flowered a little later, with the yellow-eyed blue viola 'Ardross Gem' and a deadnettle with entirely yellow leaves, 'Cannon's Gold'. I think I can claim a success.

'Apricot Delight' is a newly introduced selection of *P. carneum* which yields plants with flowers in various salmons and pinks – again, grow them and choose your favourite.

Can I also make a plea for the dainty *P. reptans*? The plant is shorter, the rootstock less woody and the delicate bell-shaped flowers a soft blue. With *Tiarella wherryi* it's among the best of the smaller perennials to pot up for a cold greenhouse to provide flowers for winter posies.

## Polygonum *(Polygonaceae)*

*CL:* Some of the perennial knotweeds, such as *Polygonum cuspidatum*, are so furiously invasive that they are apt to give the genus a bad name. But the one I should like to see in gardens, *P. orientale*, is an annual, and it is not currently available through the trade. It grows to 4 ft and has striking, deep ruby spikes on a strongly branching plant. Sometimes it self-sows, but it prefers a slightly hotter summer than we can normally provide.

Seed of *P. capitatum* is available. It is a charming half-hardy perennial of a creeping habit, with handsomely patterned purplish foliage and globular heads of small pink flowers. These are most freely produced in sun, but the plant grows more luxuriantly in shade. Although it will be frosted in the garden, self-sown seedlings appear in the following season.

*GR:* The botanists are having a rare old time with the polygonums. The notorious Russian vine, *Polygonum baldshuanicum*, is no sooner shunted into a genus of its own, *Bilderdykia* (build a dyke here!), than it's moved into a different siding – *Fallopia! Polygonum bistorta* is allocated by some, but by no means all, to *Bistorta*, while at present about the only thing that they seem to agree about is that *P. cuspidatum* has been detached into *Reynoutria* and that *P. capitatum* has been left alone. But changes continue.

*Polygonum cuspidatum* (*Reynoutria japonica*) is an evil and mischievous weed which should never be grown or, especially, allowed to escape into the wild. It is causing great damage in parts of Wales by spreading more than briskly and smothering the natural flora.

The *P. orientale* that Christopher mentions is indeed a pretty plant, and I hope that our championing of it will encourage the more enlightened seed companies to take it up. Finding a sunny, moist and well-drained spot for the plant to thrive is not always easy, but the foliage colour will be better and the production of flowers more prolific in hotter, drier sites. If you don't wish to take the chance of self-sown seedlings, cuttings will root easily.

## Portulaca *(Portulacaceae)*

*CL: Portulaca grandiflora* likes heat and sunshine in a basking position, and is a miserable failure in a wet British summer. But it is worth risking. [I'm not so sure, but global warming may help! – *GR*]

A succulent, prostrate plant, it will make 6 in or so of height and can be used at the border's margin. The flowers are satiny and in the double strain their shape is like a rose. Colours are brilliant and as varied as the annual mesembryanthemum's. Sow under glass in April or direct, in May. Transplanting is possible but somewhat resented.

## Primula *(Primulaceae)*

*GR:* There are gardeners who quiver in their boots at the thought of germinating primulas, and although some of the rarer species are rather tricky – this, doubtless, accounts for their rarity – many can be raised without too much difficulty.

Sir Thomas Beecham is supposed to have said that he'd try anything once except incest and folk-dancing. Gardeners should try anything once except Japanese knotweed and blue roses, and that includes raising primulas from seed. When you've succeeded once, you'll feel happier about trying some more. Unlike folk-dancing!

If you are buying seed from a seed company, then order early but retain the seed for sowing later. If you're feeling keen, mix it with a little damp sand, tie it in the corner of a polythene bag and leave it in the bottom of the fridge until mid-February. It can then be sown in pots of a compost made up of one part John Innes seed compost, two parts coarse sand and one part moss peat. Cover very lightly with sifted compost, and water well but delicately. Cover each pot with clingfilm and place in a shady cold frame. Many species will be up in six weeks. *Never* let the compost or the seedlings dry out.

If you already have primula plants, collect your own seed the moment the seed capsules open and sow it straight away in the way I've just described; germination will often be quicker and more complete – indeed, seedlings should appear like the proverbial mustard and cress.

*CL:* Yes, but keeping tiny primula seedlings happy through the winter is not always easy, and I myself prefer to sow in spring.

*GR:* Should you be given some old seed, or find some in an old biscuit tin, sow it in the autumn in the same way and just wait. Perhaps for ever.

This regime is one which you should find successful for the majority of the more common primulas. Other techniques which have been suggested and which have been found successful include placing the seed in a fine tea-strainer and washing it under the tap to wash chemical germination inhibitors out of the seed coat, and sowing in pots outside under a layer of grit as soon as the seed comes to hand, whenever that might be. Really tricky primulas can be raised in a compost incorporating dry, shredded sphagnum moss, with a layer on the surface too. The sphagnum creates a very moist but also very airy atmosphere.

Contrary to popular opinion, many of the commoner species don't need chilling. These include the candelabra types such as *P. pulverulenta*, *P. beesiana* and *P. helodoxa*, but *P. chungensis* and *P. japonica* do need the cold: presumably the hybrids between the two need, well, just a little chilling but not too much . . .? Some, like the British native *P. farinosa* and also the much admired *P. vialii*, even germinate better with heat. Modern primrose hybrids have mostly had the cold requirement bred out of them.

However, the regime I have outlined should give at least reasonable results with most easily available species and simple hybrids.

When it comes to recommending what to grow and what to select as companions, the choice is endless. Rhododendron-growers have an advantage when it comes to candelabra types, as they will grow in similar conditions, so it's simply (simply?) a matter of selecting the appropriate species and varieties to go with the rhodos. Gardening as I do on limestone, I hesitate to make specific recommendations. But you may find that some strains are not quite what they say: 'Postford White' may include other shades apart from the white with a pink eye, and 'Miller's Crimson' may include all sorts of reds. It entirely depends on the source of the seed.

Bog primulas look well with close relations. *P. bulleyana, P. florindae* and *P. chungensis* are striking together in their different shades of yellow and orange and different flower forms.

My favourite candelabra, the orange *P. chungensis*, and the chunkier *P. bulleyana* will self-sow among the yellow-striped *Iris pseudacorus* 'Variegata', making lively companions; ligularias such as *Ligularia dentata* 'Desdemona' are also good neighbours. The intensity of the pink *P. rosea* is difficult to place, but since a bold gardener put it with the yellow-flowered bog arum, *Lysichitum americanum*, this combination has become rather a cliché. Well, it wasn't my idea.

Polyanthus are the most useful of spring bedders, but you have to be careful about the variety you choose. In colder areas of the country the large-flowered 'Pacific Giants', the old favourites, may not be hardy – that is what comes of breeding so-called 'hardy' varieties in California. So now we must choose 'Crescendo', an F1 hybrid which has been bred for hardiness but whose large flowers are difficult to cope with close to. The more recent 'Gallant' also sounds good, with smaller flowers but more of them.

Unfortunately the number of separate colours in the 'Crescendo' series available to the home gardener is declining. Altogether there are six although some are a little variable in their shade.

To raise these, it's simply a matter of sowing in a peat-based compost in March or April if you intend to line them out, or June for growing on in pots. Cover the seed only very lightly, and keep at about 60°F. Prick out into trays and then plant out or pot up and grow cold. Plant out in their final positions in the autumn.

Try 'Crescendo Bright Red' (which is actually crimson) with white 'Mount Hood' daffodils [lovely also with the rather early, white Fosteriana tulip 'Purissima' – *CL*]; 'Crescendo Blue' among *Euphorbia polychroma*; 'Crescendo Gold' in front of 'Vulcan' wallflowers inter-planted with orange tulips; 'Crescendo Primrose' among the surging new shoots of peonies or in front of pale 'Blue Bird' forget-me-nots; 'Crescendo White' with the short, scarlet 'Red Riding Hood' tulips. 'Crescendo Pink and Rose' is, as the name suggests, something of a mixture and rather risky.

I also like the sound of 'New Lace', which is the result of crossing the traditional laced type with F1 hybrid types to produce lacing in yellow, white and sometimes pink and lilac!

Then there are the astonishing Barnhaven strains, which originated with Florence Bellis and which Jared Sinclair had been producing for many years until his retirement. In recent years the Barnhaven strains have not been at their best, but they once set the standard in hardy polyanthus and primroses. Double primroses, jack-in-the-greens, lustrous polyanthus and many more were produced by hand-pollination. If sown immediately they are received, germination of Barnhaven seed is nearly 100 per cent and plants are generally strong and vigorous.

A green-flowered strain said to have a connection with Gertrude Jekyll has reappeared; various double-flowered strains which will produce from 0–25 per cent doubles are available. But there are also far too many extremely gaudy primroses which are bred as pot plants but which are hopeless garden plants – though this is really rather a relief. If you insist on trying these outside, 'Husky' and 'Mirella' are probably the toughest, but they'll never surpass 'Wanda' and 'Sibthorpii'.

*CL:* I have one comment to make on colour in polyanthus. Nearly all have a large central flash of yellow in the flower. This associates far better with yellow, orange, red, blue or white polyanthus flowers than with pink, carmine or magenta. On the whole, single colour strains are far more satisfying to the eye than mixtures which are altogether too mixed.

Soil can become polyanthus-sick. The famous example was the huge polyanthus planting under the nut trees at Sissinghurst Castle. It became impossible to grow this easy plant there any more. So if you find that many of the plants you bedded out in autumn are dead by spring, take the hint. You can change the soil or (if you're human) grow something else.

## Pulsatilla *(Ranunculaceae)*

CR. I've often wondered why the pulsatillas are called Pasque flowers. It seemed too simple that they flowered around Easter; now I know. In the Middle Ages a dye was extracted from the flowers and used to paint hard-boiled eggs for Easter.

The Pasque flower, *P. vulgaris*, is a rare British native and I'm lucky enough to live near one of the best sites in the country. Here it grows in thin soil on the north sides of limestone quarry spoil-heaps which have been there since the sixteenth century. The big purple trumpets with their bold boss of yellow anthers shimmer in the short turf and are followed by clematis-like seed heads.

Fresh seed is essential, so it is best sown as soon as it's ripe, usually in June or July. Trim the tails off with a pair of nail scissors before sowing. Fresh seed germinates quickly and should be potted up as soon as the true leaves can be recognized. Plant in spring or autumn. Old seed will need a winter of frost before germinating.

*CL:* From commercial seed sources I get reasonable, though uneven, germination in the same year from a spring sowing.

*GR:* A lovely pure white form with pale foliage is available from catalogues, as well as a mixture of purples, reds, pinks and lilacs. A number of other species are listed, all worth growing in a sunny well-drained spot, even at the front of a border on clay soil – as long as the site has been improved. Any colours you especially like can be grown from root cuttings.

## Ranunculus *(Ranunculaceae)*

*GR:* Here's a case where fresh seed really does make a difference, and if your ranunculus seedlings never appear, it's probably because your seed was old and stale. What's more, fresh seed will often germinate without a chilling period, whereas old seed, even after a winter's cold, may yield few, few seedlings.

A couple of species are especially worth growing. *R. calandrinioides* is a very early-flowering beauty; its glaucous leaves are covered in a delicate bloom and its pure, shimmering white flowers appear as early as late January in a cold greenhouse, where it is best grown for the protection of its snowy flowers from rain. Unfortunately it's a martyr to mildew and a good air flow is essential. R. *gramineus* is altogether tougher, with emerald green, grassy foliage and big yellow buttercup flowers. This is an easier plant, for raised beds.

The highly developed double-flowered forms of R. *asiaticus* like 'Accolade' and 'Bloomingdale' are a little different. Relatively straight-forward descendants of the hundreds of varieties the Victorians grew, they can be sown between about August and October at a temperature of around 50°F. Allowing the temperature to rise above about 60°F may cause problems. Seedlings are pricked out into small pots and grown on at about the same temperature, then moved into 4-in pots for flowering in spring. A loam-based compost is usually more suc-cessful than a peat-based one.

'Bloomingdale' has the most delicate fully double flowers, petals overlapping neatly to create a whirlpool of colour, one of the most beautiful of double-flowered plants; they flower for many, many weeks in pink, dark rose, scarlet, white and yellow. This and 'Accolade' are also much more vigorous than those grown from corms, and have better flowers.

## Reseda *(Resedaceae)*

*CL:* Mignonette, *Reseda odorata*, is not a pretty plant. Its leaves are especially boring, but its warm, raspberry fragrance is an indispensable part of summer. Grow it in a sunny position (as an ingredient in a pot-grown mixture is often the best way) near to where you sit. The flowers are borne in cones and are in muted shades of brown and green. There are showier selections making larger heads, but they do not smell as strongly.

When old ladies tell you that mignonette doesn't smell like it used to, you don't have to believe them. In part they're indulging in nostalgia and a general feeling that nothing's as good as it used to be; in part, alas, it reflects an only too real loss of their own sense of smell.

This is a hardy annual of a floppy habit, and you might as well let it flop. As it transplants rather badly, sow a few seeds in a number of pots.

*GR:* I like it in a terracotta pot, with a plant or two of trailing lobelia. Take little notice of the named forms, they seem in something of a muddle.


## Ricinus *(Euphorbiaceae)*

*GR:* The true castor oil plant, *Ricinus communis*, is an old favourite for bedding out, with its big, glossy, palmate leaves, and makes quite a spectacle, reaching 6 ft in its one summer if you choose the right variety. The best are those with shining reddish-bronze foliage – a difficult shade to describe. 'Impala' is the most widely grown variety these days, reaching about 4 ft, while the newer 'Carmencita' is taller and branches more enthusiastically.

The large speckled seeds are best sown individually in 3-in pots in a propagator and then moved into 5-in pots later.

Grow 'Impala' with the tall, white-flowered *Nicotiana alata* or behind *Lavatera* 'Mont Blanc'. Alternatively go for fierier shades - crocosmias, such as the orange and yellow bicoloured 'Bressingham Beacon', and heleniums to follow. Canary creeper can be trained up through them, or the orange *Eccremocarpus scaber* allowed to fall through them from a fence behind. Mahogany 'Red Seven Star' marigolds would be welcome nearby, or 'David Howard' dahlias.

Although grown as annuals, these are perennial plants and in the Mediterranean make spreading, suckering clumps many feet across.


## Rodgersia *(Saxifragaceae)*

*GR:* These are bold-leaved perennials for moist soil in the woodland garden or by the waterside. A surfeit of moisture is far more welcome than a drought – and this should be remembered when it comes to sowing the seed.

Seed of only a few species is usually available. *Rodgersia pinnata* is a variable plant, and you won't have to be too choosy about flower colour, as seed-raised plants can range from pale pink through dark pink to white. The striking, deeply veined pinnate foliage may vary in colour too. It creates a pleasing textural contrast with hostas and complements iris foliage in both form and texture.

*CL:* A great plus point in favour of rodgersias and in contrast to hostas is that their foliage is entirely disregarded by slugs and snails.

*GR:* R. *tabularis* is now correctly known as *Astilboides tabularis* but, for fear of causing consternation so near to the front of the book, we forbore to insert it under A. This is an entertaining plant, and looks as if a rather ambitious circus plate spinner has been at work – upright and arching stems with rounded leaves attached at the centre. Grow it with irises at the water's edge.

Seed should be sown in pots of peaty but loam-based compost and left outside in full shade where it will not dry out. Germination can be unpredictable.

## Rudbeckia *(Compositae)*

*GR:* These cheerful summer-long daisies, in colours from chestnut almost through to lemon, are easy to raise from seed sown in a propagator in spring, and are treated as half-hardy annuals. All will flower in their first year, and one or two will then please you greatly by turning up again the year after.

Many of the varieties in the catalogues are of mixed origin, and some behave as genuine annuals while others are good perennials. I'll pick out three to recommend, though Christopher may disagree.

'Goldsturm', a genuine perennial, is a pale gold shade with long narrow petals making a sharp star around the dark eye. Reaching 2 ft on stiff stems, it's good for cutting and should be cut just as the buds are opening. The cut flowers dislike direct sunlight, while in the garden they love it.

*CL:* They do love it, but on the other hand 'Goldsturm' is highly tolerant of shade (provided the soil is moist) and brings its light into dark places from early August for two months.

*GR:* 'Nutmeg' is less confidently perennial, a double and semi-double-flowered mixture of darker colours – reddish-orange, rusty shades, mahogany, chestnut – including some bicolours; all reach about $2\frac{1}{2}$ ft. Grown as a mixture, they need pale or variegated foliage around them – but the best dark colours can be picked out of the mixture and grown with silver foliage such as the lacy *Centaurea gymnocarpa*. They may behave as annuals in poor conditions but as perennials in a well-drained but rich soil.

Treat 'Goldilocks' as an annual. It is a neat plant, reaching just 2 ft, with big flowers in a marmalade-yellow. The best fully-double flowers in the mixture are lovely, but there are usually quite a few semi-doubles and even one or two singles which create rather a messy effect. The slightly greenish buds give the group a curious glow.

*CL:* There are others that I grow and enjoy, and I do prefer the yellow-flowered strains as being more effective at a distance than those in which mahogany is mixed in. 'Monplaisir' ('My Joy') is tall at 3 ft, deep yellow with a black cone. It looks good in front of white Japanese anemones. 'Irish Eyes', alias 'Green Eyes', is yellow with a green disc and looks jolly with dahlia-flowered zinnias in a mixture. The double or semi-double 'Gloriosa' strain, yellow again, is handsome. Being heavy-headed, it is more unbalanced than the others, but all are the safer with a stake and a single tie to each plant.

## Salpiglossis *(Solanaceae)*

*CL:* One of the more depressing smells I can think of is the rank odour of salpiglossis in the cold rains of a miserable summer. They hate such conditions, and are not the best of garden plants because their trumpet flowers are so easily reduced to pulp; more easily, even, than the closely related petunia.

But their richly coloured and veined flowers have the quality, if not the texture, of brocade, and they are beautiful to look at in detail. The only snag is that even the modern F1 mixtures include quite a high proportion of muddy-coloured plants.

The best way, I find, to grow *S. sinuata* is in pots to stand in the comparative shelter of a patio or outside a porch. Then, if you see dead blooms that have not been shed and that will set up a botrytis rot, which will spread back into and infect a large part of the plant, you can nip them out before the damage has started.

An April sowing under cold glass of this half-hardy annual gives me excellent results, with 3-ft-tall, branching plants in 7-in pots, flowering freely from the end of July. But before that you'll see flower enough to be able to discard less worthy plants as soon as they have shown their colours. Each plant requires a stake and perhaps a couple of ties. The 'Kew Blue' strain is well worth growing. This sumptuous colour used to be included in mixtures but is not found in the F1 and F2 hybrids.

*GR:* Not so long ago a British plant-breeding company had the idea of using genetic engineering to improve the weather resistance of both salpiglossis and petunias. Nicotianas have much better tolerance of the wet, and their idea was to transfer the genes which give the waxy coating to the petals from nicotianas to petunias and salpiglossis – they're all closely related.

This thinking proved to be in advance of the scientific possibilities, so conventional breeding techniques were used instead. I remember seeing a trial of thousands of plants planted in an unsheltered spot in a windy East Anglian field, with just four or five canes marking the plants that stood up to the weather especially well. All the rest were discarded; and this was six or seven years before the variety finally appeared.

The result of many years' work was 'Casino', a dwarf variety for bedding and containers with few of the muddy shades Christopher so rightly dislikes.

## Salvia *(Labiatae)*

*GR:* There are three types of salvia – the trendy ones, the neutrals and those that are very definitely passé.

The trendy salvias fall into two groups: silvery and other biennials, and those which are a little bit tender and usually raised from cuttings.

Plants such as *S. argentea* and the very showy form of clary, *S. sclarea* subspecies *turkestanica*, fall into the first section, and are easily raised from seed sown in early summer in the greenhouse. Seedlings should be pricked out into John Innes compost with extra grit and planted out in a sunny, well-drained spot. Once settled and content they should self-sow. Plant *S. argentea* at the front of the border so that you can admire its venerable silvery-haired foliage at close quarters.

The other salvias of the moment are the tender types like the astonishing *S. discolor*, with its blackcurrant-scented foliage and blackcurrant-coloured flowers. Few, if any, of these half-hardy shrubby salvias are available as seed. If you should come across seed of any I would suggest keeping it somewhere warm and dry for a few weeks before sowing, to simulate conditions in the plants' natural habitat.

Seed of one or two of the tender herbaceous types is available, especially the exquisite deep blue *S. patens* and its paler counterpart 'Cambridge Blue'. These can be raised like half-hardy annuals and the tuberous roots kept over the winter like dahlias, to give you large, bushy plants the following year. Both are good with verbenas and argyranthemums in appropriate shades.

*CL:* I had a smashing blue and yellow bed one year, combining 'Cambridge Blue' with *Coreopsis* 'Sunray' and, in front, patches of the deep blue pimpernel, *Anagallis linifolia*.

When Graham talks about scarlet *S. splendens* as being unfashionable, I'm sure he means unfashionable with those who consider themselves leaders of fashion and for whom the acme of good taste is the white garden at Sissinghurst Castle. But given a front garden competition in a dormitory town or city suburb, I guarantee that this sage would feature prominently in the winning entry. It is interesting to remind ourselves that Gertrude Jekyll herself used it in the centre of her famous colour-graded mixed border, where red flowers took over in its hottest spot from yellow and orange. But I fancy that, at the turn of the century, it was a much less dumpy seed strain that she was growing. If this species still exists in the wild, it would be interesting to back-cross some of our modern varieties with it.

*GR:* The French may have done something of this sort, for they have bred a big bushy variety called (may they wash their mouths out with soap and water) 'Rambo'!

The neutral salvias are those like *S. superba* which, although good, solid garden plants, attract no fanatics. Many are raised from cuttings, but there are two good seed strains, 'Blue Queen' and 'Rose Queen'. Both have bracts in matching but darker colours and so remain attractive after the flowers themselves have faded. Once planted they need little encouragement, colonizing well without being a nuisance; they are good plants for new gardens. Raise them as half-hardy annuals, in which case they will flower at the end of their first year. Alternatively, sow later in the season and you will see the first flowers the following July.

The distinctly unfashionable salvias are the bedding types. Even salvia enthusiasts ignore them totally, as if simply being short, red and familiar were enough to imply their worthlessness. True, it would help if the plant-breeders created some taller, bushier varieties which were better garden plants than the squat, dumpy ones we are lumbered with, and the French have started. But if you're desperate for a red-flowered plant with dark green leaves, then 'Red Riches' and 'Red River' are the ones to go for.

Avoid the old favourite, 'Blaze of Fire'. Seed stocks are now supplied to the seed companies by many growers whose poor roguing standards ensure that the market is supplied with quite a variety of different strains under the one name – and some are very poor.

Good varieties of *S. splendens* in other shades have recently appeared. 'Laser Purple' was a lovely rich purple and has now been replaced by the excellent 'Phoenix Purple'. Hold your breath, for there are some other rather surprising colours in the 'Phoenix' series – there's white but also lilac, plus a pale and a dark salmon. Wait, don't fling the book out of the window, I've seen them and they really are surprisingly attractive.

To cap it all, you can now get striped salvias! Both the calyx and the flowers are striped with white. Red and white 'Fireworks' was the first, but now there is 'Pharaoh', also known as 'Hall of Fame', a mixture which includes pink, purple and lavender. These may be poor growers, but they are very striking. Larger plants and longer, more open spikes would be a great improvement.

These bedding salvias can be a little tricky from seed, as they need light and plenty of moisture. The best solution is to use a peat-based compost and cover each pot with clingfilm. Alternatively, cover the surface of the compost with a $\frac{1}{4}$-in layer of vermiculite, sow on the top and water in gently. The seeds need a germination temperature of 70°F and should be pricked out into 3-in pots for the best plants. They are also very prone to disease, so clean pots and fresh, sterile compost are essential.

Sow in mid-February if you intend to prick out into pots, mid-April if they are destined for trays.

*CL:* This being one of my favourite genera, I should like to invite a few more to the party. [The more the merrier. – *GR*] The varieties you see listed as *S. superba* are really selections of *S. nemorosa*. The true 'Superba' clone is sterile. As it never sets seed, it has a greater capacity for repeat-flowering, with a second flush in September, than any seed strain.

Graham has written of the true clary, *S. sclarea*, which is a biennial, but a cock-up has arisen as a result of the hardy annual *S. horminum* being wrongly described as clary. This has insignificant flowers but large, colourful bracts in pink, purple or white, atop the spike of $1\frac{1}{2}$-ft plants. Popular in some quarters, but coolly received by Lloyd.

*S. coccinea* is grown as an annual and has pure red flowers on a $2\frac{1}{2}$-ft plant. This is charming, but we could do with a little more flower power. Why don't the breeders switch their attention to it? (P.S. They are doing so.)

They have improved *S. farinacea*, which used to be too tall and gangling. Without losing its grace, 'Victoria' is reasonably compact at 2 ft. Its flower spikes and the stem supporting them are a rich bluish-purple. The foliage is pleasing too, and this is an annual that gets going rather late but remains fresh well into autumn. It looks good with a yellow rudbeckia or, on another tack, with pink mallows such as *Malope trifida*, raised from a May sowing.

The sage known as *S. haematodes* is really a variety of *S. pratensis* and it can be treated either as a hardy biennial, lining the seedlings out in their first year, or as a short-lived perennial. It carries a large, 3-ft, branching inflorescence of lavender blossom in June. This is thoroughly effective and everyone notices it, but the display is over in a fortnight.

We have lately been offered seed of *S. uliginosa*, a perennial species which flowers from August for a couple of months. Growing to 6 ft, it carries multiple short spikes on a widely branching, light and airy plant. The colour is pure sky blue with a white central flash. Combine it with pink or yellow dahlias, or even with pink *and* yellow dahlias. Pink and yellow goes against the rules (whose rules?), but with a cloud of softening blue I guarantee a delightful outcome. *S. uliginosa* is not always hardy, especially on heavy soils, so it is wise to lift a few roots to over-winter in the greenhouse.

## Sanvitalia *(Compositae)*

GR: *Sanvitalia procumbens* is a low, creeping plant with orange or yellow, dark-eyed daisy flowers all summer. Growth is especially flat and spreading, which is unusual and distinctive yet unpretentious.

The species is golden-yellow; 'Gold Braid' is similar but semi-double and less vigorous; 'Mandarin Orange' is an orange version of 'Gold Braid'.

They are not fussy as to soil but like plenty of sun. Treat them as hardy annuals and sow them where they can spread out across paths or patios or can trail down from a tub. 'Mandarin Orange' looks good in a tub with the beetroot 'MacGregor's Favourite'.

## Saponaria *(Caryophyllacea)*

*GR:* A rather disparate genus including British native wild flowers, alpines, cut flowers and hardy annuals. The trailing *Saponaria ocymoides* is one of the prettiest of the easy alpines. Its rock-hugging stems trail over a wide area and are covered with small pink flowers for many weeks in late spring and early summer. Germination is good and quick, without a cold period. *S. caespitosa* makes tight clumps of narrow leaves with relatively large pink flowers. This too germinates quickly. Give both a gritty soil.

The hardy annual *S. vaccaria* produces pink or white gypsophila-like flowers, and as these are slightly larger than gypsophila it is being grown increasingly widely as a cut flower. 'Pink Beauty' is especially pretty. Try sowing in autumn as well as spring for extra large plants. Cut just as the flowers are opening.

## Saxifraga *(Saxifragaceae)*

*GR:* A very large number of the 440 saxifrage species are the strict preserve of alpine plant growers. They vary considerably from the neat, silvery rosette and long pyramidal flower spike of *Saxifraga cotyledon*, which grows best in a rock crevice in full sun, to the clusters of small dark green rosettes and single purple flowers of *S. oppositifolia*. There's no point generalizing about germination conditions; the former requires chilling, the latter does not.

But nevertheless, for the less specialized gardener, most of the alpine types can be treated uniformly by sowing in a gritty compost and placing outside for the winter; germination should take place in spring. Although not all species require the cold period, none will suffer for it. Of the commoner species, London's pride, *S. umbrosa*, needs no heat; the mossy saxifrages like *S. moschata* demand a cold period followed by a spell in a propagator or warm greenhouse.

If you ever find seed of the delightful late-flowering woodlander from Japan, *S. fortunei*, with its starry white flowers – two long petals and three shorter – or of the similar *S. cortusoides*, they require different treatment. A moist, leafy or peaty compost which does not dry out is essential.

## Scabiosa *(Dipsacaceae)*

*CL:* The sweet scabious, *Scabiosa atropurpurea*, has a curious scent; rather musty, but I like it. It is not a fashionable annual, being slow to come into bloom and having a tall (3-ft), gangling habit that requires a stake to each plant. The breeders have let it go to pot, and seed mixtures which should include deep, velvety maroon, strong campanula blue and rich coral in fact seem to predominate in wishy-washy pink, pale mauve and off-white. You'll need to shop around for the best strain.

*GR:* This is another case where all you have to do is save seed from the deepest maroon-flowered plant, or whichever shade takes your fancy, sow it the following year, and root out other shades the minute they flower. In a few years, you will end up with seed which always produces your favourite colour.

*CL:* The pincushion flower is worth working for – so good, with thin long stems, for picking, and pretty also in a cottage garden mixture of late summer and autumn flowers. Stronger and slightly earlier-flowering plants than from a spring sowing are obtained by sowing in August, pricking the seedlings off into 4-in pots, over-wintering them under cold glass and planting them out in April. Given a mild winter, some old plants will do a second year.

*S. stellata* is not worth garden space [though flower arrangers seem to like it – *GR*]. *S. caucasica* is a hardy perennial that flowers over a long season but never much at any one time. Grow it just for cutting and on light soil. Blue is the favourite colour, but white is pleasing too.

## Sedum *(Crassulaceae)*

*GR:* Here we find one of the few annuals acceptable to alpine gardeners, indeed we find two – *Sedum caeruleum* and *S. sempervivoides*. There's also a huge number of other alpine sedums. Some of them are singularly undistinguished, it has to be said, but there are a few which excel as hardy perennials.

The dainty annual *S. caeruleum* makes spreading, branching plants only about 6 in high with clouds of bright blue flowers, plus white buds and white eyes; and there's the bonus of slightly succulent foliage which gets redder and redder as the season passes. A real gem for the cold greenhouse, it makes a rounded, sparkling blue dome in an 8-in pan, in which it can be sown direct. Grow it in a raised bed outside too, sowing where it is to flower.

With the other annual, the name tells it all, *sempervivoides* – like a sempervivum. Sharply pointed fleshy leaves make a neat rosette which then stretches into a pagoda, topped by heads of red flowers; very pretty. Sow in summer, in the greenhouse, in gritty compost, and prick out three or five to a pan for flowering the following spring.

Seed of few alpine types is available, but the uncharacteristic biennial *S. pilosum* is listed. This curiosity has a succulent rosette of leaves with silky hairs which produces heads of pink flowers in its second year.

The border types like *S. spectabile* are usually propagated by division rather than seed, though 'Brilliant' has been listed. Sow in spring in warmth, prick out, and line out after hardening off for flowering the following year. The dusky purple *S. telephium* 'Purpureum' is more often listed. But as vegetatively propagated named forms root easily (even as a cut flower they will root into the water), you do better to stick to them.

## Senecio *(Compositae)*

*GR:* Groundsel may not be anyone's favourite garden plant, but the rapidity of its germination and its capacity to flower when very small and in very poor conditions will tell you something about the altogether more attractive *Senecio elegans*.

The leaves are about the shape you'd expect from a groundsel or ragwort and irritatingly sticky, the flowers have magenta-purple ray florets with a bright yellow eye and sway atop plants about 2 ft tall.

Once there were double-flowered forms, and white, rose and deep purple; but no more. The usual hardy annual treatment is appropriate, and it might be worth trying an autumn sowing. This is not a fussy plant as far as soil is concerned, as you might guess, but it does require sunshine.

## Sidalcea *(Malvaceae)*

GR: The Europeans are getting a bit carried away with breeding new hardy perennials for the cut-flower market. Sidalceas are the latest to take their attention, with the arrival of 'Party Girl'. Now some sidalceas are rather murky in colour, but the 3-ft, relatively unbranched spikes of $1\frac{1}{2}$-in flowers are a strong rose, each with a yellow eye.

Sow in April, May or June and keep the seed-pots cool to begin with – two weeks at 40–50°F. Then move the pots into a warmer temperature, 55–65°F, and germination should take place in two to three weeks. In practice this probably means two weeks in the cold greenhouse and then into the propagator. Prick them out into individual pots, feed well and plant out by September.

Plants are unlikely to flower in their first year, but in year two they should flower from July to September. Cut when the flowers at the base of the spike have started to open, and spray them with water occasionally after arranging them to keep them fresh.

Why do we see so few wild species listed in catalogues?

## Silene *(Caryophyllaceae)*

GR: One of the first rock plants I ever raised from seed was *Silene schafta*, which has the very useful quality, for an alpine, of flowering right into October in many seasons. It's tough enough for the front of sunny borders too. The foliage may be unremarkable, but with its rather bright pink flowers on plants reaching 9 in high at most, it's great value. No chilling is needed, indeed it benefits from a little warmth at sowing time in spring.

Another perennial, this time more inclined to flop or trail, is sea campion, *S. maritima*. The foliage is slightly glaucous, the flowers white and the calyx inflated and marked with dark veins. A double-flowered form, 'Robin White Breast' may have a silly name but it flowers for longer and, what's more, flowers in its first summer after a spring sowing.

Both these species can be sown in February, if your propagator's not already bursting. Prick the seedlings out into small pots in March and by the end of April they'll be ready for planting.

The sweet william catchfly, *S. armeria*, comes originally from southern Europe but is now naturalized in a few places in the UK. An upright plant, with wiry stems and broad, slightly glaucous foliage narrowing to a point, the sharp pink flowers in their sweet-william-like heads give the plant its common name. It self-seeds in sunny, well-drained spots, and its bright flowers emerging from neighbouring grey foliage are very striking. Hardy annual treatment.

*CL: S. pendula* is a hardy annual that can be sown in early autumn for spring flowering or in spring for summer and autumn. The 'Compacta' strains grow only 6 in tall and are specially good in their double-flowered forms, of which a number used to be listed. The deep pinky-red 'Triumph' seems to be the only one at present. You can use it as an edging plant.

*GR:* There is also a quite different group of wiry-stemmed annuals, which, having migrated at various times between *Lychnis, Silene* and *Viscaria*, seem now to have settled as *Viscaria coeli-rosa* in catalogues although, correctly, they come under *Silene*.

In bold drifts in the border, in large pots or in rows for cutting I have always felt that what we all still call viscarias never quite lived up to their potential. But now that better varieties have appeared they can again be sown with confidence. For like many hardy annuals they went through a phase of neglect when the good, old strains deteriorated and no new varieties were developed.

I like their delicacy, their persistent flowering and their unusual shades – even the bright red has a certain softness about it. 'Rose Angel' and 'Blue Angel' began the revival with their strong but soft colours and continuous flowering; at about 12–15 in they are easily manageable. Now a good mixture, 'Royal Celebration', has also appeared, with these shades plus white, a good strong red and some dusky pastels.

Viscarias are best sown where they are to flower, for I've found that the root disturbance associated with pricking out sometimes upsets them. On the other hand, I think Christopher has sown them late in the season and grown them for a spring display in large pots – and this obviously entails disturbance. Perhaps he can explain.

*CL:* I have never had difficulty over transplanting viscarias, which have fibrous roots. Generally speaking, fibrous-rooted plants transplant well; fleshy and tap-rooted plants, badly.

I grow viscarias for display in 6-in pots, sowing them late August or early September in a pot under cold glass. They are not inclined to flower prematurely in the autumn, like cornflowers or heliophila, for instance, so a fairly early sowing date is safe. Prick out the seedlings, then pot them individually and have them in their final pots by late October. They are not dependably hardy, so should be over-wintered under sufficient protection not to be heavily frosted. Flowering starts towards the end of May and lasts for a good two months.

## Silybum *(Compositae)*

*GR:* This being a family book, I am prevented from making scatalogical jokes about this excellent plant. Suffice it to say that its unbelievable name is itself a good enough reason for growing the plant, irrespective of its other qualities; fortunately, it has at least one.

*Silybum marianum*, Our Lady's milk thistle, is a biennial for summer sowing outside. In its first season it produces an impressive rosette of spiny green leaves very prettily marked in white; this rosette can be up to 3 ft across so it needs space. Unfortunately disappointment accompanies the arrival of the flowers, which are fairly boring purple thistles. This is the stage to heave out all but one of your plants, which you have doubtless planted in vast drifts ('This is my silybum garden, note the exquisite marbling'), the last one being left to allow for self-sowing. Like onopordum this is a plant which makes a good present for a non-gardener, whose friends and neighbours will find the name entertaining.

## Smyrnium *(Umbelliferae)*

*CL:* The monocarpic *Smyrnium perfoliatum* is a super plant for colonizing in light shade where earlier-flowering hellebores, snowdrops, primroses and daffodils have given up. It flowers in May and is brilliant lime-green, the colour of many euphorbias, for which it is often mistaken, though it is quite obviously of the parsley tribe when you look closely. The chief contribution to this colour is made by its large, oval bracts. Its pinnate leaves are quite different and have died away by the time of flowering. I like to do a cut arrangement using this with white and purple honesty and double (or single) white poet's narcissus.

Its black seeds are set abundantly, and once you have your colony there'll be no further worries. It is the starting off that is slow and a bit uncertain if you're a manic and unimaginative weeder. From seed broadcast when ripe, all that's seen of the resulting seedlings in the following spring is one pair of cotyledons which soon die away. In the next year there is some true pinnate foliage, which also dies during the early summer. But in the third year, if not starved, the plant will flower, seed and die.

## Specularia *(Campanulaceae)*

*CL:* Venus's looking glass, *Specularia speculum*, is closely related and similar to *Campanula*; 9 in tall, hardy, annual, with upward-facing open chalices, each an inch across. The colour is violet, framing a white eye – the mirror, which is non-reflecting, but never mind. Allowance must be made for the poetry of deception.

On light soils, this pretty annual will self-sow from year to year. It will transplant from a spring sowing under cold glass.

## Tagetes *(Compositae)*

*CL:* There are two opposite schools of opinion on the enormously popular marigold: (1) that you can't have too much of it, and (2) that it should be banned from the garden without discussion. With their bright orange and yellow colouring, marigolds undoubtedly shout, and for those who want summer colour in bagfuls, they provide an easy, though unsubtle, solution. From the seller's angle, the modern F1 hybrids are ideal, since they start flowering at an early age on dwarf, compact plants so that the customer can immediately see what he's buying. The detractors of marigolds have a point, but are themselves so scared of displaying what they (and, worse still, their friends) think of as bad taste that they forgo all bright colours for fear of making a mistake. They fail to recognize the marigold's great virtues (though it has vices also, mostly of the breeders' making).

Marigolds have traditionally been split into three groups: African, derived mainly from *Tagetes erecta* and having large flowers; French, derived from *T. patula*, with small flowers that include bronze as well as orange and yellow shades; and *T. tenuifolia* (often listed as *T. signata pumila*), having a mass of tiny single flowers on a smallish bush. The frontier between the first and second groups has become blurred by hybridization into Afro-French. I should add that all tagetes hail from Mexico and are unconnected with Africa or France.

Best balance, it seems to me, is achieved when small plants carry small flowers or large blooms are borne on large plants. Large-flowered African marigolds look super on a 3-ft plant, as in the 'Climax' and 'Coin' series. Plants can be spaced 2 ft apart and there'll be enough of their pleasing, pinnate foliage visible to set off the large, intricately folded, ball-shaped blooms. Dead-heading them as they go over is a simple matter.

The idea that small gardens should grow only small annual plants is nonsense. They can accommodate stylish, large plants perfectly well but need few of them, which is an advantage. Carnation-flowered or 'Odorless' marigolds also make sizeable plants, and these lack the pungent, aseptic marigold smell which some people make a fuss about – God knows why. The rich orange F1 'Toreador' makes a $2\frac{1}{2}$-ft plant and is unbeatable in its way. At $1\frac{1}{2}$–2 ft, the 'Jubilee' series still sufficiently separates its flowers for each of them to establish an identity.

Not so the 'Inca' series, although especially beloved of the bedding plant trade for making a great splash at an early age. They achieve the deadly combination of large flowers on uniformly compact, foot-tall plants. 'Guys and Dolls' and 'Discovery' are even worse. Here we're down to 4-in-high plants carrying 4-in-wide blooms. This is grotesque.

French marigolds have smaller flowers, but even so the breeders have tended to present them on a too-bunched-up plant. Those with bronze and yellow are more effective in a garden setting where the colours are zoned than when they occur in flecks. I'm fond of the single 'Cinnabar', which is all bronze except for a thin orange margin. Plants grow a foot tall and as much across. They vary in size, which is all to the good in my (but not in the breeders') opinion. Lined up as an edging, lack of uniformity might be upsetting, but I would say group your plants, rather than line them. Let them take their place next to a *group* of 'Blue Mink' ageratum, for instance.

All varieties of *T. tenuifolia* are delightful. The pale yellow 'Lemon Gem', for instance, has bright, fresh green foliage. Grown well, these will make surprisingly big plants, a foot tall and 18 in across.

Marigold seed germinates in less than a week. If you find that your plants are ready before their positions are, get them out into a piece of spare ground and let them grow on there. Given thorough before and after waterings, they'll move remarkably well from the open ground at any time in the summer, even though already flowering. They make a good follow-on to sweet williams and other biennials.

*GR:* It's very satisfying to reach the end of Christopher's discussion on marigolds and find I've agreed with every word. I have one or two extra things to say but nothing with which to take issue.

Rigidity of attitude is certainly a problem among gardeners, especially, of course, other gardeners. For Christopher and I could hardly be said to be flexible – neither of us would have 'Inca' marigolds in the garden under any circumstances!

But as well as the 'let's have 'em all' and the 'under no circumstances' schools, there are also those who dreamily slide the most shocking marigolds into their baskets in the garden centre without really knowing what they're doing. They simply glaze over, slip into a sleep-walking mode and buy them without even paying attention to their height or colour; into the somnambulist's basket they all go. You'd think the very colour would rouse them, but no.

But if there's one thing that both Christopher and I have tried to do in our various writings over the years, it is to encourage people to think about what they do – preferably before they do it, but afterwards at the very least! So do absolutely nothing with marigolds without thinking about it first. Please.

Other varieties? I suggest you look out for the British-bred 'Mischief' series of single French marigolds. They reach about a foot in height, spread more, and the new flowers neatly overtop the old as they fade.

The mahogany with its narrow edge of gold is especially lovely, and looks equally well with silver foliage or with crisply curled parsley in front. Picking up Christopher's thought about 'Cinnabar', the tall ageratum 'Blue Horizon' could go behind.

The so-called 'tagetes', *T. tenuifolia*, with its clean-scented foliage, is so useful. You don't need many plants, as they spread so well, but the darkest, like 'Paprika', are not only slightly variable in colour – which we can happily live with – but tend to finish rather earlier than the other shades.

Marigold seed is about the easiest of all to deal with. It's big, germinates in a week indoors as Christopher says, and can even be sown outside in late spring when it will still be up in a week or two.

## Thalictrum *(Ranunculaceae)*

Marigold seed is about the easiest of all to deal with. It's big, *GR:* One of the great successes of a north-facing border in which I tried quite a few plants normally recommended for sunnier spots was *Thalictrum delavayi*, formerly known as *T. dipterocarpum*. My conclusion, having noted where it thrives in other gardens, is that it's not the sun it demands so much as moisture. In sunny, dryish spots it's a poor thing, struggling to about 2 ft; in heavier or more moist soil it thrives, making a graceful plant more than twice as tall. My north border was fairly gravelly, but being completely out of the sun rarely dried out. The thalictrum thrived.

The tiny lilac flowers with their creamy anthers are delightful close up and waft in airy sprays above prettily divided foliage, rather like that of a small-leaved columbine. It looked delightful, the thalictrum flowers overtopping the white woolly foliage of *Anaphalis yedoensis*, but this best of all silvers for shade needed rigorous reducing in spread each year.

This and other thalictrums are not difficult to raise by sowing in a propagator or cold frame at any time when you have the space between March and July; prick out into individual pots. No chilling is necessary.

*CL:* I get best germination from *T. delavayi* by sowing the seed fresh (home-collected) in autumn and leaving the container outside.

## Thermopsis *(Leguminosae)*

*GR:* Why this plant is not grown more often I really don't know. Well, having said that I have now discovered why: hardly any nurseries stock it (though Christopher's does, of course) and no seed companies list it! But that won't deter us from putting it in, as we both feel this plant deserves better. You'll have to check the lists from the specialist societies to find seed.

All the species in gardens have a rather stiff, upright habit, with dark, grey-green leaves divided into three leaflets. The flowers come in lupin-like spikes in early summer and are bright yellow in colour, catching the eye from some distance. They reach about 3 ft. *Thermopsis montana* runs, *T. lanceolata* does not.

Seed is easy to raise from a late spring sowing in a cold frame. Like many plants of the pea family, soaking and a little extra warmth will encourage the seeds to germinate before they rot or are gobbled up by mice.

## Thunbergia *(Acanthaceae)*

*GR:* Annual climbers are not so many and various that we can afford to reject any without good reason, but although *Thunbergia alata* 'Susie' is widely grown, neither the separate colours from the 'Susie' mixture nor another plant, *T. fragrans* 'Angel Wings', are seen often.

'Susie' comes in yellow, white and the typical pure orange, with or without black eyes – six variants in all, which would be very useful if available individually. More noticeable by its recent disappearance is 'Angel Wings', with its larger pure white flowers, sweetly scented.

'Angel Wings' flowers in about four to five months from an early sowing in the propagator at about 70°F. Either sow three seeds in a 3-in pot and pot on the whole lot when necessary, or prick out individually into small pots and then into larger ones before planting outside around the middle of June.

Hardening off carefully is important, as shocks can halt growth. Perhaps the best method is to plant up a container in early May and keep it protected before moving it out after the last frost. Companions in a tub might be the short-growing, dark-leaved *Ricinus* 'Mizuma' to provide support for the twining stems, the filamentous foliage and white daisies of *Argyranthemum* 'Chelsea Girl', and perhaps the palest pink petunia, 'Chiffon Magic'.

'Susie' is raised in the same way, and although not quite so delicate it still needs careful hardening off. It climbs hanging basket chains well and can even make an attractive basket on its own.

Both these varieties need a sheltered sunny site outside (a porch is ideal), and both will need protecting from the dreaded red spider mite.

## Tithonia *(Compositae)*

*CL: Tithonia rotundifolia* is a fast-growing Mexican annual, closely related to the zinnia. It revels in a hot summer, when it will grow 5 or 6 ft tall, but pines when it is chilly. It has coarse, heart-shaped leaves and single flowers of a wonderfully vital and intense shade of orange. 'Torch' is the variety to get. There is also 'Yellow Torch', but we have plenty of yellow daisies in late summer, and not so many orange. The horrible 'Goldfinger' is short-jointed and makes a squashed-up sort of plant, 3 ft tall or less and entirely lacking the tithonia's natural presence. [I quite agree, but 'Torch' is steadily disappearing from catalogues. – GR]

'Torch' looks good with white cleomes. Its tropical appearance also consorts well with cannas, castor oil (*Ricinus*) and maize. Each plant requires one stout cane. Seedlings loathe the cold, which turns them yellow. Seed germinates within four days and an early May sowing is generally soon enough, bringing the seedlings on as fast as maybe. The zinnia treatment, in fact.

## Tropaeolum *(Tropaeoliaceae)*

*GR:* Few gardeners have much respect for nasturtiums, and this blinds them to their good qualities. For although at their worst they can look coarse and colourless, at their best they're a treat.

The climbing types, based on *Tropaeolum majus* and *T. peltophyllum* (*T. lobbianum*), can develop large, over-dominant foliage at the expense of flowers if badly grown. And well-grown, in the case of climbing nasturtiums, means more or less starved. That sounds harsh, but the problem is that if fed and watered too well the leaves grow large and the petioles grow long, effectively hiding the flowers. The conditions at the foot of a privet hedge often prove to be ideal, the hedge of course also providing support. This is not such a problem with the far more delicate canary creeper, *T. canariense*. Its leaves are much smaller and neatly divided, and it is ideal for training through an old mature rosemary.

The fat seeds of these climbers can be sown where they are to flower, although it is better to raise plants in pots in a cold frame and then plant them exactly where you want them; you won't need many.

There is also a semi-trailing variety, 'Gleam', in various shades, but I find its impatient urge to turn into a climber irritating.

Better are the genuinely bushy types, like the semi-double 'Whirly bird'. But I prefer 'Alaska' and 'Empress of India', both of which make rounded plants about 12 in high. 'Alaska' is unusual in having its foliage speckled and striped with cream, which is carried in the seed unlike most variegations. The flowers come in nearly a dozen shades of orange, yellow and cream, some with apricot and peachy tints.

I gave up growing 'Alaska' at one time, partly because it kept being listed as a crop failure in catalogues and partly because plain green-leaved plants kept appearing. Now it has been reselected for small, 100 per cent variegated foliage and a neat height of just 8 in; what's more, seed supplies now seem pretty reliable.

One seed company is now selecting out the different colours, so they should soon be available separately. If this fails, you can take cuttings of those you like best. A bed of 'Alaska' makes an undulating carpet through which dark-leaved cannas or dark ricinus can erupt.

By contrast, 'Empress of India' has deep blue-green foliage and the deepest crimson flowers on equally rounded plants. This is a very special plant and should convert the most steadfast nasturtiophobes. Good around a variegated weigela.

Sadly, the double-flowered 'Hermine Grashof' sets no seed and must be raised from cuttings.

*CL:* Of the dwarf nasturtium seed strains, I am particularly fond of 'Whirlybird', especially when you can find it in separate colours. The flowers are without their usual spur, which is a slight shame, but you soon forget it, and the shining merit of all 'Whirlybirds' is that they hold masses of blossom well above their foliage, even on well-nourished soil, so they make excellent bedders. As they develop so quickly, I use them as a follow-on to biennials, or to plants like lupins or perennial dianthus that I have treated as biennials and discarded in early July. To this end, sow one or (for safety) two seeds in each of a number of pots in early June and plant them out a month later. I've had them flowering into November, so that it has seemed a crime to have to sweep them aside. 'Jewel' is another well-presented dwarf strain.

It has to be said that nasturtiums are by no means trouble-free, being afflicted by black aphids and by cabbage white caterpillars. The latter can be picked off. A spray against the former often kills the plant as well as the pest.

## Ursinia *(Compositae)*

*GR:* Annuals from South Africa always seem to be orange – dimorphotheca, tripteris, venidium, arctotis and ursinia certainly are. Ursinias are flamboyant plants with fine foliage and orange, or yellow, daisy flowers on plants about 15–18 in high. Unlike many South African annuals, ursinias usually have the good grace to keep their flowers open all day, rather than closing up the moment the sun shows a hint of dimming. They're easy to raise in warmth, though they are tough enough to be sown outside in April.

Sun and good drainage are essential, but staking may be necessary especially if plants are grown in rich conditions. Good in terracotta pots.

## Venidium *(Compositae)*

*CL:* These are South African daisies of the osteospermum/ gazania/ursinia/arctotis persuasion. *Venidium fastuosum* is a half-hardy annual with grey-green foliage covered with silky-looking hairs, tacky to touch. It rises to 2 ft, collapses under its own weight, but rights itself sufficiently not to need support. The daisies are sizeable, about 4 in across, orange with a purplish zone at the base and a large disc, shining black like a healthy dog's nose. It is a handsome plant, with a long flowering season ended only by frost.

Well-grown seedlings can be spaced at $1\frac{1}{2}$ ft.

*GR:* The creamy 'Zulu Prince' has recently appeared, and this unusual shade is enhanced by the colouring at the base of each ray petal, where there is a small black triangle edged in fiery orange. Its grey foliage is an improvement on most *fastuosum* varieties and it flowers well into the autumn, with plenty of buds still to open in late September.

'Zulu Prince' also makes an impressive cut flower on its long stems, and whereas in the garden the flowers close when the weather is dull, cut them and bring them indoors and they will be open in ten minutes.

## Verbascum *(Scrophulariaceae)*

*CL:* The mulleins have spiky inflorescences, simple or branching, and are beautiful midsummer-flowering biennials or perennials. Our native Aaron's rod, *Verbascum thapsus*, is biennial and looks best as a rosette of grey felted leaves in its first year. The flowering spike is not showy.

*V. bombyciferum,* another biennial, is a far better garden plant, with silvery leaves that are elegantly cut. To see them flatteringly, which again is in the seedlings' first year from an April sowing, they need siting near a border's margin. Will it then be disconcerting when they flower at 6 ft in their second summer? I think not. Verbascums are plants that do not block the view. You can see past them. Height at the front òf a border prevents the ultimately stodgy arrangement of shortest at the front, tallest at the back (or in the middle, in the case of an island bed). Although quite good in yellow flower, there are better species for this purpose and you might choose to replace it before flowering starts. It masquerades under various better-selling names than the clumsy *V. bombyciferum,* such as 'Arctic Summer', 'Silver Lining' and 'Silver Spire'. They're all the same.

*GR:* I'm not convinced, for though I'll grant you that the flowers are just the same, I've found that 'Silver Lining' will wait for two whole seasons before flowering, in its second year making impressive widely spreading white rosettes.

*CL:* The grey-leaved, biennial *V. phlomoides* was grown by Gertrude Jekyll. Another 6-footer, it is sparsely branching and has rather large yellow flowers. Mullein flowers, incidentally, wilt in the heat of the midday sun. In hot weather they are at their freshest in the mornings.

Unfortunately this last species has often been confused with and misnamed *V. olympicum*, which is a far superior plant. Seven feet tall, this species rises on a single stem to 3 or 4 ft; the main spike then branches freely into obliquely held side-spikes which comprise a symmetrical candelabrum of great magnificence. It is biennial, and flowers in July and into August. For best results, sow in a pot in April, prick off the seedlings, then line them out at 18 in for the summer. Move them to their flowering positions in the autumn.

*V. chaixii* is a reliable perennial, with green leaves and narrow spikes, to 6 ft, of yellow flowers with purple anthers. Mine have seeded themselves among pink border phloxes, which causes the 'colour harmony' school to turn their heads aside in horror and shame (for me), but I enjoy the contrast. More subtle is *V. chaixii* 'Alba', in which the purple stamens stand out in contrast to a white flower.

There are nowadays some excellent mixed colour seed strains of *V. phoeniceum*, a 2-ft, early summer perennial (albeit short-lived) with large flowers for the size of the plant. It looked very good in a cold Scottish garden underplanted with purple, mauve and white *Viola cornuta*. Its own colour range includes white, pinky-grey, lilac-pink and purple, in dense but slender spikes.

Verbascums have two enemies. Powdery mildew can become most unsightly on the foliage and prevents it from functioning properly. Protect with a systemic fungicide. The mullein shark caterpillar (which also attacks *Scrophularia*, the figwort) is a handsome brute but will decimate both flower spikes and foliage if unchecked. Fortunately it is day-feeding and easily spotted. The caterpillars hatch from the first week in June. If you conscientiously scan your plants, twice a day for ten days, and squash newly emerged larvae between finger and thumb, there'll be no further trouble. Don't plaster the plant with an insecticidal dust such as derris. You'll kill the plant, from suffocation, as well as the caterpillar.

*GR:* The big problem with verbascums is that they cross with each other so enthusiastically. If you grow more than one or if your neighbour's are different from yours, buy fresh seed each year rather than save your own. [Sometimes the crosses are good, as when *V. olympicum* acquires the purple stamens of *V. chaixii.* – *CL*]

## Verbena *(Verbenaceae)*

*GR:* A number of modern seed-raised bedding plants have been developed from older varieties raised from cuttings; the geranium is the prime example, and the verbena is another. 'Silver Anne', 'Sissinghurst' and 'Loveliness' are varieties which the seed companies have yet to replicate, but many developments have taken place, even if progress has not always been in the right direction.

The tendency has been to develop a compact habit rather than the more spreading growth which typifies the older varieties. There has also been a regrettable increase in susceptibility to powdery mildew, which often curtails flowering and also creates a spectacle on a par with a rust-ravaged antirrhinum.

Yet another problem which has emerged concerns germination, with many varieties showing poor emergence. This is not due to seeds being infertile (or 'dead' as we say in the trade), but because there are certain germination inhibitions which the breeders have yet to remove.

The causes of this germination inhibition are interesting. Under the outer shell of the verbena seed there is a waxy layer, coating the internal part of the seed. Although moisture and oxygen can penetrate the outer seed-coat, they are sometimes held up by this coating of wax. And without the necessary complement of water and oxygen, germination cannot take place.

This problem can be lessened by choosing for breeding work those plants in which the waxy layer is least developed, and also by growing the plants from which seed is collected under cover in controlled conditions.

The right germination conditions are also important. Seed should be given bottom heat, creating an even temperature of 65°F, shaded to prevent temperature fluctuations, and germination should take place in two to three weeks. It pays to grow verbenas on the dry side and not to feed them too generously.

So far the best variety for germination is 'Romance', giving up to 85 per cent.

The 'Derby' series of varieties and the new 'Novalis' series are the best of the bushier types, with a good mixture of colours, although the 'Derby' series is slightly biased in favour of pink shades – a colour which is rather outliving its appeal. Both these are compact and will probably need spraying against mildew. The older 'Showtime' has a wider spread, with strong reds and purples as well as white.

One other variety of verbena worth mentioning is 'Polaris'. Christopher will doubtless be enthusing over *V. venosa*, but 'Polaris' is a unique grey-blue flowered version which is lovely with blue hostas or the green-flowered *Nicotiana langsdorffii*. Like its purple-flowered predecessor, 'Polaris' has tuberous roots which can be stored for the winter like dahlias.

*CL:* Sorry, Graham, but I find 'Polaris' disappointing – dirty white and indefinite in colour, best seen at dusk (or in total darkness!). *V. rigida* (syn. *V. venosa*), long popular with parks departments, is a shouting shade of purple, but as the flowers are small, its loud voice is not amiss. Growing only 15 in tall, it mixes well with the yellow poppies and glaucous foliage of hunnemannia. It self-sows freely.

So does the 6-ft *V. bonariensis*, which is a softer shade of purple. A real winner, this, if you live in the south, but in the north, where it doesn't ripen seed, it tends to die out. It is a short-lived perennial, not altogether hardy. Although so tall, you can plant it or let it sow itself at the front of a border because it is a see-through plant, with quite tiny leaves. The square stems are green and do most of a leaf's work in the way of photosynthesis. It flowers from July to November, being at its best in September.

If, among the bedding verbenas that you raise from seed, there is a colour that specially takes your fancy (the 'Derby' strain includes a very pure white), you can easily keep it going as a half-hardy perennial by taking cuttings each autumn and over-wintering them under frost-free glass.

## Viola *(Violaceae)*

*CL:* Within this genus are the groups we know as violets, violas and pansies. Violets are generally propagated vegetatively. If grown from seed, this is best sown, fresh, in autumn and containers placed in a cold frame or plunge bed where frost can reach them. Germination is slow. Spring sowings are often a total failure.

The distinction between violas and pansies is even more tenuous than when you could trust pansies to have masks and violas to be plain-faced. But violas are generally smaller-flowered and tougher and they withstand high summer temperatures better. 'Blue Heaven' is a prolific viola that I have long grown to associate with the orange flowers of *Geum* 'Borisii' in May. The small-flowered 'Prince Henry' is a dead loss, scarcely visible even at close range, but the yellow 'Prince John' is cheerful and effective. [Both are sadly susceptible to mildew. – GR]

Pansies can, if regularly dead-headed, flower through the summer, but there are better bedding plants for that season. [Why, when there are so few spring bedding plants and so many for summer, do breeders try and turn pansies into summer flowers? Grow them for spring. – GR] Their great strength is in providing colour in autumn and winter as well as spring. In spring they are excellent carpeters to tulips. In their own right they'll flower long before the tulips. Then there's the tulip and pansy climax, and after that you can change your bedding.

Self colours usually work best for bedding of this kind, rather than mixtures, and plain rather than masked flowers, although a black and yellow pansy will offset yellow tulips handsomely.

Mixed pansies with masked faces look confused at a distance but come into their own in tubs, troughs and window boxes, which will be seen at close range. The 'Swiss Giants' are popular for this purpose and, being open-pollinated, are less expensive than the F1 hybrids.

The latter, however, make exceptionally strong, long-flowered, heat- and cold-resistant plants, and the F1 'Universal' strain, whether in a mixture or in separate colours, has astonished the world, if not the universe. Bred for cold winters, it will, in our climate, stand these unprotected and be flowering again as soon as frost and snow let up. Universals do detest a really wet winter, some colours more than others, which is an argument for growing a mixture. The duds will not show up in blocks, as they do if the varieties are grown in separate groups.

*GR:* What has astonished the world almost as much as the 'Universal' pansies themselves has been the sophisticated marketing campaign which has been used to ensure that no one grows any of the similar varieties! So if you come across 'Reveille' or the superb 'Ultima' (in twenty-six colours!) don't eschew them. You may already have grown them, as some garden centres sell any winter-flowering pansy as a 'Universal'.

*CL:* Pansy seed can be sown at almost any time, according to when you want your display. July is probably best for a long-flowering season with a long-flowering strain like 'Universal' and 'Floral Dance'. Given a mild winter, these will bloom non-stop from autumn onwards, with a climax in spring.

Once sown, it is important that pansy seed should never dry out. It is apt to germinate poorly under hot conditions. If I'm sowing in July, the hottest month, I place the container, covered by a sheet of glass, beneath trees and keep it thoroughly watered. Germination takes about two weeks.

*GR:* One of the most interesting developments in recent years has been the increasing range of pansies in unusual colour combinations. (These are sometimes less tough than those in more familiar shades, so are better in containers where you can control conditions. Give them shelter and a well-drained compost (not pure peat), or keep them in $3\frac{1}{2}$-in pots in a cold frame until spring and plant up in early March.)

So in catalogues you will now find the butter-yellow 'Flame Princess', each flower with a blotch varying in shade from brilliant red to a deep rusty colour. It's good with 'Cantata' tulips in orange-scarlet, and if I could find a pure white *kaufmanniana* or *greigii* type I'd be tempted to try that.

Many are best grown alone. These include 'Rippling Waters' in purple with a narrow white edge, 'Brunig' in deepest mahogany red with a yellow edging, 'Love Duet' in palest pink or palest lemon with a deep pink blotch and 'Jolly Joker' in orange with purple edges! Some of these defy you as you search for companions, but you can give up and still feel you've done the right thing.

'Bowles' Black' is a pansy too, a variant of the wild pansy and akin to it in its straggliness and its small flowers. If you have other pansies around it will be difficult to prevent 'Bowles' Black' from becoming anything but black, as it will cross with almost anything. Grow it away from other varieties and rogue out anything less than black, or it will drift to purple, even in isolation.

## Xeranthemum *(Compositae)*

*GR:* Their small 'straw' flowers and tall straight stems recommend xeranthemums for drying, and this is the purpose for which they're usually grown. The flowers are more or less double and come in soft pinkish tones, and they can be sown in rows in a sunny spot in April and thinned out. Cut the flowers when they're fully open.

## Zinnia *(Compositae)*

*GR:* In Britain, zinnias can be tricky plants to grow well, though as our climate becomes more Mediterranean, as the experts keep telling us it will, they will doubtless become less difficult.

Zinnias have a hard time here in Britain. They suffer from root disease, often exacerbated by root disturbance and also by wet conditions, not to mention lack of sunshine. So, given that the climate in Harrogate is unlikely to resemble that in Barcelona for some years to come, this is how I suggest you go about growing them. The large-flowered types in particular need the following treatment; some of the smaller more spreading ones are less fussy.

Sow the seed in April, individually, in small peat pots or segmented trays with each compartment about $\frac{3}{4}$in across. Use a peat-based compost, but if the one you happen to have to hand looks as if it might not be well drained, add some grit or perlite. After sowing keep the seed at around 60°F. When germination has taken place and the roots start to penetrate the walls of the peat pots, move them into 3-in pots. Then grow them on and harden them off before planting as usual.

Choose a site that is in full sun and well drained, but don't worry if it has not had the benefit of lashings of compost; reasonable fertility is enough. Plant out in late May or early June, water in well with a liquid feed added, and then don't water them again unless it's obvious that the plants are suffering badly.

The less expensive varieties, especially the smaller-flowered doubles like 'Persian Carpet', can also be sown where they are to flower and thinned out.

In wet seasons the large double-flowered varieties will suffer from botrytis in the flower-heads and also in the flower-stems; not just in the neck but also sometimes where the flower-stem branches from the main shoot. They may also collapse as a result of soil-borne disease.

Of this group probably the most reliable are 'Belvedere' and 'Bouquet', and of the smaller-flowered, more spreading types, 'Thumbelina', 'Classic' and 'Persian Carpet'.

*CL:* I don't sow my large-flowered zinnias till the first week in May, at which time they germinate in four days. I don't pot them singly until the pricking-out stage, when the seedlings are a week old. Zinnias are supposed to transplant badly, so I was interested to find, at the Buchart gardens on Vancouver Island, that they actually transplant them almost fully grown and when already in full bloom. Every bed, there, has to be a blaze of colour, right from the start.

As Graham says, we do have to bank on a good summer to succeed with zinnias, which are so prone to fungal diseases, but, accepting this risk, I like to grow the large, dahlia-flowered types with flat rays. When they succeed they look so prosperous. Far easier, yet effective and having a long season, are the dwarf, bushy kinds, of which I grow the bronze, gold-tipped 'Chippendale'.

# List of Seed Suppliers

**J. W. Boyce**, Bush Pasture, Lowercarter Street, Fordham, Ely, Cambridge, CB7 5JU

**D. T. Brown & Co.**, Station Road, Poulton-le-Fylde, Blackpool, FY6 7HZ

**Thomas Butcher**, 60 Wickham Road, Shirley, Croydon, Surrey, CR9 8AG

**John Chambers**, 15 Westleigh Road, Barton Seagrave, Kettering, Northamptonshire, NN15 5AG

**Chelsea Choice Seeds**, Regal Road, Wisbech, Cambridgeshire, PE13 2RF

**Chiltern Seeds**, Bortree Stile, Ulverston, Cumbria, LA12 7PB

**Samuel Dobie & Son**, Broomhill Way, Torquay, Devon, TQ2 7QW

**Mr Fothergill's Seeds**, Kentford, Newmarket, Suffolk, CB8 7QB

**S. E. Marshall & Co.**, Regal Road, Wisbech, Cambridgeshire, PE13 2RF

**Suffolk Herbs**, Sawyers Farm, Little Cornard, Sudbury, Suffolk, CO10 0NY

**Suttons Seeds**, Hele Road, Torquay, Devon, TQ2 7QJ

**Thompson & Morgan Seeds**, London Road, Ipswich, Suffolk, IP2 0BA

**Unwins Seeds**, Histon, Cambridge, CB4 4LE

**Gruydt-hoeck**, Postbus 1414, Groningen, Holland

**North Australian Plant Exports Pty Ltd**, 247 Tower Road, Suite 12, Montgomery House, Casuarina, NT 3792

**Southern Cross Seeds**, Templestowe Road, Lower Templestowe, Vic 3107

**D. Orriell**, Seed Exporters Unit, 11/10 Golfview Street, Nt Yokine, WA 6060

**Thompson & Morgan Seeds**, Erica Vale Australia Pty Ltd, PO Box 50, Jannali, NSW 2226

CANADA

**Albion Seed**, PO Box 492, Bolton, Ontario, LOP 1AO

**Apache Seeds Ltd**, 10136–149 Street, Edmonton, Alberta, T5P 1L1

**Buckerfield's Ltd**, 1640 Boundary Road, PO Box 7000, Vancouver, BC V6B 4E1

**William Dan Seeds**, West Hamboro, Ontario, LOR 4A2

**McFayden**, Box 1800, Brandon, Manitoba, R7A 6N4

**Ontario Seed Co. Ltd**, 16 King Street South, Waterloo, Ontario, N2J 3Z9

**W. H. Perron & Co. Ltd**, 515 Labelle Blvd, Chomedey, Laval, PQ, H7V 2T3

**Robertson-Pike**, PO Box 20000, Edmonton, Alberta, T5J 3M3

**Seed Centre Ltd**, Box 3867, Station 'D', Edmonton, Alberta, T5I 4K1

**Stokes Seeds Ltd**, PO Box 10, St Catharine's, Ontario, L2R 6R6

**T. & T. Seeds Ltd**, PO Box 1710, Winnipeg, Manitoba, R3C 3P6

**Thompson & Morgan Inc.**, 132 James Avenue East, Winnipeg, Manitoba, R3B 0N8

NEW ZEALAND

**Arthur Yates & Co.**, PO Box 940, Auckland

**F. Copper Ltd**, PO Box 12–347, Penrose, Auckland 1135

UNITED STATES OF AMERICA

**W. Atlee Burpee Co.**, Warminster, PA 18974

**The Country Garden**, Route 2, Box 455A, Crivitz, WI 54114

**Chas. C. Hart Seed Co.**, PO Box 9169, Wethersfield, CT 06109–0169

**Nichols Garden**, 1190 N. Pacific Hwy, Albany, OR 14240

**Harris Seeds**, 615 Moreton Farm, 3670 Buffalo Road, Rochester, NY 14624

**Park Seed Company**, Highway 254 N, Greenwood, SC 29647–0001

**Stokes Seeds**, 1036 Stokes Bldg, Buffalo, NY 14240

**Thompson & Morgan Inc**, PO Box, 1308, Jackson, NJ 08527

**Moon Mountain**, Box 34, Morro Bay, CA 93442

# Index

Index entries in **bold** type refer to main entries in the A-Z of Garden Flowers.